Essential Guide to Handguns

Firearm Instruction for Personal Defense and Protection

STEPHEN R. REMENTER
BRUCE N. EIMER, PH.D.

Looseleaf
Law Publications, Inc.

43-08 162nd Street
Flushing, NY 11358
www.LooseleafLaw.com
800-647-5547

Library of Congress Cataloging-in-Publication Data

Rementer, Stephen R.
    Essential guide to handguns : firearm instruction for personal defense and protection / Stephen R. Rementer Bruce N. Eimer.
        p. cm.
    Includes bibliographical references and index.
    ISBN 1-889031-65-8   13-Digit ISBN 978-1-889031-65-1
1. Crime prevention.
2. Firearms--Use in crime prevention.
3. Pistols.
4. Self-defense--Equipment and supplies.
    I. Eimer, Bruce N., 1953- II. Title.

HV7431.R46 2005

683.4'3--dc22

2004024915

First Printing - 2005
Second Printing - 2009
Third Printing - 2009

Cover Design by *Sans Serif, Inc.* Saline, MI

Table of Contents

Table of Contents (Continued)

About the Authors

Stephen R. Rementer** is a Vietnam combat veteran and 30 year veteran of the Philadelphia Police Department. He is a certified police firearms instructor, SWAT team professional, bomb disposal technician, and industrial radiographer. He has handled 1400 live explosive devices and has successfully completed uncountable tactical assignments in his law enforcement career. He is a licensed blaster and bomb disposal technician in Pennsylvania. Currently, Mr. Rementer is a licensed private detective who specializes in dignitary protection, explosives interdiction, and corporate security consultation. With his wife Linda, he teaches civilians, both corporate and individual, firearms defensive techniques at their Pennsylvania Lethal Weapons Institute. He is also active in training and qualifying security personnel and retired law enforcement professionals.

Mr. Rementer is a Glock Certified Armorer and a Smith and Wesson Certified Armorer. He can be reached at Pistol People, Inc., 2167 State Road, Bensalem, PA 19020. Tel: 215-245-SAFE. www.pistolpeople.com.

Bruce N. Eimer, Ph.D.** is a board certified, licensed clinical psychologist in Pennsylvania. He is a Life Member of the National Rifle Association (www.nra. org), an NRA Certified Pistol and Personal Protection Firearms Instructor, and a Glock Certified Armorer. Dr. Eimer is also a contributor to Concealed Carry Magazine (www.concealedcarrymag.com), and a member of the International Association of Law Enforcement Firearms Instructors.

Dr. Eimer has been a practicing psychologist for over 20 years and is the author of three textbooks for clinical practitioners and two self-help books for the general public: **Coping With Uncertainty: 10 Simple Solutions** and **Hypnotize Yourself Out Of Pain Now!** www.newharbinger. com). Dr. Eimer can be reached at Alternative Behavior Associates, P.O. Box 6, Huntingdon Valley, PA 19006. Email: dr.eimer1@comcast.net.

Dedication

To Dominic Germano, United States Secret Service; my mentor, who exemplifies integrity and dedication.

To Tony Curcio, my lifelong friend and brother in honor and honesty.

To Don Imus, a truly inspirational, passionate, complex leader in media and American values, by opening our hearts and minds. His gifts in every conceivable area are incalculable.

To my loving wife Linda, my spiritual and personal foundation.

To my children, my inner strength and pride.

Stephen R. Rementer

To Allison, for teaching me valuable lessons about firearms safety.

To Marisa, for being herself.

To Andrea, the love of my life, for letting me play and keeping me grounded.

To Mom, for picking me up when I am down, and teaching me the meaning of love.

To Dad, for teaching me to be unrelenting and loving.

To Oskar, for making our family whole.

To Brooke, for loving Oskar.

Bruce N. Eimer

We also dedicate this book to the memory of all of the victims who have not survived violent criminal confrontations and who suffered terroristic abuses and humiliations at the hands of monsters, as well as to those with the survival instinct who found themselves capable of rising to the occasion and not succumbing. We also dedicate it to all of the brave men and women who risk their lives daily to preserve, protect and defend our society and our freedoms.

SRR / BNE

iv

Acknowledgments

e gratefully acknowledge our publisher, Looseleaf Law Publications, Inc., for seeing the value in and helping us develop our original idea, and for having faith in us when we were *"not yet gun-writers."*

We give thanks to all of our extremely helpful and supportive editors at Looseleaf Law. Without their talents, skills and dedication, this book wouldn't exist.

We gratefully thank Paul Benjamin for taking all of the digital photographs that constitute the illustrative figures in this book. Paul's generosity and unselfish devotion to whom and what he believes in place him at the head of our honor roll. Paul, you are a very talented and kind human being.

We also wish to gratefully acknowledge and thank all of the topnotch companies who helped us evaluate and report on their firearm products and accessories by providing or loaning us samples to test and evaluate. These companies constitute our "honor roll." The list is pretty long. They had faith in us, as at the time we were unknown entities; "not yet gun-writers." All the organizations and manufacturers who contributed in our written process are indeed world class. Their products speak of quality, durability, accuracy and affordability. They include:

The best portable OC Pepper Spray manufacturer in the world: Spitfire.

The best tactical folding knife manufacturers in the world: Benchmade Knife Company; Columbia River Knife and Tool; Emerson Knives and Cold Steel; Kershaw Knives; Spyderco Knives.

The best knife sharpener makers in the world: Edgecraft; Edgemaker Company; Great American Tool Company (Gatco); Lansky Sharpeners; McGowan Manufacturing Company; Spyderco Triangle Sharpmaker Kit.

The best tactical light companies in the world: Insight Technology; Mag Instrument, Inc.; Streamlight; SureFire.

The best integral laser sighting systems in the world: Crimson Trace Corporation; LaserMax.

The best handgun manufacturers in the world: Beretta U.S.A. Corporation; Glock Inc. USA; Hechler & Koch; Kahr Arms; Kel-Tec; Kimber Manufacturing; North American Arms; Para-Ordnance; Larry Seecamp of L.W. Seecamp Company; Sigarms, Smith and Wesson; Sturm, Ruger and Company.

The best semi-auto handgun magazine manufacturers in the world: Chip McCormick Corporation and Mec-Gar Corporation.

The best handgun ammunition manufacturers in the world: Cor-Bon, Federal Cartridge Company; Fiocchi USA; Speer; Winchester Ammunition.

The best holster makers in the world: Jerry Ahern of Ahern Enterprises; Aker International; Lou Alessi of Alessi Leather; Lefty Lewis of Bell Charter Oak; Bianchi International; Tim Wegner of Blade-Tech; Josh Bulman of Bulman Gunleather; Gregg Garrett of Comp-Tac; Matt Del Fatti of Del Fatti Leather; DeSantis Holsters and Leather Goods; Jim Murnack of FIST, Inc.; Gould & Goodrich Leather; High Noon Holsters; Kim Fiedler of Don Hume Leathergoods; Greg Kramer of Kramer Handgun Leather; Michaels of Oregon; Tony Kanaley of Milt Sparks Holsters; Mitch Rosen of Mitch Rosen Extraordinary Gunleather; Ken Null of K.L. Null Holsters; Mike Meredith of Pocket Concealment Systems.

The best concealment handgun-toting leather outerwear in the world: Coronado Leather.

The best revolver and pistol grip accessories in the world: Jack Barash of Barami Corporation; Lyman Products Corporation; Pearce Grips; Tyler Manufacturing & Distribution Company.

We also gratefully acknowledge and thank the following individuals for all of their help and support and their feedback in the various stages of our manuscript: Dana Alexandrunas; Paul Benjaman; Tony Curcio; Andrea Eimer; John Farnam; Paul and Cindy Labonski, Lt. Dave Spaulding; and Linda Veitz Rementer. We also thank Dana for modeling for us. Her form and stance are exemplary.

I thank my wife, Linda Veitz Rementer, for putting up with me during this awesome project and for providing support and help in allowing herself to be drafted as our photographer's model. We thank Linda for being our model, and also for all of the helpful and informative feedback she has generously provided us. Linda is the best firearms instructor in the world. She makes it safe and easy. *Stephen Rementer*

I thank my wife, Andrea Nock Eimer, for being there for me as usual; my daughters, Marisa and Allison for understanding Daddy's busy, and my Mom, Cecile Eimer, for providing support and understanding every step of the way here. *Bruce Eimer*

Foreword

Today a deputy in my agency was shot. He was assigned to a court security detail, working hard to make sure that the citizens of Montgomery County, Ohio, were safe as they went about their daily routine of conducting legal business. A man walked through the main entrance of the court building, but was stopped by deputies when he set off a metal detector located around this same entrance. As our deputy attempted to run a handheld metal detector around this man, he grabbed the deputy's .40 caliber semi-automatic pistol from his holster and shot him with it. He then exited the building – firing shots as he went – through the same entrance that he had just entered. As he cleared the door, he was confronted by two other deputies who shot him. It was over in less than one minute. The deputy survived but the suspect died in the hospital.

Routine in the big cities of America you say? Well, maybe. But it certainly makes one stop and think a minute about where one is truly safe. If not in the halls of justice, then where? The fact is that while the U.S. is statistically a very safe country, the average person has no idea when and where violence will occur. As I write this, the country is still reeling from the aftermath of the Beltway Snipers. Over and over again, people state that "I just can't believe that this has happened," or "I can't believe that this is happening to me," when violence strikes. The response of the public when something like these sniper attacks occur is to hunker down and wait for the police to handle it. In the case of the Beltway Snipers, law enforcement did an outstanding job, but anyone who thinks that it is up to the police to protect them is naive at best and stupid at worst.

The fact is the police are only required to protect society as a whole. As a matter of fact, the courts have stated that law enforcement is not required to protect citizens as individuals. This being the case, who IS responsible for our individual protection? The answer to this is simple...YOU! You must prepare both mentally and physically to protect yourself and the ones you love. No one is likely to do it for you.

Since you are reading this book, it is obvious that you have come to this same conclusion and you have decided to take your self-preservation into your own hands. You could not have found a better way to start than by reading this book. Stephen Rementer and Bruce Eimer have put together one of the best primers that I have ever read on how to begin your personal defense program. While the title calls this work "an Essential Guide," it is actually an encyclopedia of what you need to know to get started preparing your own personal defense plan.

Mr. Rementer is a skilled veteran of the battlefield and the street, having seen combat in Vietnam and then spending thirty years with the Philadelphia Police Department. Mr. Eimer is a board-certified psychologist who has written three books in the field. They have combined their diverse backgrounds into a question and answer guide that you can rely on. There is in-depth coverage of everything from how to select and clean your personal sidearm, to how to properly select OC spray. But they do not stop there. They then go on to give solid advice on how to use these weapons for personal defense. Listen well to what these two gentlemen tell you and then work hard to make what they have said part of your personal defense package. It may just help you get through a tight spot and if nothing else, will give you the confidence, through knowledge, that you need to go out in public and not hide in fear. After all, a life lived in fear is not living.

Dave Spaulding, author of
Handgun Combatives and
co-author of *Defensive Living*

Introduction

W ith violent crime on an upswing and the advent of terrorism, every adult should be prepared with a personal defense plan. Having taught personal defense skills for over 35 years, and coping, self-reliance and personal recovery skills for over 27 years, we learned that people looked to us for answers as instructors and we dedicated ourselves to finding the answers when we did not know them. It cannot be a "me" or "I" ego game. It has to be a "they" or "us" mission. It doesn't matter which socio-economic or ethnic background the student or client comes from. The fears, questions and experiences are usually very similar. Breeding confidence is probably the best accolade that any instructor can receive.

Our mission has been and continues to be to employ our experiences, training and imagination to interpret, train and solidify the individual egos of the students and clients we meet, and to help them develop their defensive and coping skills.

We incorporate flexible and practical ideas, methods, skills, outlooks, and experiences in the field of combat handguns and defensive techniques and make them available to the professional law enforcement officer and the concerned general public. The vast majority of the populace will never become law enforcement officers, and hopefully never regularly come into contact with the variety of violent criminals that others have. Therefore, writing this book is the best way to communicate those aspects of our experiences that can prepare the reader to prevail and survive.

The focus throughout is on the *safe* use of combat handguns as a defensive tool. At a time when airline pilots are being trained to "pack heat," and there are more legally armed citizens than ever with concealed carry weapons permits, the need for an introductory guide that covers most of what needs to be covered in basic handgun and firearms training is evident. However, it is also intended to serve as a reference that beginning, inter-mediate and advanced handgun owners can turn to again and again.

Please note that this book is not a substitute for hands-on, live training and supervision by a certified and qualified firearms instructor. It is an adjunct. It is not intended to teach anyone how to shoot. That is a skill that can only be learned through systematic, appropriate, and individualized live instruction and supervised practice. For some, this Guide can serve as an introduction to the field, for others, it provides a good review on fundamentals as well as offering our unique perspective.

We have strived to provide the reader with the most accurate and up-to-date information available. However, neither we nor our publisher can obviously control how readers use this information, twist or distort it. Therefore, we do not and cannot take any responsibility for how the information in these pages is used.

We state the *facts* just as they are—*facts*. However, since so much in the defensive firearms and handgun combatives field constitutes *opinion* and *preferences*, we take the liberty of presenting our opinions, preferences and biases which are honest, as they are the products of our own real experiences.

Our focus is on SAFETY.

You can only benefit from the concepts and techniques we teach if your focus is on the safe use of handguns. You can only absorb the facts and information herein if your intentions are good and you, most importantly, must put into practice the safe use of handguns and *all* firearms. SAFETY comes first *and* second *and* last.

The safe use of handguns for protection, law enforcement, security, personal and group defense requires a thorough knowledge of the material covered.

However, after carefully reading and digesting this material, in conjunction with competent firearms training and instruction, it is recommended that the defensive handgun student read Dave Spaulding's *Handgun Combatives* (2002: Looseleaf Law Publications) next. Massad Ayoob's *The Gun Digest Book of Handgunnery (5th Edition)* (2002: Krause Publications), the NRA's *The Basics of Pistol Shooting* (1991), Ayoob's *The Truth About Self-Protection* (1994: Bantam Books), Gila Hayes' *Effective Defense* (2000: Firearms Academy of Seattle), Chris Bird's *The Concealed Handgun Manual* (2000: Privateer Publications), John Farnam's *Farnam Method of Defensive Handgunning* (2000), and Boston T. Party's *Boston's Gun Bible* (2002) are also all considered essential reading, and also constitute references that no safety-conscious, serious defensive handgunner should be without. We do provide a comprehensive reference and recommended reading list at the back of the book.

I have to admit that this book would probably not have happened were it not for the insistence of my eager colleague, friend, and co-author, Bruce Eimer, a clinical psychologist. This project has been a unique opportunity to collaborate with him, a civilian and professional, who has a dedicated interest in the responsible use of firearms and safe shooting for self-defense and survival, and understands the clinical aspects of aggression and fear. He shares my genuine desire to help people survive and we both want to make a dent in the insidious effects of crime in our society.

Crime is terrorism on a small scale. It is devastating to all, just as terrorism is to the world.

As a clinical psychologist, Bruce's professional life has been dedicated to helping people alleviate distress and suffering by developing and exercising inner strengths and psychological coping skills. A practical personal defense plan and the skills to implement it can overcome the limitations of age, gender, psychological hang-ups, and physical abilities.

There is no question about the fact that firearms are a *great equalizer* or *neutralizer*. Understanding their safe use, applications and limitations is a tremendous responsibility to be taken seriously. A firearm is a tool to be used for good. "Good" is defined as survival of the innocent, law-abiding citizen, and as the freedom to live one's life without the fear of being brutalized by vicious criminals. Firearms, and specifically, handguns, are not a panacea. However, they can be indispensable in most people's personal defense plans.

Adequate hands-on training by a qualified instructor is essential for learning how to safely operate and rely on a handgun as a self-defense tool. This cannot be obtained from a book. There is a vast difference between a literary effort and actual physical and psychological preparedness. Learning to shoot a handgun is not what it's all about. There is knowledge and techniques that must be mastered before one can safely make use of a handgun in one's personal defense plan.

We encourage readers to seek their training by shopping around and conversing with prospective trainers and students. Note the atmosphere in each training environment to determine who will meet your needs best. You have to *feel comfortable* to absorb information and learn.

These efforts apply to all who need to develop the skills to defend themselves against the everyday threat of violent confrontation. Devotion to duty is not enough. Preparedness, awareness, and survivability assure continued devotion to duty.

We are firm believers in the United States Constitution and personal self-defense. This is a right protected by our constitution.

The right to exercise self-defense is basic to a free society as opposed to a totalitarian one. However, with that right comes responsibility to be a good citizen, obey the law, respect other people's rights, and treat others as you wish to be treated.

As Colonel Jeff Cooper so well states, "Firearms, most particularly personal firearms, are Liberty's teeth, as pointed out by the Father of Our Country." This is because of the awesome power firearms provide to those who own and use them effectively and safely. Owning a firearm can provide you with the power to fight back and prevail against a personal attack. However, it is your responsibility to develop the necessary knowledge, skills, and discipline required to safely use firearms.

If you are a civilian, it is not adequate to simply purchase a handgun, or as a law enforcement professional, it is not adequate to be issued a sidearm and expect to be able to **safely** use it in a violent confrontation without essential training, continuing education, and ongoing practice.

A Disclaimer and Note of Explanation

Neither the authors nor the publisher have any financial interest or stake in any of the companies or products that we recommend.

Nor do we take any responsibility for how the products we describe and mention are used. We do not offer legal or medical advice. Nor do we claim to teach how to shoot from this book. However, we *do* claim to offer useful information for educational and informational purposes only. As you shall see, we impart this information carefully, clearly, and responsibly, peppered with a little bit of humor to keep the read from being too dry. Just like a firearm, a good read needs some lubricant to enable the reader to stay awake and continue to turn the pages.

Let us all face facts. All firearms are **lethal weapons**! Their legal purpose for defensive use is to stop aggression. However, in actuality, the way you stop a criminal aggressor who is armed, and intent on doing you serious bodily harm, is to neutralize his efforts first!

A word about the criteria we used to include recommended products in this book.

Our objective in writing this book is to strengthen your survival. It is not a shooter's catalogue of firearms and accessories, nor is it a compendium of articles from gun magazines or trade publications. As such, we considered it to be our duty to report to you what equipment we use that works and also to explore current products in the marketplace to find some within each category of handguns and accessories that can strengthen your survival.

With this objective, we tested various products. We do not mention or report on those products that we tested and evaluated if we found that, in our opinion, they were: impractical, not worth the price, defective, flawed in some basic way, lacking in quality, functionality, durability, or reliability, not well suited for their intended purpose, or if we came to the conclusion that they did not work as intended or advertised. We also eliminated products when we found a product's manufacturer or authorized customer service organization to lack customer responsiveness or courtesy. What good is a product if the manufacturer does not stand behind it, or if the manufacturer gives the customer angina?

Now, if we were writing an article for a magazine focusing on reporting our evaluation of a specific product, it would be our obligation to report both the good and the bad. However, we weren't writing a magazine article. Our goal as far as products are concerned is solely to report to you what we use or would use ourselves or would recommend our students use. Thus, we only recommend products in this book that we have full confidence in, have used, and feel good about. We admit that we are biased. We are partial to survival.

1

Gun Myths

▶ **Do guns kill people or do they save lives?**

More often than not, weapons save lives. However, due to the fact that our media is so often anti-gun, the positive aspects of self-protection often go unreported. The scholar, John Lott, wrote a data-based, honest book about this curious phenomenon of selective news reporting entitled, "More Guns, Less Crime." Nevertheless, the literature published by various firearms presses and, sometimes unfortunately, self-interested magazines, often does describe situations where civilians have successfully defended and saved themselves or others with a firearm. Our personal experience has been that some students we have trained have come back and described situations where their knowledge and unimpeded access to a usable firearm have deflated a situation that could have easily gotten out of hand quickly, or worse, become lethal.

Firearms training and knowledge is a proactive as opposed to reactive response to your personal security and defensive needs. No serious trainee ever wants to take a life or use a firearm inappropriately. On the contrary, such individuals consciously choose NOT to become a statistic.

The fact is that a firearm used appropriately by a trained individual can level the playing field when such an individual is faced with the threat of a physical confrontation neither sought nor expected, that could result in his or her imminent, grave bodily harm. Most citizens believe that the police are a buffer between criminals and society. However, evidence has shown that most often the police are reactive only when they receive a report of prior or ongoing criminal acts.

Most law abiding citizens have a false sense of security and are unprepared for true criminal aggression. The "trained" law abiding citizen has a better than even chance of survival when faced with the brutality of a violent criminal attack. This is made possible by having the self-protection and self-defense skills provided through comprehensive firearms training.

It is important to highlight the fact that a firearm is just a tool that can be used appropriately or inappropriately just like any other tool. Without adequate preparation, any tool is value-less, or worse dangerous. As we currently are experiencing today, even tools that no one previously thought could be dangerous, have been used to wreak havoc on people and institutions. Specifically, take a look at the computer.

Fifteen years ago, before the current epidemic of computer viruses and widespread hacking, who would have thought that a computer techie could be dangerous. Today there is little doubt about the power that such skills can have in the wrong hands. Malevolent computer hackers have become a threat to the very fabric of our society; for example, to nuclear and other power generator installations, financial institutions, and military and law enforcement agencies.

A firearm does not have independent aggressive action because it does not have conscious thought. Therefore a gun cannot shoot anyone or "go off" unless there is someone who misuses its capabilities.

Throughout recorded history, society has produced numerous effective and deadly protective implements and lethal tools. Oftentimes, the people with the weapons were the source of power and the people without them were their victims. Firearms neither increased nor diminished human's ability to destroy one another, but did allow average people to prepare for common or individual defense. The invention of firearms did not alter human beings' violent propensities.

No one and no entity has the right to legislate away from us our rights to protect ourselves and our loved ones.

▶ **Don't more guns mean more crime?**

The majority of firearms are legally purchased and owned by responsible, law abiding, individual citizens. Unfortunately, the firearms we as a society cannot control are those on the black market where criminals have to go to arm themselves in order to avoid the legalities of legitimate purchase.

Percentagewise, the firearms used in crimes are mostly attached to the underground market. In a small number of cases, illegal usage of firearms by registered owners usually occurs by untrained or psychologically unbalanced individuals who shouldn't even own a butter knife! The numbers of firearms produced in reality do not correlate with the numbers of crimes actually committed. It is only when an isolated event gets reported by the news media and purported to be a sign that firearms are the most destructive element of our society that undue attention is raised about the need for gun control (e.g., the Columbine school shootings, Washington, D.C. area snipers, etc.)

It is important to recognize that in many of these cases (e.g., Columbine), the perpetrators had other lethal weapons as well, such as explosive devices, knives, and so forth. Few people have gone on record arguing for bomb or knife control!

The majority of statistical studies have shown that the legal availability of guns is actually correlated with a lowered incidence of reported violent crimes (Lott, 2000). These studies have revealed that in the United States, states with rigid restrictions on law abiding citizens' access to firearms (i.e., gun control laws) have a higher incidence of violent criminal activity than do states that have laws that allow for registered concealed carry privileges. In fact, other studies demonstrate that countries that have taken away citizens' rights to own firearms (e.g., Canada, Great Britain, Australia, Japan) actually have higher rates of violent crime per capita than do countries where such regulation is not legislated.

Totalitarian regimes flourish in countries where only the government, the military and the police are permitted gun rights (i.e., Cuba, Iran, Iraq, North Korea). In such societies, citizens are clearly at the mercy of the state. For the best example of this, one has only to look at the bureaucratic net that was woven in Nazi Germany during the 1930s when Hitler was building his power. The end result was the ultimate in fascist governments, mass genocide, and the elimination of a generation.

Because violence is so horribly distasteful, law abiding citizens need firearms to prevent and deter violence, and survive it if it is unavoidable. Therefore, carrying a handgun as a viable defense measure makes good sense. You should never draw a firearm unless absolutely necessary, nor should you draw your gun unless you are ready to use it. No bluffs, please! The goal should always be to defuse a situation as quickly as possible without violence before the situation can turn violent.

Carrying a firearm is a responsibility that should not be taken lightly because it is often the *last resort* for defusing and surviving a situation rather than escalating it. Responsible gun owners recognize and understand this. Thus, they are *peacemakers* and not outlaws as some would have us erroneously believe. So, for law abiding and responsible citizens, carrying a firearm for personal defense and protection is a sensible thing to do. One carries a gun as a tool to be used only when needed.

People who legally carry concealed handguns are not cowboys. They value and cherish human life and do not denigrate it. In fact, assuming the responsibility of legal gun ownership highlights how important it is to be in control at all times. One must celebrate human life and detest aggression and violence.

▶ Do gun control laws stop criminals from getting firearms?

Absolutely not! The underground marketplace is still the viable source of goods for criminals and those who are desperate that it has always been. One has only to look at the failure of the United States government to control the distribution, sale and use of illegal drugs. People who are determined to use any illegal commodity usually find a readily available source despite government regulatory restrictions.

The most compelling issue that distinguishes firearms from other regulated or prohibited commodities is that firearms are capable, in the right hands, of repelling criminal attack, violent confrontations, and promoting personal survival. Therefore, in many overly regulated (i.e., Big Brother) states that discourage firearm ownership and prohibit legal carry privileges, many law abiding citizens are faced with a dilemma. That is between carrying illegally to protect themselves and finding themselves criminal violators, or surrendering themselves to opportunistic criminal attack. This then creates a breeding ground for black market enterprise. The fact is that when legal avenues for obtaining desired products (whatever they are) are closed by the state, then this opens up opportunities for other sources to profit. The question is do we want to see criminal organizations control the sale and distribution of firearms?

If a state wants to regulate firearms ownership, as states do with drivers' licenses, the best way to demonstrate genuine concern for the public good is not to make criminals out of its citizens but rather to make sure its citizens are properly trained. This can be easily accomplished by having people attend and complete a qualified course of instruction before firearm privileges are granted and/or licensed. This can be easily legislatively mandated by any state government that is genuinely concerned about the welfare and safety of all of its citizens.

It is important to remember that many organizations purposively choose names that mislead the public. For example, there are organizations that have the words "public safety" or "safety" in their name, yet they do nothing to teach people how to live safer lives. They are, in fact, ultimately dedicated to taking away people's rights and property!

On the other hand, other organizations, such as the National Rifle Association (NRA), are dedicated to running organized educational programs to help people enjoy self-defense safely. In fact, there are firearms manufacturers that have devoted large sums of money to public safety awareness and education (e.g., Sturm Ruger, Glock, Smith & Wesson, and so on).

▶ Do I have a right to own a firearm?

YES. However, along with that comes a lot of responsibility. It is essential to know the laws of the state you live in. Proper training with a topnotch instructor to develop good instinctive training and know the tool's limitations in order to prevent self-inflicted or accidental discharges. We point out that to get to the point of having "instinctive training," you have to really work at it. Conscious and deliberate practice makes skills automatic, subconscious and instinctive, and helps you stay safe.

▶ What does the United States Constitution really say about gun ownership?

The founding fathers of the United States who designed the U.S. Constitution's Bill of Rights had direct experience with the European tactics of oppression. As such, they specifically designed and appropriately positioned the Second Amendment as one of the most important amendments to the Constitution as part of the Bill of Rights. It specially mandated the right of the *individual citizen* to keep and bear firearms to combat oppression, tyranny and injustices so often perpetrated in the European theater.

In our opinion, what the founders wrote in the U.S. Constitution's Bill of Rights should be set in *concrete* and not violated by any special interest groups in whatever name they choose to interfere with the founding fathers' original intent. The founding fathers realized that a citizenry that was prohibited from arming itself was at the mercy of any government that took away that right, and that any government that did so was not "by and for the people." So, the purpose behind penning the Second Amendment was to make sure that all law abiding citizens of the new republic of the United States could defend themselves from tyranny or aggression stemming from either internal or foreign sources.

▶ Do I have a right to carry a firearm?

In our opinion, CERTAINLY! With few national exceptions, most state governments in the U.S. have realized the urgency and direct need of the populace to be able to protect themselves in criminal and other aggressive situations. This comes with the realization that there is not enough police to protect its citizenry on a 24 hour-7 day a week basis. One can live with the illusion that the police are out there defending us, but the realities are often tragically different. In fact, the courts have ruled that the police have no legal responsibility to protect individual citizens from criminal attacks. The legal, court-adjudicated responsibility of the police is to "keep the peace" and "protect the public."

It is interesting to note the following contradiction. Anti-gun organizations (gun banners and "gun grabbers") argue that the Second Amendment to the U.S. Constitution only gives gun ownership rights (read *the right to self defense*) to an organized militia (read *organized state governments*). This was certainly not the intent of our founding fathers who sought to protect the citizenry of the Republic against further and future tyranny! After all, why would the founding fathers want to substitute one form of tyranny for another? These same anti-gun groups disseminate the erroneous belief that the police are there to protect the individual! They clearly have it backwards!

> *The police are legally responsible for keeping the peace and protecting the "public." That is why the Second Amendment stipulates that the right to self-defense (read the right to bear arms) is an individual right.*

Defensively it could be related that where citizens are legally armed with concealed weapons permits, a notable crime drop is immediately realized (Lott, 1998). However, untrained people with firearms permits are more often than not more of a hazard to themselves than an actual criminal attack.

It is essential to know the laws of the state you live in. States like New Jersey that have no carry permit privileges actually endanger their population rather than protecting it by putting citizens at the mercy of criminals who don't obey the law. With that said, it is important to recognize that citizens like Bernard Goetz, the NYC subway vigilante, took protective measures to an extreme, violating NY State's laws. Perhaps if he had had the opportunity to legally obtain a carry permit, the incidents that led eventually to his subway criminal actions might have been prevented or at least diminished without the tragic outcome for all concerned. Society doesn't need morons, vigilantes or emotionally disturbed people with firearms. The majority of citizens should be able to protect themselves from the few who would otherwise prey on them and do them violent harm.

2

Choosing to Take Responsibility For Your Own Safety

▶ **Who is ultimately responsible for protecting me and my loved ones?**

We are all responsible for protecting ourselves – education is power and power is the first thing that the criminal intends to take away from you! The responsibility for acquiring knowledge of defensive measures lies strictly with you and your immediate family.

Statistically, urban dwellers are in greater jeopardy of criminal assault than are suburban or rural dwellers. However, the simple fact is that suburbanites also travel to the city and should not allow themselves to be caught unaware and unprepared should the need to defend themselves arise.

Just as in the animal kingdom, sheep and herds have a false sense of security. The proverbial "wolf" always eyes the weakest herd members and usually succeeds in eliminating them. If you look like food, you are more likely to be eaten.

Expect the worst and hope it never happens. Without adequate preparation, your chances of survival are markedly reduced. Therefore, a useful exercise for you to do on a regular basis is to practice mentally going over "what if" scenarios in your head. What if the worst happens? What will I do? For example, what if two armed men break into your home at 2:00 AM? What would you do? Mentally and physically rehearsing strategies and tactics can give you the edge you need to survive.

▶ **Where do I start? Where should I get information about self-protection?**

A good place to start is the National Rifle Association's (NRA) web site (www.nra.org). The NRA has supplied academic support materials for firearms instructors for years to guide students through the various phases of competent firearms training.

The NRA also is probably the most prominent and legitimate organization dedicated to the preservation of your gun rights in the United States and is true to the Second Amendment. It is dedicated to firearms safety education and awareness programs. Now, we realize that this may sound like propaganda, but it is the truth.

The former President of the NRA, Charlton Heston, has personally spoken with Steve. We have both listened to his views at length. He is a truly gifted speaker, writer and defender of the U.S. Constitution and his arguments in favor of a legally armed citizenry are solid, data-based and factual regarding legally armed citizens, gun rights and self-defense.

Books and the Internet are useful sources of information, however, the accuracy and timeliness of this material needs to be validated. We provide a list of recommended references at the end of this book.

▶ **How do I evaluate the quality of the instruction?**

Your instructor/instruction should have certain qualities:

1. A genuine concern for the students as opposed to money issues.
2. Tactical experience gained through years of service in bringing an unprepared populace up to speed.
3. Presentation of various pertinent literature.
4. Personalized training as opposed to militaristic boot camp training.
5. An attitude that views the student as an equal in all aspects rather than as a subject. This facilitates the possibility that the student can eventually become as good, or better, than the instructor.
6. Egos should be put to the side and focus should be placed where it belongs: on survival.
7. A thorough working knowledge of firearms, their components and operation. This is essential for communicating and teaching the skills needed for survival preparedness.
8. The ability to demonstrate non-lethal measures so that you have alternatives. Responses may happen in milliseconds but one always has to have alternatives that are not lethal.

9. He or she should recommend that you shop around for products, if he or she is legitimate and dedicated to you as a student. Think about it for a second. Are you going to place your life or the lives of those you treasure in the custody of someone who lacks integrity and only thinks about making a buck?

10. Evaluate the quality, attitudes and behavior of the students. Are they a model for how you want to act in the area of personal defense and the use of firearms? Are they sexist or racially motivated? Are they a good role model, are they professional? How do they evaluate the quality of the instruction?

11. Is the training provided in an atmosphere of fun in addition to education to help you relax so you can absorb the information better? Or, is it combat footage from a bad Audie Murphy movie?

▶ **How do I avoid getting bad information?**

Swelled egos are your first vital concern. Know-it-all attitudes will make themselves apparent within the first two minutes of a conversation. If you hear a lot of "I"s, if an instructor is pretentious or insulting, or if you are asked to accept information on faith alone, you are bound to come up short. So fly out of there. If you sense any degree of condescension or worse yet, intimidation, you know you enlisted in the wrong army. If the information being provided is based on experiences in the Civil War, our suggestion is that you have a good time by watching "Gone With The Wind" one more time, and don't waste your instructional time.

Competent training requires at least 20 hours over a spread out period of time in order to comprehend and maintain the information in one's muscle memory; the most important muscle being the brain to absorb and retain the information. A one or two day class firing about 5000 rounds will not facilitate long-term retention of the important information by most trainees. Good training requires building blocks, not shock. The best reflection of an instructor should be his or her students. Finally, more expensive does not equal better training.

▶ Who are people with self-serving agendas?

Honor above profits is our first consideration. An instructor that you can go to on a continuous basis for updates, clarity and genuine interest reflects best on our own selection of attributes. Facilities that demand that you purchase a particular firearm or other tool to complete their program makes them invalid by what appears to be just common profiteering. Everyone's defensive needs are different and as such, a "true instructor" will always seek to fit the tool to the individual as opposed to fitting all individuals to the same tool.

Retail isn't always the best source of self-protection tools such as firearms. You will be better prepared to seek good equipment once you have learned how to intelligently examine whatever you are looking to purchase. Just stay away from the "monkey syndrome." This refers to being sucked in by the glitter of a lot of shiny objects in the display case to pick up and play with, which are often lacking in quality. Remember that the most profit is usually made on inexpensive items. True quality usually cannot withstand a large mark-up. As is true with most things, with defensive weapons such as firearms, you typically get what you pay for. This doesn't mean that you must surrender your firstborn to get a quality firearm! Quality can be had at a reasonable price if you are in the know.

This book might have been titled "From Oz to Reality." What we mean is that there are a lot of myths floating around that can easily get you killed. If you find yourself with the "wrong" instructor, you can easily be sucked into spending a lot of hard earned money on useless equipment and training.

In our excursions into the world of tactical defense training and retail services, we have discovered that integrity is not an automatic watchword or a given. When you purchase training, it is important to steer clear of instructors whose egos or self-serving agendas (i.e., monetary profit) supersede your personal needs.

3

People Who Should
Not Own Guns

There are **people whose personality, intellectual deficiencies or lack of common sense** make it impossible for them to understand the grave responsibility that goes along with gun ownership. Perhaps they get so confused at times that they are unable to pay attention long enough to learn how to safely operate a firearm. *These people should not own guns.*

There are **people who lack the necessary judgment and impulse control that would enable them to exercise appropriate restraint** when they get hot under the collar. These people present a risk to themselves and others should they own a firearm. *These people should not own guns.*

People with severe attention deficit and hyperactivity disorder should probably not own a firearm. They can turn into a danger to themselves or others.

People who lack the necessary intellectual capacity, patience or character to apply themselves to learn what they need to learn to take on the responsibility of owning a gun, should not own a gun.

People who are convicted, violent felons, or who have major anger management issues and very short fuses should not own guns. Obviously, all efforts should be made legally to prevent psychopaths and sociopaths and criminal personalities from owning guns.

Then, there are **clinically depressed people** who are at risk of committing suicide. They should be convinced to give up their firearms at least temporarily until their depression is well under control. While they remain clinically depressed, *these people should not own guns.*

Then, there are **people who are so smug, stupid or ignorant** that they believe that it is okay to purchase a gun and not take any lessons on how to use it.

There are many **people who think they know everything** they need to know about using a gun—just aim at your target and pull the trigger. The hell with all the complicated and boring stuff! WRONG! Hopefully, after reading this book you under-stand the substantial body of knowledge that is necessary for you to develop that goes along with responsible gun ownership.

Owning a gun is not a game. Anyone who is not willing to put the time into learning how to operate and maintain his or her firearm, should get a dog or an alarm system. *These people should not own guns.*

Then there are **people who** feel so uncomfortable with fire-arms that they **will never go to the range and practice.** Many of these folks are unable and unwilling to take a human life in self-defense even if it means getting raped or murdered. Their belief system makes them morally opposed to self-defense. They would rather the State defend them. They live under a dangerous illusion, and they should not own guns. They will not learn how to use their gun. They will not develop the mental readiness and preparation for using a gun in self-defense if the situation warrants it. It is a shame.

People who are show-offs and braggarts and who can't keep their mouths shut about serious and personal matters **should not own guns.** If they let the world know that they own a gun, who knows what could happen?

Here are two real cases (disguised identities) from the authors' personal files:

One of us had a neighbor who wanted to be taken to the range. He came calling one day and asked to see the author's gun collection. The author denied having a gun collection which was the truth. In a lapse of judgment, the author agreed to take this neighbor to the range. Much to the author's surprise, the neighbor met the author with two of his neighbors and his son in his truck. He was telling those neighbors what a "gun nut" and marksman the author was!

At the range (the author should have walked away right then and there), the neighbor was unwilling and perhaps even unable to focus and listen to instruction. He just wanted to be allowed to shoot. Then he wanted to purchase the range gun (a sub-compact low caliber pistol) at a bargain price so that he could keep it in his bedroom drawer as a home defense weapon. He wanted to be able to use it to blow off an intruder's head, especially if the intruder took one of his family members hostage. On the line at the range, this gentleman kept fumbling with the gun but wouldn't pay attention to instruction on how to operate the pistol.

*He just couldn't keep the gun consistently pointed down range. He kept turning around with the loaded gun in his hand, unwittingly pointing it at the instructor and at the office behind the range. **This person should never own a gun!***

In this case, one of the authors was teaching a basic NRA firearms class at the range.

*One of the students who registered for the class kept talking about "close calls," people that were out to get him, and situations in which he had the opportunity to blow someone's brains out but didn't. He limped and carried one of those sword canes with him. His affect was stilted and he looked very angry at times. He never seemed to be paying attention to the instructor. He seemed as if he was in another world. He dropped out of the class after two classes. **This person should never own a gun!** He wanted permission to kill people! We don't give that. We don't abide by that or recommend it! **This person should never own a gun!***

4

Psychological Preparedness

▶ **What is my best personal defense tool?**

Your best personal defense tool is your mind and the information you feed it. That includes what you extract from your training in mental preparedness and the use of techniques and equipment.

The street has no mercy. In a true defensive plan, one must always be flexible and adaptable. Unpredictability demands flexibility and that means survival. You have to develop good mental preparedness and condition your attitudes and responses to keep you alert, attentive and aware of your need to stay alive; that is, keep your eye on the ball.

The key to a sound body and survival is a sound mind. A sound mind is a mind that is conditioned and prepared for the worst, but that reflects the best. A head-in-the-sand, ostrich attitude will not facilitate survival. A victim self-image or belief system is reflected in victim behavior and criminals are experts at spotting victims.

Like the wagon trains in the Old West, a defensive ring today encompasses 360 degrees all around you, 24/7. You must develop confidence in yourself and your ability to handle emergencies. This begins with cultivating an ongoing, automatic awareness of your surroundings and being able to instantly detect threats, react appropriately, overcome and prevail. Each one of us who wishes to be responsible for our own survival needs to develop a "little Marine" within us. This little Marine is the part of us that says *semper fidelis* which means "always ready to defend" and "always faithful."

Fear is okay and is usually justified. We call it personal awareness and mental preparedness. If you condition yourself to ignore or squelch fear signals coming from your body and your mind, then you are in effect turning off your internal warning mechanism and neutralizing your natural instinctive survival mechanism.

When faced with a survival threat, we all experience the "fight, flight or freeze syndrome." This is unavoidable and a biologically programmed response. What training is meant to do is to condition us so that in an emergency we instantly know whether fight or flight is the more desirable option, and never freeze like a deer in a set of headlights at night.

Through my military and police experiences (SRR), I have experienced many a time when I had a gun pointed at me or was being shot at. I am here today because I reacted through training not allowing the crippling responses that biologically impair one from prevailing and surviving. The bottom line is that fear is a normal response but it should not be crippling. Defensive training works and kicks in with mind and muscle memory as long as you've committed the time and energy to developing a personal defense plan and you've rehearsed and practiced it to the point where it has become automatic and subconscious.

We cannot emphasize enough the importance of having a well rehearsed action plan when it comes to your self-defense and a positive mental attitude that spells S-U-R-V-I-V-A-L.

▶ **What mental tools go along with responsible firearms ownership?**

Security is the pinnacle of preparation. A responsible citizen is an asset and an irresponsible citizen is a detriment to society. Irrational beliefs lead to irrational behaviors and responses. People and organizations that promote unrealistic ideas about what can be accomplished with a firearm are at odds with serious survival. There is no dearth of idiots out there who have the bells and whistles to draw people's attention but who can seriously mislead people into thinking that they are equipped to handle situations that they definitely are not. Substantive training and equipment and a realistic understanding of what you can and can't do is what leads to substantive responses.

A Clear View of Your Defensive and Security Needs

The first mental tool that promotes responsible firearms ownership is *a clear view of your defensive and security needs*. This is developed by becoming intimately familiar with your surroundings, your personal risk profile, threat level, and developing knowledge about yourself. Then you have to employ that knowledge. Preparedness comes from employing that knowledge regularly. Your education, upbringing and professional and social status influence no one in your personal defense. Should you choose not to take responsibility for your own personal defense, who then will? The police? Doubtful!

Anyone whose personal possessions could be an object of desire for those who would act to take them if they believed they could get away with it, are at risk of a violent assault and need to be prepared to defend what they have. For that matter, anyone whose hard work has allowed them to accumulate any degree of visible personal success must be prepared to sacrifice what they have or defend it should the need arise. But remember; there is no guarantee that sacrifice is any more effective than defense. In fact, giving in or surrendering to a violent criminal is no option because it leads to greater escalation of the imbalance of power. Criminality, as we shall discuss below, is all about *power.*

Harry typically gets up at 3:00 AM every day and goes to the local café for his morning cup of coffee. He had a feeling one morning that he should carry his firearm. No more than 10 seconds after he pulled up outside of the café, he was approached by two males stating that they had a gun. They ordered him, "Give it up, old man!" With his options limited, Harry decided to defend himself or most probably be killed. He pulled his Glock 23 .40 S&W caliber pistol and told them to drop their weapons. At that point, totally surprised at his response, his assailants ran way. Harry didn't have to kill anyone or chase anyone. He re-secured his firearm, called the police, and briefed them about the incident.

How many events like this one occur every day that go unreported? We continually ask ourselves this question. However, it should be noted that Harry had the training and resolve to use his firearm to assure his survival if the need had arisen. Trust the hairs on the back of your neck. If something gives you the intuition to do something that you normally would not do, trust that feeling. It has saved numerous people's skins. Listen to those "vibes." They are a biologically programmed inner defense response mechanism.

Restraint

Appropriate restraint means the ability to exercise good judgment about the threat level you are exposed to and measure the level of response required. Time of day, distance from your assailant, ability to get help, and your ability to prevail should be your major influences. Remember that no matter what criminal activity takes place, under law, an overt action must be taken by the assailant before you can legally react with lethal force.

You must be psychologically capable of exercising appropriate judgment and restraint or else you shouldn't own a gun. Don't develop "gun muscles" where through pure ownership of a firearm you start to feel invulnerable. Nothing can be further from the truth. Just like "canned courage," "gun muscles" only lead to disaster.

Owning or carrying a firearm is not a panacea, nor is it a license to use it by becoming judge, jury, and executioner. If you cannot convince 12 people looking at the same critical situation with which you were confronted, that lethal force was your only viable defensive option, then you do not pass go and you go straight to jail.

With firearm ownership comes the responsibility of doing everything you can to avoid confrontations. Carrying a firearm with a concealed carry permit gives you a life and death power that should not be unleashed during normal day to day activities. Carrying a firearm constitutes no license or excuse to provoke confrontations that could escalate. For example, "road rage" demonstrates that the largest weapon that a driver can have is not a firearm—it is a three to four thousand pound projectile!

An elderly couple were driving on a business highway and inadvertently cut in front of two thugs behind them. At the next traffic light, the two thugs jumped out of their vehicle and whacked on the couple's hood causing numerous dents. The elderly man was armed with a snub nosed revolver but chose not to produce it. He realized that it was not legal to shoot anyone over property, so he drove away. His appropriate response was to get the thugs' vehicle registration number, the make, model, and color of their vehicle, as well as a description of the two assailants, and make the appropriate report to the police. One of the insurance companies reimbursed him for the damages to his car, and the thugs were eventually jailed on charges of vandalism and making terroristic threats.

Self-Control and Good Judgment

These qualities are developed and refined from good training and confidence in one's self. Having had a painful childhood is not a viable excuse for exercising poor self-control or judgment in confrontational situations. Self-control and judgment refer to using what you know is right and your ability to remain in charge of your own behavior to control your actions when under stress. Remember that projection and delivery are everything. They enable you to outwit and overcome. The ultimate meaning of what you say and do are determined by the outcome. We must make a choice when confronted with a situation that requires a response. It is at these critical junctures that we must exercise good self-control and judgment.

> *Ilene is a mentally gifted, physically attractive female who lives in a well-to-do section of the state. She chose to be trained, after an unsolicited stalking incident. Prone to working late hours at her business, Ilene normally put in a 12 to 14 hour day. Following successful completion of her basic firearms training, she reported that one evening after work, as she was exiting the inner hallway of her building, she became aware that something was not right. Instead of proceeding outside, she chose to return to her office and call 911. The police arrived and discovered a serial rapist hiding in the bushes in the parking lot by her car. Ilene survived this incident well by listening to her intuition and exercising appropriate judgment by not putting herself into a position where she would have had to deal with a violent confrontation.*

In a confrontational situation, it is imperative that you take control and command. Command presence is an absolute. Police departments base their direction and authority upon it. They give orders to people on a daily basis on how to get out of the line of fire. Command presence is a necessity to remove you and others from danger.

On a smaller scale, if you are in your residence or in a vehicle on the road and you are accosted aggressively and being threatened with imminent bodily harm, *you* must give commands to your children, to your spouse, or to your parents, etc., should the emergent need arise. In order to survive another day and protect your loved ones, you must be prepared to take action while giving confident direction to others who may otherwise be zombies or panic stricken. Panic will get you killed. Someone must take the responsibility. There are no other choices at this point. A weak-kneed person is probably a dead person. Without command and control the situation at the very least is tenuous.

Prior to anything ever taking place, you should ask yourself these questions about how you are going to respond to a variety of "what if" scenarios. You should write your answers down for each scenario, review them, list your options and then mentally rehearse and prepare well before an incident takes place. Then, if a similar incident occurs, you will instinctively run through your checklist and be prepared.

Ask yourself these 6 basic questions, and by doing so, you will help yourself through most possible scenarios:

1. *Who am I facing and what are they armed with?*

2. *What are my responsibilities and what are my actions going to be?*

3. *Where is my best defensive posture taken from?*

4. *How can I prepare myself well ahead of an incident? What training and what defensive tools will I need?*

5. *How am I going to best defend myself in a particular setting in which I am involved, unfamiliar and uncomfortable?*

6. *How am I going to better prepare myself and my family for the future once we've survived an incident?*

Ability to De-escalate

The ability to de-escalate refers to ceasing your lethal response *once you are sure that the threat and aggression have been contained and/or ceased.* This is an important part of your total defense plan. We are not the aggressors. We are the defenders. Our right is to survive and not to punish. The latter job is for a judge and jury.

Jennifer arrived home in the early evening hours and heard some noises in the upstairs area of her residence. She readied her firearm, a SIG Sauer Model P239 9 millimeter semi-automatic pistol. Calling out, "Who's in here?", she attracted the intruder, who approached her with a large knife, while growling what he was going to do to her. As he continued to advance, she fired two shots into his chest which dropped him to the living room floor. She limited her response to only what was needed to effectively stop the assault. She did not walk up to the fallen and still assailant. She did not continue firing at him. She kept him in her view at all times, gun trained on him, while she maintained her cover and concealment. She dialed 911 and kept the intruder at bay until the police arrived. One can only ask what would have happened if Jennifer wasn't armed and mentally prepared. Events like Jennifer's happen every day throughout the country. Some end tragically and some end with a fortunate outcome. Fortunately, Jennifer was prepared.

You Have the Right to Defend Yourself and Survive!

If Jennifer saw that her assailant was still capable of and actively attempting to do her serious bodily injury or worse, then she would have been justified in firing additional shots to stop him and render him harmless. No one has the right to violate, assault or kill you.

Keep in mind however, that Jennifer later did have to justify her actions to the authorities. She didn't make any statements to the police until the next day *with her lawyer present.* If an overzealous, anti-self-defense prosecutor had decided to press charges (the DA didn't), she could have been forced to justify each and every shot she fired! The assailant/would-be rapist-murderer did die of his gunshot wounds. The would-be rape/murder victim, Jennifer, survived.

Understanding of the Pertinent Laws of Your Jurisdictions

Being that most statutory laws are written for lawyers by lawyers, they are often confusing to those of us without a law degree. Ordinary citizens can easily misunderstand the many statutes pertaining to our rights to self-defense. Fortunately in most states, good, legally savvy authors have chosen to interpret the laws of particular jurisdictions. These documents can be usually obtained without undue expense of time, money or energy at your local library or on the Internet.

It is essential that you familiarize yourself with your local laws. The laws of every state can be similar but different. As a law-abiding citizen, it is imperative for you to understand these differences in order to avoid legal trouble and preserve your rights. You cannot assume anything. If your state has granted you a legal right to carry a concealed firearm, that does not mean that you have the right to carry your weapon in any other state unless there is legal reciprocity or you have obtained a permit to carry concealed in that other jurisdiction.

It is your responsibility to know the laws and obey them. Ignorance is NOT bliss and certainly not a viable excuse for breaking the law! Severe penalties can result from misuse of any lethal object. The consequences can affect the rest of your life.

The basic premise is that nearly all states recognize the fact that you cannot react with lethal force unless a forcible felony has occurred. **The operative word here is *force*.** These crimes include: murder, attempted murder, aggravated assault causing serious bodily injuries (i.e., requiring hospitalization or worse), manslaughter, kidnaping, rape, involuntary deviate sexual inter-course, arson endangering occupied structures, robbery (a crime of person as opposed to "burglary" which is a crime of property), etc. The point of using lethal force is to avoid dying, but the law holds you to the fact that you have to be able to articulate the events surrounding that imminent attack.

Most states recognize the fact that warning shots are dangerous and not permitted. To shoot to wound is not a viable option. When you draw a weapon from a holster and point it at someone, that is understood to mean that you intend to shoot *that* someone in defense of your own or someone else's life. **You are not allowed to draw a weapon to scare someone.** That is illegal. An overt act has to be taken by the assailant. Later, we shall get into how you can obey the law and yet act defensively within the milliseconds that you have between being threatened and being overwhelmed when you recognize that you are in a life threatening situation.

Fear and Threat Management

Fear should be respected because it is a signal that something is wrong. Therefore, it can be an aid to our survival. However, while fear should not be a controlling factor in your life, it does expose the necessity of preparedness in the face of immediate danger. Fear enhances our senses and can motivate us to be more aware of and vigilant towards our environment.

In our book, *Coping With Uncertainty: 10 Simple Solutions*, my colleague, psychiatrist Moshe Torem, M.D. and I, discuss how healthy fear management can help you to cope with and minimize unnecessary anxiety (Eimer & Torem, 2002. Oakland, CA: New Harbinger Publications). Controlling fear is healthy and necessary for adaptation and survival. Submitting to it is crippling.

Aggressors use fear as a catalyst in their attack to exert power over and intimidate their victims (i.e., "prey"). Unmanaged fear in the face of a criminal attack is a cue to the assailant. It fuels the perpetrator's aggression and motivates the carnage of a vicious criminal attack. Fear is a double-edged sword. It either cripples you, or motivates you to survive. Wield it to *your* advantage against the threat!

By drawing on our internal strengths, even in the face of overwhelming odds, we can use our fear as a motivator to help us transform ourselves from victim to victor. This is the true definition of a hero: *being in the wrong place at the wrong time and having the fortitude to stand up to the unavoidable circumstances, muddle through them, assessing the threat and responding in the best way he or she can.* This is where training and preparation *really* count.

Survival cannot be based on misinformation. It is based on competent preparedness. Unmanaged fear produces misinformation which clouds our assessment of the danger and our judgment. All the technical and tactical self-defense training in the world is worthless unless you develop your internal strength, prepare to handle the worst, learn from mistakes, critique them, and add to your personal database of survival tools.

Preparedness

Whether you are a police officer on the beat or a civilian in your home, being prepared effectively reduces your chances of becoming a victim. When a person is suddenly faced with a violent confrontation, a massive dose of stress hormones, including adrenaline are released into the bloodstream. These hormones activate the "fight-flight response" and prepare the person to take survival-oriented actions. However, a high level of arousal can also cloud judgment.

Appropriate prior training and mental preparation are necessary to counterbalance the judgment-clouding effects of the fight-flight response. Without adequate mental and physical preparation for a violent confrontation, the fight-flight response can become a "freeze response" which doesn't lend itself to making it through any day.

Preparedness and confidence steadily build your everyday life into one of clarity. You become a formidable defender when you are confidently prepared. This enables you to sensibly and effectively approach all life issues, i.e. everything from your next raise, to traffic jams, to your defensive needs. Our primary goal is to educate you on how to build your internal strengths, common sense, options for effective and legal responses, and most pertinent of all, to empower you to continue to contribute to society. We want you to stay healthy, mentally and physically.

Healthy fear management is just good common sense. Using fear as a source of information and energy makes it possible to use the immediate moment to invoke appropriate counter-measures to the immediate or imminent threat. It assures that you will fight or withdraw tactically as opposed to freezing in the face of the threat. Whatever your response, at least it will be conscious, enlightened, and tactically sound. For example:

Mary is a business owner who was held at point of shot-gun at her business counter. She was ordered to sur-render all of her money. She complied. The assailant's second demand was that she proceed into the rear room. At that point she made a conscious decision that ultimately saved her life. She felt that, if she complied, then she was going to die. She didn't argue. She led the assailant to the rear room and suddenly grabbed and secured his shotgun taking him prisoner. She dialed 911 and held him until the police arrived.

Mary assessed her risk and responded to reduce it. She took her best option. It turned out that her response was a lower risk than complying would have been. The assailant had murdered other shop owners before in the same way. However, Mary had prepared for this scenario and she was able to carry it off.

Survive For Yourself and For Those You Love

In violent confrontations, one usually experiences sheer terror and havoc. This is when you realize that there is no one to save your life but *you*. It helps to think about not just protecting your life, but also others' lives and the lives of your loved ones.

It is essential to have the determination and the will to survive, that you are not going to let some "s-o-b" take your life. This helps you totally refuse to relinquish control to the "a--hole" who is confronting you.

It is intentional that we use these derogatory terms to describe an opponent in a life or death situation. That is because thinking of your opponent in this manner helps you keep focused on a positive outcome and stay determined to pre-vail and survive. We are actually reapplying the intimidation technique so often used by the criminal element. This is turning a negative into a positive and using the right strategy for that particular moment.

After a lethal confrontation, prosecutory lawyers may say that we de-humanized our adversary. We didn't. The assailant wasn't human in the first place! He was an animal: inhumane and intent on destroying us. We have to respond to the threat to maintain control of our fears during the confrontation and survive. It is important to focus on the fact that we didn't start the attack. We took whatever measures needed to competently finish the situation, control the outcome and survive (a.k.a., *adapt and overcome*).

You Are Precious. It is important to focus on the fact that you are irreplaceable and valuable. That in and of itself will fuel an instantaneous response, energizing your defensive efforts when you realize that you will not let someone take your life or that of innocent others; period, end of story!

Adrenaline. Adrenaline energizes the determination and will to survive. That is why a lot of soldiers and police officers are sometimes called "adrenaline junkies." In these occupations, this reaction becomes automatic and self-preserving. In other words, a police officer can go from issuing a traffic ticket to a shooting in a matter of seconds. Without adequate mental preparation, you can become a statistic. It is all about trans-forming the fear into something positive.

A Critical Incident's Aftermath. No matter how outrageous the situation is, your training is automatic and your fears produce adrenaline which mobilizes you to respond to the serious situation you find yourself in. In other words, all of your training prepares you to outwit and overcome. However, this does not mean you are invincible or immune to psychological consequences after a critical incident. After all, no matter how well trained you are, you are human and have human frailties.

Therefore, it is imperative to seek appropriate help and support after a critical incident. The purpose of seeking help is to effectively cope with the normal reactions you are going to have as a human to outrageous circumstances. You want to prevent your post-critical incident reactions from mushrooming into a post-traumatic stress reaction.

Unfortunately, this necessity for the continued health and well being of our police officers is often overlooked. The people who do not get help and support in the aftermath of a critical incident (e.g., a line of duty shooting or worse) are the ones who often are at most risk for developing serious adjustment problems after the fact. Such adjustment problems can make any professional unfit to handle the accumulated stress and continue to function on the job.

One positive long-term outcome of surviving a critical incident is that you automatically develop a greater appreciation for the sanctity of human life—especially your own. Some people confuse having "balls or guts" with the "will to survive." Macho issues really do not figure prominently in tales of survival. What does figure prominently is the will to survive above all else. It is also helpful to remember that the most dangerous foe in the natural world is a female protecting her offspring.

Healthy fear management is an ongoing life style and way of coping because we are human and we all feel fearful at times. So, it is important to continually build up your confidence to counter negative thinking and critical voices in your head that we all have from time to time. This is done by talking positively to yourself and being your own best friend and personal coach. Develop confidence in the tactical techniques you are practicing.

- **Keep Your Techniques Simple**. Simple is better than complex. Remember the acronym, K.I.S.S. which stands for *Keep It Simple and Survive*! In a clutch, you will be able to implement simple methods because they will be reflexive. Complicated techniques lessen your chance of surviving when milliseconds can make the difference between victory and defeat.

- **Practice Mental Imagery Regularly**. Visualize and feel yourself coming out victorious and surviving. Believe what you are mentally rehearsing and feel the positive difference that building internal strengths develops.

- **Trust The Hairs On The Back Of Your Neck!** When a dangerous situation is unfolding, you will be able to trust your intuition just like you can trust your family dog. Dogs have instincts on which humans have relied for millennia. Trained animals as well as people respond more reliably and efficiently in high stress situations. We don't expect you to live your life as a pistolero as most working people cannot. But, a defensive plan deserves a percentage of your lifestyle dedicated to it to insure that you will be able to enjoy the fruits of your chosen profession.

Just like a caveman relates to a dinosaur, once a couple of your friends have been eaten, you don't have to visualize the dinosaur or wait to see one to know that it can cause instantaneous expiration. The smart caveman will seek the security of his cave once he hears the thump of the T-Rex's footsteps. Facing reality doesn't make you a coward. It makes you an intelligent survivor. We recommend that you choose to retreat from a dangerous situation when you can, versus entering into a violent confrontation. It serves the same purpose because your survival has been maintained.

- **Stay Mentally Positive.** Do not let life beat you down. Physical exercise like mental preparedness enhances your response capabilities to every situation. So, get regular physical exercise even if it's just doing a few sit-ups in your living room or den periodically or taking 15-minute walks in your neighborhood. Walking has been proven to be just as effective as running for maintaining a healthy body through physical aerobics. A healthy mind and healthy body go together and clears your focus. Focusing on negativity is self-destructive. Focusing on the positive is strength and power.

Open-Mindedness and Flexibility

Many police academies have static curriculums that are slow to change and update. Often their instructors have been off the streets for years and, too often, their egos reflect that. Such situations do not create the best possible energies for training new police recruits. Society changes daily and criminality changes daily. So, too, effective, valid instruction and instructors need to be continually updated.

Many lives ultimately will rely on instructors' viewpoints and methodologies. Often, the first instructors that new recruits are exposed to make lasting impressions that stay with them for the rest of their careers and lives. Too many young men and women go out into society as police officers unprepared for the critical job they have to do, and ill-equipped to make the responses that need to be made in critical situations. Perhaps a better process should be designed for screening training instructors because of the overwhelming effect they have on the people they teach.

What You Can Do. Gather all the information you can from whatever source it comes from, and screen it. Keep yourself open to learning as much as you can about survival and ways to assure it. Do not be afraid to place theories to the test, re-evaluate ideas, put viable new ideas into practice, and make reasonable and necessary changes.

As a new recruit or a practical, survival-oriented civilian taking firearms training, ask yourself:

1. *Does my instructor keep updating his or her knowledge and skills?*

2. *Does he/she show genuine concern for me?*

3. *Is he/she willing to adapt new information and techniques to the requirements of different situations?*

4. *Does he/she critique actual combat occurrences and attacks? Does he/she critique students honestly?*

5. *Do I feel confident asking questions? Does the instructor's reply communicate that there are no "stupid questions"?*

6. *Does my instructor claim that his/her philosophy and views are the only valid doctrine in the world? If so, how well prepared and equipped is my instructor for his/her life circumstances? And, how well equipped is he/she to help me with my own unique, personal defensive needs?*

Flexibility. Flexibility is being able to adapt and adjust to changing times. On the other hand, rigidity is associated with stagnation, denying the existence of a problem and holding on to your point of view regardless of what is happening around you.

It is important to continually re-evaluate how you are practicing and training to make your tactics and methods better, more flexible and attuned to the changes occurring in your environment. Flexibility is conducive to a healthy body, ergo it is healthy for an open mind.

Acceptance of One's Limitations

Limitations relate to such things as physical ability, age, gender, and cultural background. Some of these factors can be readily changed, while others (such as gender and cultural background) cannot. Factors that can be changed include: physical condition by working out, education, perception of your risk profiles by doing research about what is going on around you and what dangers you face. Ergo, limitations are only restrictions we place upon ourselves unconsciously as opposed to learning more and more survival methods and opportunities.

Preparedness

Preparedness involves being inventive. For example, if it means you have to fake a heart attack to get to your weapon, or fake that you're going insane to get an advantage over your opponent, or fake fainting to get to the ground, do it!

By using your imagination you can overcome a series of adversities and this makes you more apt to survive, plus it might win you an Oscar!

Preparedness means being able to transfer skills from one setting into another to assure your survival. For example, most women are not afraid to yell at their husbands, but in a clutch tactical situation, they may become submissive. Therefore, our advice is: if you are assaulted, treat your assailant the same way you treat your husband! More seriously, what we are saying is that you must be prepared to seize control of the situation. Control is better in your hands than in the hands of the criminal.

Today we receive more trash mail than we'd like, for example, simulated credit cards, etc. To prepare yourself for getting robbed, it works to carry a phony billfold with you containing only these phony cards. That way, should a criminal demand your money, throwing your expendable billfold on the ground can telegraph to you immediately whether your assailant is after your money, you, or both. At any rate, by temporarily redirecting your assailant's attention, you've controlled the situation by creating a temporary distraction and buying yourself more time to react as the situation dictates.

Respect for Life

It is not our intention to create gunslingers seeking opportunities to put their skills to work becoming the local sheriff of
their community. Healthy training and assessment usually lends
itself to quite the opposite: a greater respect for life. Primarily
the lives you should respect the most are your own and those of
your loved ones. However, keep in mind that we don't seek to be
vigilantes. Remember "Death Wish" was just a movie and not a
license to really become Charles Bronson. As civilians or law
enforcement professionals, we are still everyday people subject
equally to the law and our responsibility to society.

Surviving daily life doesn't mean we have to be victimized. It
does mean we have to be prepared. We don't advocate starting
confrontations. We advocate avoiding them, if possible, but
ending them if necessary.

Life is a God-given gift and only God should be able to take
it away.

Guns are lethal weapons. Weapons in the hands of vigilantes, emotionally disturbed people, and the dregs of society
are not conducive to fostering the value of life. With firearms
ownership comes the responsibility of greater awareness so that
we can put respect for life first.

▶ **How can I prepare myself physically and psychologically for
defending myself and my loved ones should the need arise?**

Begin by making a list of your vulnerabilities in your vehicle,
home, travel routines, etc. Then, research and educate yourself
about ways to remedy these vulnerabilities. For example, most
ATM locations usually face a dark parking lot; so, avoid them.
Some retail and convenience stores now have ATMs in populated
and well-lit areas, exponentially reducing your threat of attack.

Your Vehicle. Drive with your doors locked and windows up.
If you are stopped by a stranger, crack the window, don't open
it. If you are stopped in traffic, leave enough space for your
vehicle to make an exigent departure should the situation
dictate, for instance, a car-jacking. If you are in a parking lot,
and you see suspicious people milling around, don't get out of
your car or park. If someone strikes the rear of your vehicle on
a dimly lit highway, don't stop to exchange insurance
information! Contact the police via cell phone if you have one or
drive to the nearest police station or firehouse. This ploy is
common to rapists and car-jackers today. Always remember that

your car is a 4,000 pound projectile that you can use in your own defense.

Your Home. Walk around the exterior of your home looking for obvious vulnerabilities; for example, bad window or door locks, cracked panes of glass, etc, and then correct them. Keep all of your doors and windows locked. Maintain your privacy. Most Peeping Toms' behaviors will usually escalate and manifest to that of rapists and violent criminals if given the opportunity to repeatedly see things that stimulate their sick desires. Therefore, have adequate window treatments to keep wandering eyes where they belong—in the gutter.

Window air conditioners should be secured internally so that they cannot be extracted from the exterior easily giving criminals access to your interior through your windows. If someone is going to break into your home, make them work for it. Don't leave ladders and tools laying around open areas. This is an invitation to burglars and other felons. Employ good lighting and a good recording of Rin Tin Tin wouldn't hurt, either.

Shrubbery should be continually maintained so it does not provide a welcome hiding place for criminals. Criminals love the darkness. So security lighting should be mounted high enough so it cannot be tampered with. Gates and fences should be secured and locked internally and externally. Fencing is good for privacy but it also creates a blind for criminals. So, install motion detectors specifically in areas where external fencing creates security problems on your property. Don't leave keys around. Also, don't surrender your home keys along with your car keys to parking valets. Keys are easily copied and tag numbers expose the address of your residence.

Motor vehicle and other personal information is more readily available today on the Internet so you are in that sense more vulnerable than you once were, hence the importance of bolstering your home security. There is a reason they call your home your castle. It is supposed to be the most protected and secure bastion for you and your family. Therefore, many are considering bringing back moats and alligators in addition to the usual home security measures. Seriously though, home surveillance systems with video camera capabilities have dropped drastically in price, making them more readily affordable to people who cannot join the millionaires' club. These systems enable the homeowner to monitor the exterior and interior location for wanted and unwanted guests; an important aspect of home security. You are better prepared to defend against what you see coming.

Often physical security is something you do not see the value in until it saves your life once.

A Floor Plan. Draw up a floor plan of your house. It will expose vulnerable areas—i.e., blind spots and weak points where a home intruder can hide or spring up unannounced. The best defense is a prepared one. So, create a map of your home and know your best defensive position. Let the criminal come to you, don't go to him. Consider making your bedroom a "safe room."

Don't assume that your rear exit is the safest one. A criminal who invades your home usually has an accomplice in the rear to look out for the police and/or prevent your escape.

Supplemental lighting (i.e., quality flashlights) is essential for a twofold reason. As a tactical measure, it blinds your adversary temporarily giving you a tactical edge. It also illuminates hiding places to help you fend your adversary off. Laser pointers have the same effect in inducing temporary blindness and additionally give you an aiming point in your defensive posture, which we shall go into detail later.

Depending on the structure of your residence, you may want to consider purchasing an emergency ladder to allow you exit through a second floor window.

Take Inventory. If your home or business is ever burglarized, you want to be able to account for every set of keys, so that you are not vulnerable to a second attack because the criminal has a set. In your own home, survival tools include household cleaners, kitchen knives, pots and pans, broomsticks, baseball bats—whatever you can have available for your immediate self-defense needs. You invalidate your home security plan if you let strangers into your home without checking credentials. A peep-hole is a great idea at your front, rear or side doors. It allows you to inspect person(s) approaching. Apply the basics of street training—observing body language, verbiage, intimidation or over-persuasiveness, clothing that could conceal weapons, bulges where there shouldn't be, and observance of general physical appearance and gestures. In other words, you must assess the totality of the circumstances so that you can react appropriately.

Have Discussions. Discuss and train your children about your home defense plan as if it were a fire drill. If you tell them that the "boogie man" could enter their house, you are going to create panic and screaming. Such behaviors are unwanted and anti-survival. They need to be eliminated in order to have clear perceptions and awareness of the movements of a home intruder.

Change Your Routines and Develop Safe Habits. Don't establish predictable patterns (e.g, time of day, routes, stops, etc.). Don't let your neighbors know your husband is going to be out of town on business for a week unless you can count on them to assist you should there be a problem. Remember that cute little Jimmy who lives across the street may now be a drug addict who is looking for the right opportunity to break into your home and commit a robbery, burglary, rape or whatever. Announcing your vulnerability spells D-I-S-A-S-T-E-R.

Check elevators before you enter one. Scan areas before walking to your vehicle. Before getting into your vehicle, look inside it, under, around and behind it. Park in well-lit areas and avoid dark corners.

When shopping make sure your arms are not full so that you are able to reach your defensive measures (e.g., pepper spray, keys, knife, gun, etc.). A common criminal practice in our area is that assailants will sometimes lay under your vehicle waiting for the opportunity to sever your Achilles tendon while you unlock your car, beginning the victimization process. If you are a woman, watch for any vans that park near your vehicle with darkened windows. Use common sense to avoid being abducted or worse! The definition of a criminal is a violent opportunist.

Physical Fitness. It is desirable to maintain as good a body condition as is feasible for you. If you do nothing else, watch a Richard Simmons video—at least you'll exercise your abdominal muscles as you laugh yourself silly.

▶ **What does living in fear do to me? How do I know if I am living in fear?**

Living in fear is crippling. You know this if you start avoiding common things you once enjoyed because the elements have changed around you. Training and self-esteem without putting yourself in harm's way can allow you to continue your normal activities confident in the belief that you prepared as well as possible for taking back control of your life. This allows you to continue living normally. Any fear can be overcome with the right outlook. Nothing has changed other than your preparation. Your dignities and freedoms are irreplaceable. If you let your fears of criminals confine you to your residence, then you are the one serving a sentence. Let's reverse that.

▶ **Why is the need to feel safe the most basic of all human needs?**

Abraham Maslow, the famous psychologist theorized that there is a hierarchy of human needs with the most basic needs having to be assured and fulfilled first before other needs. The basic needs are survival needs that include food, water, and shelter. In our opinion, Maslow erred in positioning the requirements for safety and security as being much less urgent than these former needs. It is important to remember that without an effective defensive posture you are not going to keep your food, water and shelter very long!

Maslow's "higher," less urgent needs also included such things as the need for achievement, success, acquisition of material wealth, etc. He also included self-esteem midway up his hierarchy. We would reposition this need lower and, therefore, more basic and essential on the hierarchy because good self esteem goes hand-in-hand with self defense, self protection and self-realization. To visualize that, one has to only look as far as any totalitarian regime that maintains total control through the use of fear, intimidation and informers. Here, we would also include abusive relationships between spouses or partners, as well as the problem of stalking. Both examples are crippling and destructive as well as life-threatening. Maslow lived in an ivory tower at Harvard University in a different era that was much less exposed to the raw realities of the criminal element. We live in reality.

▶ **How do I go about building personal awareness and safe boundaries?**

Maintaining appropriate distances to preserve your personal space is a priority. Up close and personal is not better in a defensive plan. Maintaining distance allows you time and space to evaluate, control and prepare, and extends your reaction time—a.k.a., your implementation of your personal defense plan. Distances under 21 feet of your defensive bubble reduce your survival chances. An intent, physically fit attacker with a knife can traverse 21 feet to your throat in less than 2 seconds. It is to your advantage to monitor and maintain this space as a 360-degree protective bubble around you. This is where remaining static can be to your detriment. Flexibility and movement are valuable tools in your self-defense plan.

Some authors over-complicate your defensive needs with exotic formats, models and schemes. The bottom line is that by remaining aware and keeping appropriate distances you'll be able to easily determine when you are in harm's way and react appropriately. Unlike the game of "twister," you want to stay attentive to your situation. Trying to recall theory and the elements associated with it can get you injured or killed.

▶ **What are the signs of an impending criminal attack?**

If you stay attentive and alert to your surroundings, you'll stay alive. The criminal's intended actions are often telegraphed by specific visual and auditory signals. Like a wolf pack, the criminal predator will often move in a circle to select and assess the intended victim. Once the predator selects a victim and picks a vulnerable spot, the attack begins. These include places where a victim is unlikely to get immediate help (e.g., subways, alleyways, dimly-lit areas, lonely parking lots, at home alone, etc.).

Criminals will often recruit other criminals to assist them in their terroristic robbery efforts; i.e., the "wolf pack syndrome." Where they would not operate alone, the wolf pack will be especially brazen and dangerous in circling, intimidating and victimizing their prey.

It's interesting when you watch the predator in preparation for an attack. As a "granny team" member with the Philadelphia Police Department, I (SRR) had that opportunity. Certain behaviors are not readily visible to *uniformed* police and unprepared civilians. Criminals preparing to attack often engage in predatory behavior such as masterminding cut-off procedures to reduce the intended victim's escape avenues. They consolidate their tools whether it be a knife, gun, screwdriver or whatever, as they get ready to launch their attack.

Escalation of Viciousness

If you're a "granny officer," once a robbery is in progress, a common call sign to summon assistance from your back-up officers is, *"Please don't hurt me! Please don't hurt me!"* It should be noted that those two sentences **actually encourage** the criminal aggressor to become more vicious—stabbing, punching, kicking, beating, or shooting the granny officer who is prepared to deal with such violent behavior through prior training and preparation. Now, imagine yourself as a civilian walking and being that same victim! You determine your percentage chances of survival.

One more point is important to emphasize and repeat. Criminals are by nature opportunists. They are most likely to strike when your guard is down. Don't give them the opportunity and you won't become a victim. Another thing criminals will do in selecting their victim is they will assess how much persuasion and insistence it takes before the victim gives in or acquiesces. Letting the criminal get a foot in the door could mean death. Don't let him in and don't give in no matter what!

The point is: *don't relinquish your power!* Stay in control. Transferring power to the criminal aggressor can easily lead to your demise.

▶ How do I identify the signs of the menace?

Forget about the eyes being the window to the soul. It's the hands and what's in them that can cause your demise! Seriously, you must look at both. You must keep your cool. Maintain distance. Look, listen, feel, and visualize various approaches and retreat avenues. Have a solid defense plan already prepared, and be ready to respond quickly.

The criminal predator often stares into his victim. However, at first, before the attack, he may avoid direct eye contact and appear fidgety. You must pick up on body language. The predator ready to pounce will telegraph his state of readiness through body language. *The key is his exclusive focus on **you** as his prey.* When you are prepared to pick up on this, you can *feel* the sensory and motor language and the vibes as the hairs stand up on the back of your neck.

Verbiage as intimidation is a common tool to throw you off guard. Verbiage is just that—words. The age-old adage, "Sticks and stones may break my bones but words can never hurt me," applies as long as you don't let yourself be intimidated into a submissive posture.

It's the physical threat and its implementation you should be most concerned with. Nobody we've met yet has an "S" on their chest. So, tactical retreat (a.k.a., escape) is always a real option to be considered and not to be thought of as cowardice, especially when you are alone and do not control the immediate environment. In such instances, tactical retreat to an environment you are comfortable in, such as the interior of a car, the wall of a building, or the interior of a store makes sense. Standing alone is a bad plan unless you have no other options and are backed into a corner.

Physical aggression is telegraphed by posture—aggressive stances and actions. For example, staring, following or tailing, violating personal space, distraction and manipulation can all be precursors to a person-crime in progress. Keep your eyes and ears open and you will negate 90 percent of the criminal's tools. Remember the adage that God gave us two eyes and two ears and one mouth so that we could hear and see 4 times as much as we say.

▶ **How can I best reinforce my memory of the descriptive particulars of a criminal event?**

We've supplied, as a training aide in Figure 4.1, a Suspect Description format, which will enable you to practice how to take and record a detailed description of a person, weapon, and conveyance on a regular basis. Please feel free to make copies for your personal use and distribute them. It makes a great tool for teaching children as well as "granny" about strangers and survival.

Don't rely on your short-term memory because short-term memory, as is the case with long-term memory, is unreliable and hence easily contaminated. Recording the events on paper will be an effective way of capturing the incident. Such recording can act as evidence should you have to testify to its contents 8 months to 2 years down the road. Additionally, time and date the document and secure it in a safe place. It doesn't do any good to prosecute a criminal if you are not going to be able to get a conviction.

SUSPECT DESCRIPTION

FILL OUT AS BEST AS YOU CAN
GIVE TO THE FIRST POLICE OFFICER ON THE SCENE

Sex	Race	Age	Height	Weight	Weapon type

Hair

Glasses type

Complexion

Scars/Marks

Tattoos

Hat (color, type)

Tie

Shirt

Coat

Trousers

Shoes

AUTO LICENSE, MAKE, COLOR

DIRECTION OF TRAVEL

ADDITIONAL INFORMATION:

_____

_____

_____

_____

_____

_____

Figure 4.1

5

Basic Tactical
Self-Protection Tools

▶ **How can I use a flashlight tactically to enhance my personal defense?**

Flashlights have various tactical uses depending on the situation. Obviously, if you are a SWAT cop, your tactical equipment needs are going to be vastly different on the job than those of the home defender. In this book, we will not be going into SWAT tactics. Our focus is on personal defense and protection; staying safe and surviving.

For the home defender, house clearing is not conducive to survival and is highly discouraged. If your home is invaded, your first order of priority is to make sure your loved ones are all in one safe place. Typically, the master bedroom makes the most sense as the *safe room* in the house. This is the place in which to barricade yourself and your family and from which you should promptly call 911. It should be your home defense "command center."

In such a scenario (i.e., a home invasion), you should have a big rechargeable flashlight such as a Maglite rechargeable (or the D-cell battery "Louisville Slugger" size Maglite), or a Streamlight "UltraStinger". The flashlight should always be placed in such a fashion that it does not illuminate you, the defender, either by holding or by shadow or by backlighting you. So, the light should be capable of being rolled across the floor to illuminate the entire room or area **in front of you** so as not to back light you and thus, expose your position should the bad guy(s) break through the door to your safe room.

God forbid, before such a thing happens, when you hear the bad guys outside your safe room, you should bark in a commanding voice something like, **"Leave these premises immediately. We are well armed (or, we have guns) and the police are on their way! Do not enter or you will be shot!"** Of course, you should also be "armed" with a cellular phone so you don't have to worry if the phone lines were cut.

In Chapter 11, we shall cover basic principles of low light tactics. However, please keep in mind that no matter what type of light you choose to purchase, always have extra bulbs and batteries on hand. Check your equipment periodically (ideally quarterly) to make sure it is functioning properly. The goal in using a flashlight for illumination is to help you see the bad guys and if necessary to blind them. If your equipment is not functioning properly, such as for example, due to dead batteries, that will leave you in the dark and bad guys love the dark! This is not conducive to S-U-R-V-I-V-A-L.

▶ **How can I choose a flashlight for enhancing my personal defense?**

Two main considerations in choosing a good flashlight are structural strength and illumination output. Blinding your adversary is a tactical advantage either in aiding your escape or camouflaging your movement. Checking under and around your surroundings that are capable of hiding a criminal is, of course, of value. While there are a wide variety of flashlights on the market, it has been our experience that three leading companies far outshine the competition and illuminate the market.

Mag Instrument, Inc. (909-947-1006; www.maglite.com) makes an excellent, reliable and affordable flashlight. The "Maglite" can be purchased readily at retail outlets such as K-Mart, Home Depot, Sam's Club, BJs, or Walmart. Mag Instrument, Inc. has been the preeminent supplier of defense flashlights to law enforcement, security and civilians for years. As such, Maglites have saved numerous lives.

"Maglites" come in several sizes ranging from AAA miniature handhelds that can be carried in a hip holster to multiple D cells which are the size of a Louisville slugger. All Maglites are made of lightweight aircraft strength aluminum. Many provide sufficient illumination and structural integrity that make any of them formidable weapons, both visually and as a blunt striking tool. A feature of all Maglites is their focusable beam which allows you to adjust the light spread from pinpoint to wide angle. Figure 5.1 shows the Maglite Rechargeable.

"Streamlight" (800-523-7488; www.streamlight.com) makes a wide array of products that are so high in their illumination outputs that you'll probably have ships docking at your residence. Like a lighthouse in a storm, Streamlights are a valuable tool and effective combat deterrent. They are either rechargeable in your home electric outlet or from your vehicle cigarette lighter by way of the supplied AC vehicle adaptors. They are very reliable, of sturdy construction, and their size make them readily manipulative.

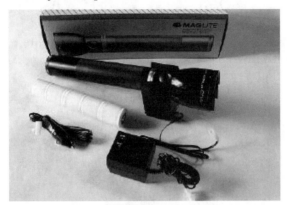

Figure 5.1

Streamlight's "Scorpion" and "Stinger" lines have proven themselves extremely effective for checking (i.e., "clearing") your residence (an activity not recommended if avoidable!), when camping or if you are just walking your dog at night. They provide a viable tactical alternative for blinding an adversary, canceling out his night vision and readily increasing your performance in a tactical defense situation.

We experimented with these products and happily found that each one of the models we tested was effective, reliable, and sturdy. No corner of any room we searched was left unillumi-nated. However, please do not shine any Streamlights at your own eyes. You'll see black spots for two hours! Seriously, these lenses are so bright that you really don't want to test them on your own eyes. That is what makes them so effective for tactical defense use. They will definitely blind an assailant even with some seriously cool dark shades.

Also, these lights become very warm to hot depending on duration of use. Do not touch the lens cap. Don't let the small size of the little "Scorpions" fool you into underestimating their power. Their power is really unbelievable and they pack a real sting. Size makes them convenient tools for belt pouch or clip-on carry.

The bigger flashlights in the Stinger series are even more powerful. The largest one in the series, the "UltraStinger" lends itself to bedroom home defense. It conveniently plugs into a charger in any electric outlet and can be easily removed from its holder and rolled across the floor to create a wide beam of illumination. Other Stinger models can be used for safe room or bedroom home defense also, but because they are more portable in size, they can be conveniently and defensively used in your vehicle. They come with an adapter charger that plugs into your vehicle's cigarette lighter.

All of these Streamlight products are valuable tools that are well worth their price and will last a lifetime. Figure 5.2 shows the Streamlight product line.

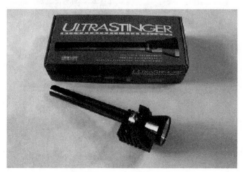

Figure 5.2

"SureFire" (18300 Mount Baldy Circle, Fountain Valley, CA 92708. 800-828-8809; www.surefire.com) manufactures the most hard core tactical flashlights on the planet. Their wide product line sets the upper limits for maximum power with minimal size. Every one of their lights has a nearly flawless white beam, ultra-high light output, and is extremely rugged. SureFire lights also have "tactically correct" (also read ergonomic) on/off and momentary switches. This takes the form of a tailcap momentary switch and a lock-out tail-cap that allows the light to be locked in the OFF position, thus preventing the possibility of the light being accidentally turned on during storage or transportation.

SureFire lights are constructed of either lightweight, hard anodized aluminum or Nitrolon, a proprietary polymer, both of which have superior durability and impact absorption. Their lights are built with shock-isolated lamp assemblies to protect them from impact damage. And, all of their lights operate on disposable lithium batteries that have a ten-year shelf life! Because of their small size, SureFire's line of lithium-powered lights are great for any application where size or weight are a significant concern: for example; camping and hiking, personal defense, work-related carry, and so forth.

Whether you're a homeowner, home defender, traveling salesperson, mechanic, cop on the beat, SWAT professional, or Special OPs military professional, SureFire is sure to have a quality, high performance light to meet your unique needs. You can choose among their high performance personal lights, advanced rechargables, special operations lights, and mountable weapon lights.

Price is not a consideration. Their highly affordable G2 personal light, at around $34.00, is powered by two lithium batteries (10-year shelf life) and is made of Nitrolon, a proprietary polymer compound that is lightweight, corrosion-proof and non-conductive. This lightweight, five inch long SureFire light offers a sure grip in any weather, and is three to four times brighter than a typical 2-D cell flashlight. It also features unique switching originally developed for law enforcement—twist for constant on, or depress the tailcap button for momentary illumination or emergency signaling.

On the other hand, you can purchase their top-of-the-line C3 Centurion which is powered by three lithium batteries and produces 105 lumens of shocking power light output.

Their rechargeable, highly portable, 8AX Commander, 110 lumen flashlight features premium aluminum construction, rugged military specification, hard anodized, precision machined aluminum, and an optically coated, tempered Pyrex lens window. You can have a fully charged battery in the light for your use while a second rechargable battery is charging in your SmartCharger. Like all of SureFire's lights, the 8AX Commander features SureFire's unique switching originally developed for law enforcement—twist for constant on, or depress the tailcap button for momentary illumination or emergency signaling.

Last but not least, SureFire's quality weapon-mounted lights feature grip, activated switching that requires only one hand to operate, and a trigger guard mounted adapter rail.

It is no wonder why SureFires are the choice of the US Navy SEALs and other elite military and law enforcement units in the United States and around the world. Their motto reflects their commitment to excellence: "Failure is not an option and there can be no compromise." It's a SureFire to be sure.

▶ **How can pepper spray be used to enhance my personal defense?**

Pepper spray is an effective, non-lethal tool in your personal self-defense arsenal. It is a product commonly used in law enforcement that works on the olfactory and mucous membrane systems of the body—eyes, nose, mouth, and lungs. Pepper spray will most often incapacitate a subject in seconds. The sprayed subject starts coughing spasmodically. The subject's eyes reflexively flutter closed from the inflammation and stinging, thus disabling sight. As a self-defense tool, pepper spray can be used within a range of 10 feet or closer to enable escape in a violent physical confrontation.

These physiological effects can create a panic in the assailant subject at best, and at least, temporarily incapacitate him giving you time to escape. So, it takes you from the terror of an attack to surprising the offender and impairing him tactically.

Pepper spray comes in variously sized canisters and percentages of the active ingredient which is oleoresin capsicum (OC). We recommend a preparation with a percentage strength of at least 10% OC that puts out at least 1,000,000 Scoville Heat Units (SHUs). The pocket or pocketbook sizes enable you to carry it with your keys and have it available as an assailant-stopping tool when you are getting into your vehicle, opening your home's front or side door, etc.

It is important to note that wind can blow pepper spray irritant back toward your eyes. While a little pepper irritant will not impair your vision enough to prevent your effective escape and survival, a lot can. Therefore, turn your face away to protect your eyes when you are spraying upwind. This will help you get away from the blow-back. However, it is also important to recognize that in defending yourself against an attacker, your adrenaline will be flowing. You will be so pumped up (which is an adaptive survival response) that you will be resistant to a little blow-back of the pepper spray irritant.

However, this resistance also applies to the criminal aggressor! So, be prepared to spray and flee. Also remember that you are unlikely to have a reason to spray an assailant who is more than 10 feet away from you. The use of pepper spray is a close quarters surprise escape tactic. It gives you a precious moment to escape. Seize that moment and survive!

A subject who is prepared for a shot of pepper spray can withstand it and keep fighting. It is important to remember this so that you do not succumb to "psychogenic shock." If you are exposed to the spray's blow-back, or if the assailant sprays you, you do not have to fall down and submit! You can persevere and prevail. However, this also applies to the aggressor. So, the key element is surprise. Once you have surprised the aggressor, use your time wisely—escape!

Most manufacturers of the pepper spray tool in their instructions, tell you what the optimum spraying distance is (often around 5 feet depending on the size of the canister and the type of propellant used to disperse it). This actuating distance can keep an assailant from getting up close and personal. Also, if possible, you should move at cross angles to the wind or laterally to avoid blow-back.

For a law enforcement professional who has a sidearm, pepper spray is strictly for non-lethal resolution of criminal conduct. It creates the opportunity to move in and make a successful arrest. For civilians, it creates the opportunity to escape and secure help.

Spitfire (800-SPITFIRE; www.1800spitfire.com) is a quality company that manufactures and distributes a very intelligently designed, powerful, concealable pepper spray product. Their unique canister design has a positive safety that reduces the chance of an accidental discharge. It is also designed to fit the natural shape of the human hand so that the delivery dispenser can be pointed at an attacker with the thumb of your strong hand. Figure 5.3 shows the Spitfire canister and packaging.

We talked with Walter Cardwell, the President and founder of Spitfire, Inc. True to his Texas heritage, he exemplifies the characteristics of being humble, dedicated and a self-made American. He literally spent hours of his corporate day enlightening us with a thorough overview of the ins and outs of pepper spray.

Figure 5.3

Mr. Cardwell's love for his wife led to his developing the truly unique pepper spray delivery system that far surpasses the closest competition. He pointed out to us that he focused on women's needs primarily in designing Spitfire. Mr. Cardwell shares our values of integrity, honesty and honor.

Pertinent to the requirements for a viable pepper spray delivery system is the fact that a statistically significant number of attacks occur from behind and in very close quarters. Men are not usually attacked for purposes of sexual assault. As a result, for men, that isn't typically a main concern. Women, however, are 10 times more likely to be attacked and, therefore, do have that concern. Thus, the needs of a woman for self-defense are unique.

Because a rapist usually tries to avoid witnesses and intends to engage in an act that is going to keep him at the scene for awhile, he will seek a lone female, grab her from the back to restrain her and keep her quiet. That means the woman has to be able to defend herself, if surprised by an enemy she may not necessarily be able to see. Thus, her aiming or accuracy in using a tool such as pepper spray has to be intuitive or instinctive; ergo, the design of Spitfire. Cardwell points out that one needs to be able to deploy pepper spray instinctively and accurately no matter from what direction the assault emanates. Figure 5.4 depicts a typical attack posture and resulting defense technique.

Figure 5.4

Mr. Cardwell points out that instinctive deployment of pepper spray at close range is a matter of the physiology of your hand, wrist and eye-hand coordination. So, holding the old style pepper spray canister with your wrist cocked and elbow bent, brought up to eye level is counter-intuitive and unnatural. If on the other hand you extend your forefinger or thumb and point, you can point directly at someone's eyes wherever they are. It becomes a natural extension of your hand and forearm. The Spitfire canister is ergonomically designed to lay in your hand allowing you to naturally point in the direction of attack so that your point of aim corresponds to point of impact. By setting the canister horizontally in your hand similar to a flashlight or hose nozzle, you don't have to be concerned with aiming because it is an automatic and natural reaction.

You push the trigger button forward and then press down when it is at its most forward position. A built-in automatic reset to the safety position occurs upon trigger button release. This safety spring-back mechanism is also unique to the industry. This prevents accidental discharges, a valid concern with most other pepper spray delivery systems.

Many pepper spray dispensers are inaccurate and limited ergonomically. Cardwell's simple test says that if you stand in front of a mirror and try to dispense the spray at the reflection of your head, you'll probably find that you cannot accurately do so. The chemical may be able to do its job, but without a reliably accurate delivery system, you will not disable your attacker. A pepper spray's effectiveness therefore relies on accurate delivery of the chemical agent to your attacker's face and head area where all of his mucous membranes are located.

In the darkness, where a visual cannot be made of the pepper spray stream, directional delivery is essential. Cardwell points out that the defender can have Spitfire in a "close ready hip position" from where it can be instantly and instinctively deployed. For example, a defender can have her "weak hand" up saying "Stop!" as a distraction and then deploy Spitfire with her "strong hand" from the ready waist level at the attacker's face. In addition, she can be turning her side toward the attacker so as to camouflage her strong shooting hand and begin her tactical retreat.

Flexibility in defensive fighting is essential to your survival and depends on your choice of tools. If you are grappling on the ground, it is necessary to be able to hold a pepper spray dispenser between your thumb and forefinger like a knife. So, Mr. Cardwell makes the point that Spitfire was designed and developed for a woman at night grabbed from behind with no one else around. Women can carry Spitfire with their keys in a close ready position when they feel vulnerable. Then, they can instinctively instantly react if the need should arise. Similar to firearms training, the key to success is all about accuracy and delivery with a good caliber bullet. Spitfire exemplifies those characteristics.

The Spitfire comes packaged with a practice canister to allow you to develop your defensive skills. The dispenser that supports the pepper spray canisters is reliable and refillable. The Spitfire's chemical spray is 10% OC concentration at 2,000,000 Scoville Heat Units (SHUs), which is police strength.

Spitfire also provides the user with a way to evaluate the canister level of active OC chemical agent so that you don't come up empty in a clutch (a.k.a., shooting blanks). It is called the "float test." The procedure is performed by simply dropping the pepper canister into water at room temperature. If it floats up and breaks the surface, refill it. If not, it is good to go. Spitfire pepper canisters work best for about 24 months. One should periodically check the expiration date printed on the canister and perform the Float Test regularly. Inexpensive pepper canister refills are available wherever you buy Spitfire.

In addition, Spitfire snaps free from your key ring for use in situations without turning off your car. You can orient it into its firing position by feel as you pull it free for quick spraying. It can then be snapped back together again for reuse.

In sum, pepper spray is an inexpensive tool that is available in most retail outlets. It makes a great stocking stuffer for the holiday season to give to those whom you care most about and Spitfire is the best non-lethal pepper spray product out there for assuring your survival.

▶ How can a cell phone be used to enhance my personal defense?

Short of hiring a security guard from Pinkerton's, a cell phone is your most mobile bet for continuous communications. It can provide a real lifeline when you need it most. Just dial 9-1-1.

It's a little known fact that even if you have terminated your service on an existing cell phone, as long as you keep the phone charged, "911" is always in immediate access. A cell phone is only as good as its carrier, so make sure yours has a strong signal.

▶ **How can a pen be used to enhance my personal defense?**

Any sharp or pointed object can be used as a self-defense tool in a clutch situation. A pen of course is such an object. We recommend no particular pen manufacturer. We leave it to the reader's imagination and discretion to ponder the myriad of ways for implementing effective "point" placement. However, a fountain pen has a sharp metal point. Leave the rest to your imagination.

There is also a specific product design that is worthy of mention. Imported from various sources is a knife-pen configuration which easily lends itself to portable defense and surprise counter-attack should the need arise. By simply removing the pen's cartridge holder and inverting it into the handle, you have a reliable 2½- to 3-inch blade that can surprise an offender and get you out of a lot of tight situations with a jab to the eye, up the nose, or straight into the eardrum. So, if you are attacked, reach out and touch someone in a pointed way. Figure 5.5 shows two pen-knife examples.

Figure 5.5

▶ **How can keys and other pocket or belt tools be adapted as a self-protection tool?**

Any pointed or hardened object such as keys, a screwdriver, a kubaton (a jabbing tool), a dog chain, or a belt buckle, held in a tightly clenched fist can offer whipping, slashing and jabbing options to your already expanding self-protection arsenal. A belt with a heavy buckle can certainly be used as an improvised "Mace" to clear and maintain a defensive radius. Blinding and bruising the offender are equivalent to buying yourself more time to use other defensive measures or to just tactically retreat and escape with your life. It is important for you to realize that in a pinch you can turn almost anything into a tool to help you survive.

▶ How can I safely use a knife for self-defense and protection?

Without years of dedicated martial arts or commando training, do not consider *knife fighting* a viable option in your self-defense plan arsenal. In close quarters combat (CQC), "mano a mano" with a practiced knife fighter, you probably don't have a good chance of winning the fight. However, the in-close slashing, jabbing and stabbing capabilities of a quality, carry-able, tactical folding knife do indeed supplement your close-in defensive options. If given the chance a skilled knife fighter can leave you seriously injured, if not dead, before you can respond. Your best defense is preventing the attacker from entering your defensive radius of 7 yards. Don't feel wimpy...it has been shown that even armed police have trouble with such foes.

But, remember, don't throw your knife. Forget the Jim Bowie movies and cartoons. Hold on to your tools. The security of your life means securing your tools. So, don't throw them away!

▶ How can I protect myself using sticks, canes, hands, feet, etc.?

A readily usable addition to your defensive toolkit is a sturdy, quality cane which offers a myriad of protective capabilities such as jabbing, hooking, striking, batting, tripping, etc. A broom handle, shovel, Louisville Slugger, hammer, ax, and plunger handle are some of the items which may be available in your home and which can be used to assure your survival in a clutch situation. Don't forget the golf club which can assure that you par your survival! If you are attacked near an automobile, you can also snap off an antenna and use it as a blackjack to jab at or whip your assailant.

A good smash with the heel, pointed toe of your shoe or boot onto an assailant's in-step can cause severe pain and/or cripple him. Also, don't forget what a well-aimed, good kick in the groin can do to cripple a male opponent. It's an instantaneous one strike and you're out!

Your hands also offer a viable multifaceted defense or combat tool. It's like opening a Swiss army knife—you can jab, poke, punch, tear, scratch, rip, squeeze, choke, twist, and even open bottles. Bottom line—don't give up the fight!

▶ What is a floor plan?

A floor plan is a reconstruction of the existing layout of your house—locations of entrances, windows, doors, skylights, exits, stairways, routes to and from safe rooms and family rooms, furniture, etc. Floor plan development is essential because no one knows the layout of your home better than you do. Use this knowledge to your tactical advantage. Recognize that any home intruder is at an immediate disadvantage on *your* turf. Another reason for plotting a floor plan is to eliminate any security deficiencies that may exist within your residence.

"Fatal Funnel of Fire." This term describes a triangular or funneled shaped area that covers the space funneling out from the point (or apex) where you are situated to the furthest and widest span from where an assailant could appear. It should be treated as a "no man's land." However, while you are not setting a trap since the fatal funnel exists already, the criminal knows that he is not allowed in this space, by violating it, he will have committed a fatal tactical error (a.k.a. "checkmate").

So, this space should be used tactically. You best control it from its apex. In other words, your best strategic response in the event of a home invasion is to stay put behind cover and concealment at the apex, and thus, make this funnel "fatal" for the home invader. This is also known as maintaining control of your defensive perimeters. A common and often **fatal** mistake is for the home defender to attempt to "clear the house" and locate the intruder. That's the most dangerous job and should be left to professionals, i.e., the police.

Thought also should be given to keeping a second set of house keys on a fluorescent key ring in your bedroom alongside your recharging cell phone. This will come in handy to throw out your window to the responding police when they arrive. (You have called "911," right?) Doing so can eliminate the dynamic entries that often demonstrate themselves with broken windows or doors torn from their hinges.

Never, repeat, *never* meet the police with *any* weapon in your hands. You know who the good guy is, but you cannot expect they will. Establish a code word with the police dispatcher; something to which the offender could not relate, and have the responding police call it out to you to let you, the homeowner, know the area has been secured. Several additional thoughts to keep in mind:

- Taped conversations with the 911 radio dispatcher often lend themselves as recorded evidence for securing convictions.
- Should you yell for help from a window, yell "FIRE!" Everyone jumps and immediately calls 911 when they hear "FIRE!" Also, everyone loves firemen. We wish we could say the same for everyone's feelings about police officers! In every social event Steve has ever attended, the first comment he's usually blasted with refers to a traffic violation!
- Consider your 911 dispatcher the calvary when your wagon train is surrounded.

▶ **Why should I get to know my neighborhood?**

Getting to know your neighborhood is important today because Mr. Rogers doesn't live here anymore. Today, we need a better response than Officers Tooty and Muldoon on *Car 54, Where Are You?*. Nowadays, getting to know your neighborhood means finding escape routes in the event of an emergency. It also informs you about who you are best able to reach out to, should the need arise. You want to know where your family can be the safest while awaiting the arrival of the authorities. You also want to know who and what areas to avoid. Additionally, if it's possible to get together with a few good neighbors to establish some sort of "Town Watch," all of you would be ahead of the game, or as otherwise defined, there's "strength in numbers."

6

Basics of Handguns Choosing and Handling; Maintaining

In this chapter, we cover the basics of handguns. The central importance of *safety* is emphasized throughout this chapter and throughout this book. We impart essential knowledge one needs to know in order to safely own and responsibly use a handgun, whether it be for the shooting sports or for personal defense, or both.

How Safety Begins. Safety starts by becoming well educated. As we stated earlier, power is knowledge, and knowledge is the basis for positive responsibility. The first step in safe firearm ownership and handling is accepting the responsibility for managing your safety and the safety of those around you. You must have the requisite knowledge.

Having a good informative book like this to read. The second or concurrent step is to take quality basic training from a competent NRA certified firearms instructor at a clean and safe shooting range. As part of this training, you will learn about the different types of firearms, their purposes, how they work, and you will become educated as to which one, or ones, are right for you.

Purchase Quality Equipment and Training. The next step involves purchasing a *quality* handgun. You are unlikely to go wrong with any of the products of the manufacturers we recommend in these pages. The watchword is *quality*. To be safe, you must have superior, dependable and reliable equipment. Such equipment is predictable and durable. That means it will do what it's supposed to do and not do what it isn't supposed to do.

You should only purchase from a reliable, educated dealer who knows about the equipment he or she sells and is willing to explain your choices, help you make an informed choice, and then introduce you to the basics of operating and maintaining your chosen firearm. Such a dealer is one who cares about you, the customer, and is a person to whom you can go back if you have a problem related to your firearm purchase. Remember the dealer's responsibility to be of help to you doesn't stop at the time of purchase, as long as you accept and manage your responsibilities.

Read the Operator's Manual. Next, after your purchase, you must read the manufacturer's operator's manual that comes with your handgun cover to cover. You must get to know your equipment well. You must know what it is capable of and what it cannot do. You must understand its mechanical operations and its limitations. You must learn how to use your gun and how to maintain it. You learn this by reading the manufacturer's operator's manual, working with a professional instructor, and reading this book.

Learn the Basic Rules of Safe Gun Handling. You must learn the basic rules of safe gun handling. Since they deserve repeating and further elaboration, we repeat them and go into them in more detail later on in this chapter. However, for starters, you must know that:

1. *You must treat every firearm as if it were always loaded* until you have checked to see that it isn't, or you have cleared the gun (more about this later). You never take it for granted that a gun is unloaded without checking that the gun is in fact not loaded. Then, every time you put a gun down, each time you pick it up again, you must recheck. Accidents have happened because someone was handling an "unloaded" gun, then put it down after being interrupted or distracted, and then picked it up again and didn't check it because he or she assumed it was unloaded.

2. *Guard the trigger!* Never put your finger on the trigger until you are ready to shoot. This is one of the most important safety rules. Guns do not discharge accidentally all by themselves unless someone or something pulls the trigger.

3. *You NEVER point the muzzle of a gun, loaded or unloaded at anyone, or in the direction where anyone might be*, including at yourself, *unless you intend to destroy the thing you are pointing at.* This must become a habit. You must always become aware of where you are pointing a gun you are handling.

4. *You always work with an unloaded gun when you are familiarizing yourself with the gun*, its operation, cleaning it, and/or readying it for storage. Ammunition

should always be kept separately from the firearm. The only time your gun should be loaded is when it is on duty. More about this later.

5. *No ammunition should be around when you are cleaning your gun.* All ammunition should be cleared from the cleaning area.

6. *You must make the appropriate arrangements to safely store your firearms.* It is your responsibility to prevent unauthorized access to them. That is why all new guns now come with trigger locks. Use them! Your firearms must always be locked up when not in use.

7. *You must obey all laws pertaining to firearms in your jurisdiction and state.*

8. If you are going to carry a gun (if it is legal in your jurisdiction) and you have a concealed carry permit, *you must learn safe carry techniques and use a safe, reliable holster.*

9. *You must always think SAFETY FIRST AND FOREMOST.* Guns are not toys. They are lethal weapons. To own a gun demands that you are capable of exercising the appropriate judgment to THINK AND PRACTICE SAFETY FIRST. Safe gun handling requires knowledge, self-control, focus, common sense, positive intent, positive thinking, good ethics, and positive responsibility.

10. *You must never allow yourself to get sloppy or lazy with your guns and gun handling.* You must maintain your firearms in good working order. That means keeping them clean and well lubricated by field-stripping and cleaning them regularly according to the manufacturer's factory specifications as explained in their operator's manual.

11. *You must always respect your firearm and respect other people's rights.* You must never do anything reckless or stupid or careless with your firearms to endanger yourself or anyone else.

Additional Safety Considerations

1. **Never** eat or have food or drink around when you are at the shooting range OR when you are cleaning your weapon. You don't want to ingest toxic lead residues, baked-on carbon deposits, grains of unburned gun powder, toxic cleaning solvents, etc. Grains of unburned gun powder look like pepper, but don't use them to spice up your food!
2. **Always** wear eye and ear protection when you are shooting or entering the range area! Even if you are not shooting you must protect your eyes and ears at all times from flying shrapnel and the crack and bang of gunfire.
3. **Only** use a holster for the specific gun the holster manufacturer made that holster for! If you ignore this rule, you are increasing your risk for an accidental discharge! It is sometimes tempting to holster a handgun in a holster built specifically for another gun because it seems to fit. But does it really? You may likely find that you cannot draw your gun very smoothly, or that the holster does not retain the weapon very well!

▶ **What is a handgun?**

A handgun is a concealable, portable firearm made by numerous manufacturers that can be fired with one or two hands, although two hands is the preferable mode of operation. It is the least effective of firearm defensive tools when compared to its big brothers, the shotgun and the rifle. Its most viable attribute is its concealability and portability due to its size.

▶ **What is a revolver?**

A *revolver* is a handgun that operates on a system of geometric progressions–that is, a system of springs and levers. It rotates a round of ammunition in a cylinder located between the barrel and the firing pin.

▶ **What are the parts of a revolver?**

A revolver has 4 main component parts:

1. The **barrel** contains rifling on its interior surface; also known as the lands and grooves. They give the bullet (a.k.a., the projectile) spin, trajectory and accuracy as it

is propelled out of the gun towards its target. The top front of the barrel is also the platform for the front sight used for aiming the revolver.

2. The **frame**. The barrel is threaded to the frame. The frame supports the internal mechanism (also called the "action") which encompasses the hammer, the firing pin, the trigger and the handle or grip. Integral to the frame is the trigger guard which surrounds the trigger and prevents outside forces from arbitrarily contacting the trigger. Also attached to the left side of the frame above the trigger is the cylinder release latch. This mechanism enables the operator to release the crane and cylinder to its loading or unloading position. Located on the rear of the frame's top strap in front of the hammer is the rear sight.

See Figure 6.1 for a picture of a typical double action revolver. It depicts a Smith & Wesson Model 66 stainless steel .38 special revolver with a 4-inch barrel.

Figure 6.1

Supported within the frame are the third and fourth main components; the crane and the cylinder.

3. The **crane** acts as a hinge for opening and closing the cylinder.

4. The **cylinder**, situated between the barrel and firing pin, contains the chambers which hold the ammunition, or "rounds." Cylinder capacities range anywhere between 5 to 9 rounds depending on the revolver's caliber, although the most common capacities are 5 or 6 rounds.

Located within the cylinder are two components that aid in the operation of unloading. These are the ejector rod and the star. The ejector rod attached to the star is a spring loaded mechanism that when pushed rearward ejects the empty casings (i.e., spent shells) from the cylinder.

▶ **How does a revolver work?**

There are two basic modes of operation of revolvers; *single action* and *double action*. These terms refer to the actions of the firearm and not *your* actions as the shooter.

Single Action. When you pull the hammer manually to its rearmost position so that it locks in place, it is said to be "cocked" in *single action* mode. Visual inspection of the trigger indicates that it also has moved to a rearward position much closer to the frame indicating that it will take much less pressure to release the hammer, thus firing the firearm. *Single action* refers to the fact that when the hammer is manually cocked and the trigger is pressed, it releases the hammer, thus the trigger is doing one action.

Double Action. *Double action* is the second basic mode of revolver operation. By pressing the trigger rearward, it *simultaneously* (1) cocks and (2) fires the firearm, hence the term "double action." That is, the hammer is cocked and released by squeezing the trigger all the way rearward, thus the trigger is doing two actions.

Internal to the revolver are two main components which complete these operations. On the recoil plate end of the frame which lies to the rear of the cylinder, a rectangular window holds in place a metal projection called the "hand." In either single or double action modes, the "hand" attaches itself to the "star" and its metal cutouts called "ratchets" which project rearward from the center of the rear face of the cylinder. These ratchets rotate the chambers in the cylinder which is situated between the barrel and the firing pin; ergo the term *revolver*.

▶ **How do revolvers vary?**

The most prominent attribute on a revolver that varies is the length of the barrel. It may range anywhere between 2 and 8 inches in length. What has to be recognized about barrel length is that the longer the barrel, the less recoil produced when the revolver is fired and the greater accuracy of the revolver at distances. In addition, weight is a second consideration; the heavier the weapon, the less the recoil.

Two-inch barrel length revolvers are commonly known as "snub noses" or "snubbies" and are the least accurate of revolvers at distances over 20 feet. They are colloquially called "belly guns" because they are well-suited for close-up work. As such, they lend themselves to deep concealment.

Four-inch barrel length revolvers are most common to police and military sidearm standard issue. They offer the best of both worlds; relative concealability and accuracy. Six-inch guns and longer are most often used by hunters, competitive shooters and for home defense.

Revolvers also vary in terms of having either exposed or internal hammers. Internal hammers tend not to get caught or snagged on clothing when drawn for personal defense. Thus, they are well suited for "deep cover" snubbies which can be carried in a pocket. Smith and Wesson, the world's premier manufacturer of quality revolvers, produces numerous examples of exposed, protected or shrouded, and internal hammers. After market customization work can also be done to remove the spur on the external hammer of a revolver. This is called bobbing the hammer.

Internal hammers are only double action as compared to the exposed hammers which can be operated in single or double action. "Shrouded hammers" have the same physical features as the revolver with an internal hammer, the only difference being the hammer is only 95% covered (i.e., shrouded) allowing both modes of operation.

The other variable is weight. Lightweight revolvers lend themselves to concealed carry. Smith and Wesson has several. These reliable weapons are either constructed from pure stainless steel, aluminum, titanium or scandium alloys; the latter two being the most lightweight and newest of Smith and Wesson's offerings.

▶ What is a pistol?

A handgun that has any mode of operation different from that of a revolver is called a *pistol*. Some examples are semi-automatic pistols, derringers, and single shot breech loaders such as the "Thompson Contender." Today, too many instructors intertwine the terms *pistol* and *revolver* using these terms generically. This is inaccurate because they have totally different operating modes. In addition, pistols encompass the category of semi-automatic handguns. All semi-auto handguns are pistols, but not all pistols are semi-automatic. For example, derringers are single action pistols that are not revolvers. They are usually one or two shot (single or double barrel) single action pocket handguns. To operate them, you have to cock the hammer before you squeeze the trigger and fire the gun.

▶ **What is a semi-automatic pistol?**

A semi-automatic pistol is a pistol that is either *spring recoil operated* or *gas operated*. Both mechanisms are driven by ammunition pressures. A semi-automatic pistol is automatically *self-loading* after each shot until both the magazine and barrel chamber are empty. However, when you fire a round by pressing the trigger, you cannot fire another round until you let the trigger go (so that it can reset) and then press it again. The semi-auto's mechanical operation is described in more detail below.

▶ **How does a semi-automatic pistol work?**

A semi-automatic pistol usually has 4 main component parts. These are: (1) the magazine, often called the "heart" of the pistol, (2) the frame, (3) the slide, and (4) the barrel/guide rod assembly.

The magazine has 4 component parts. These are:

1. The **tube**, which is the frame of the magazine that supports all of its other components;

2. The **follower**, which supports the rounds and, on a quality semi-auto pistol, locks the weapon out of battery once the last round has been discharged.

3. Below the follower is the **spring**, which supports the ammunition weight and pressures rounds upwards to be fed by the follower into the chamber each time the weapon is charged.

4. Finally, the **floorplate**, which secures the bottom section of the magazine tube and the components contained therein. A magazine's operation can be best compared with that of a Pez dispenser.

In Battery/Out Of Battery

At this point, the terms *in battery* and *out of battery* must be discussed. Starting with "out of battery," which means the slide is locked to the rear and the weapon cannot be fired until the slide has been released to its most forward position, which is called "in battery."

To put a pistol "*out of battery*":

1. Pull the slide back to its most rearward position, if there is **no** magazine in the magazine well, push up on the slide stop lever (the mechanical lever that locks the slide rearward out of battery) to lock the slide in place rearward.

2. Pull the slide rearward on the slide's friction grooves (i.e., the serrations at the rear of the slide that allow gripping), if an **empty** magazine is fully seated in the magazine well in the grip, until the slide locks in place in its rearmost position.

Some blow-back operated, semi-automatic pistols and inexpensively manufactured pistols will not lock out of battery once the last round is fired because they do not have a slide stop lever. Thus, some inexpensively made pistols cannot be charged from the out of battery position because that feature is lacking.

Note. You do not want to lock a slide out of battery if there is a loaded magazine in the magazine well. The reason is that when you go to put the gun back into battery (read on), it will chamber a round.

To put the gun "*into battery*" there are three operational methods:

1. If there is **no magazine** inserted, pull the slide rearward by the slide's friction grooves as far as it will go, thus disconnecting the slide stop, and then let the slide go forward. This allows the compressed internal spring of the guide rod to propel the slide forward to the in battery position.

2. If there is an **empty magazine** inserted, pull the slide slightly rearward by the slide's friction grooves and press downward on the slide stop lever. This disconnects the slide stop when you let the slide go while still holding the slide stop lever down.

3. If there is a **loaded magazine** inserted, pull the slide rearward and then let it go forward. Putting the gun back into battery in this way will chamber a round.

Note. The *incorrect* way of loading from the out of battery position is to just press down on the slide stop lever and let the slide go forward from its own momentum. It will work, but repeatedly doing it in this way will cause material fatigue to the slide and the lever mechanisms. That is because the semi-automatic pistol needs the heavy spring action that is produced by the correct method of pulling back on the slide to allow the compressed internal spring of the guide rod to propel the slide forward to the in battery position and reliably chamber a round.

Each and every time you load from the out of battery position in the **correct** way, you are manually duplicating the automatic slide spring action that occurs during the regular firing sequence of the semi-automatic pistol. The gas pressures in the chamber and the pressure of the recoil spring assembly automatically rack the slide again by sending it rearward and then propelling it forward back into battery chambering another round.

In other words, when a semi-automatic pistol with a round in the chamber and a backup round in the magazine is fired by pressing the trigger, the sequence of automatic mechanical operations is identical to our correct manual loading procedure!

Thus, a semi-automatic pistol is *self-loading*, and so, it will not fire a round until you, the operator, let the trigger go (or reset) and then press it again. In contrast, a fully automatic pistol is automatically self-loading once you press the trigger, period. Once you press the trigger, the gun will fire the chambered round and then automatically chamber and fire all of the remaining rounds in the magazine until the magazine is empty of rounds.

Blow-Back Operation

On semi-automatic pistols, *blow-back* operation is defined as follows: The circulatory gases produced by the ignited ammunition propel the slide rearward ejecting the empty cartridge casing. In blow-back operated slides, the pistol's barrel remains stationary and is attached to the frame (a.k.a., receiver). Blow-back systems do not incorporate an *extractor* but they do indeed have an *ejector* in place.

Recoil Spring/Locked Breech Operation

With recoil spring operated extraction in a pistol, it is the compression of the guide rod spring assembly in the slide *in addition* to the extractor that unloads and reloads the pistol mechanically. Empty cartridge casings are ejected from the ejection port and the pistol reloads mechanically as a result of recoil spring tension as opposed to compressed gases from the ignited ammunition. In the recoil spring operated pistol, the barrel is confined between the recoil spring assembly and the slide, and thus, the barrel is free floating which means that it is not stationary but instead, mechanically moves with the slide.

In the "in battery" position (slide forward), the barrel's breech (rear end) is locked by the connection between the barrel lug (on the underside of the barrel) and the locking block on the receiver or frame.

Single vs. Double Action

Similar to the actions of revolvers, semi-automatic pistols come in both *single action* and *double action* modes.

Single Action Semi-Automatic Pistols. As with a revolver, with a *single action* semi-automatic pistol, you have to first cock the hammer before you can press the trigger to fire the chambered round. However, unlike a single action revolver where you have to hand load your rounds into the cylinder's chambers, with a single action semi-automatic, you have to rack the slide to chamber the top round from the magazine and thus, "charge the weapon." This cocks the hammer, thus readying the single action pistol for the first shot.

The most common single action semi-auto pistol design is the "1911 design" which was pioneered by the visionary gunsmith, John Moses Browning in collaboration with Colt

Firearms in 1911. The original Colt Government Model 1911 and its numerous re-designs, copies and iterations since 1911 have a manual mechanical safety located on the frame or receiver under the rear of the slide. When the hammer is cocked, this safety must be engaged by pushing it into its uppermost position so that the pistol is safely *"cocked and locked."*

In addition, these models also have a "grip safety" on the backstrap under and behind the manual mechanical safety. It is necessary to compress this grip safety inward into the backstrap with a full grip to release the hammer and fire the weapon once the manual mechanical safety is disengaged and the trigger is pressed. Many quality 1911 style single action semi-autos also have an internal firing pin safety mechanism to prevent an accidental discharge should the weapon be dropped.

Once the first round is fired, the slide is cycled, the next round in the magazine is chambered, and the hammer is automatically cocked, thus readying the pistol for the next shot. To fire that second chambered round, the operator simply has to press (squeeze) the trigger. All subsequent rounds are chambered, fired, and cycled in the same way until the pistol is empty. To put the pistol into "safe mode," the manual mechanical safety must be engaged.

Major Manufacturers of Quality 1911 Style Single Action Semi-Automatic Pistols

Colt Manufacturing Company	800-236-6311 or 800-962-COLT	www.colt.com
Kimber	800-880-2418	www.kimberamerica.com
Para-Ordnance Manufacturing, Inc.	416-297-7855	www.paraord.com
Springfield Armory	800-680-6866	www.springfieldarmory.com

We strongly recommend that you peruse their web sites.

Double Action Semi-Automatic Pistols. In a *double action* semi-automatic, the trigger performs two tasks. It cocks the hammer or internal firing mechanism for the first shot, and also releases the hammer or the internal firing mechanism.

In a *double-action-only* semi-automatic, the trigger will cock and release the hammer or internal firing mechanism on the first shot and all consecutive shots. The slide will chamber a new cartridge after each shot, as it does for the other types of semi-automatic actions, but it will *not* cock the hammer or internal firing mechanism. The cock and release action is accomplished by pulling the trigger for each shot. In this way, the action of the trigger is similar to that of a double-action revolver. However, in most double-action-only semi-automatics, the hammer cannot be manually cocked to a single-action position as it can in a double-action revolver.

Due to the large variety of mechanical designs available for semi-automatic pistols, always be sure to carefully read and understand the instruction manual. If questions still exist, be sure to consult a knowledgeable person.

Trigger pull or pressure is much heavier with double action than with single action. What this means is that with a DA pistol, the trigger pull is much heavier in the first double action shot. Then, after that first shot is fired, the trigger pull or trigger pressure required to take the remaining single action mode shots is much lighter.

Despite the differences in their mechanical operations, pistols and revolvers ultimately accomplish the same thing. A revolver's loaded cylinder rotates within the space between the barrel and firing pin, while the forward motion of a semi's slide strips a live round off the top of the magazine and feeds it into the breech end of the barrel, allowing for either single or double action firing.

Differing from a revolver in unloading and recharging, the semi-auto's slide has an internal attachment called the extractor. The extractor removes the spent casing from the barrel's breech moving it rearward to a secondary component called the ejector. The ejector redirects the empty casing through a cutout on the slide commonly called the ejection port. So, differing from a revolver where you manually unload the spent casings from the chambers of the cylinder, a semi-auto expends the empty cases out and away from your body. The semi-auto loads, fires, extracts and ejects the empty casings and reloads with one pull of the trigger. That sequence of operations continues until the magazine's rounds have been exhausted, hence the term semi-automatic pistol.

▶ **What's the difference between a semi-automatic and an automatic pistol?**

The two terms are often confused. A fully automatic pistol is commonly known as a submachine gun. Submachine guns are called such because they strictly fire handgun calibers, hence the "sub" prefix. They can be rifles, carbines (i.e., short-barreled rifles), or handguns. Light machine guns on the other hand are rifles or carbines and always fire rifle calibers. They are magazine fed. Heavy machine guns are fixed to either a tripod or an armored vehicle and are always belt-fed.

Fully automatic means that when the trigger is pressed, the weapon will continuously fire until the trigger is released or the magazine is exhausted.

▶ **Should I own a handgun?**

Since you are reading this book, you probably either already own one (or more), or you are considering the purchase of a handgun. But let's consider a few issues. Because you are taking the time to read this guide, you are willing to face the facts. You, our dear reader, are probably not the initial aggressor if you agree with our philosophy of self-defense and survival. So...how important is your life to you and what measures will you take to protect it?

Education is power and power leads to a defensive perimeter that is extremely hard to penetrate. Firearms are but one avenue in a totally personal decision. This is why we have also taken the time to explain other sources of non-lethal protection that you can feel confident about. The measures you choose may eventually determine the life or death of yourself or a loved one. Make your decisions based on information not emotion.

You are only trapped as long as you believe you have no choices. Once you recognize there are choices out there, you are no longer trapped. Indecision, especially about survival, is not conducive to survival. In general, it is, at the least, non-productive and, at the worst, it can be crippling.

It is important to recognize that owning a firearm is a right granted by our forefathers in our Constitution, but along with it, comes awesome responsibility. One must become educated enough about personal self-defense, about firearms in general, and the particular firearm one chooses. Plus, there are legalities attached to owning and carrying a firearm that must be understood thoroughly enough to obey the law and be responsible. As stated earlier, ignorance is not bliss, and is no excuse for a mistake. With firearms, mistakes can be lethal and disastrous.

▶ What are the basic rules of handgun safety?

Contrary to what some "anti-gun," "gun-control," and "gun-ban" advocates and politicians would have people erroneously believe, accidental deaths involving firearms actually constitute only a minuscule percentage of all deaths ruled as accidental. In fact, in 1999, the figure was 1%, based on the National Safety Council's 2000 report, "Injury Facts." In many of these cases, the ways in which the news media reported these tragedies could lead some people to believe that the firearms somehow discharged by themselves!

The truth is that firearms cannot "go off" or discharge by themselves—someone has to be careless or irresponsible to cause an "unintentional discharge" and a tragic gun accident. That's why safe firearm handling and gun safety must be the first consideration whenever someone handles a firearm. Safety must become ingrained and habitual for anyone who chooses to own a firearm.

We have developed an acronym for being and staying S-A-F-E-S-T. It will help you to remember the basic, rules of firearm safety so that you ALWAYS employ these rules automatically *every time* you pick up *any* firearm. It takes a nanosecond to make a mistake, but a lifetime, or never, to recover from one.

Stay *S-A-F-E-S-T* and stay alive!

Safe direction.

Always point the muzzle of any firearm in a *safe direction*. Never point the muzzle of a handgun or any firearm at anything you do not intend to destroy.

Always loaded.

Treat every firearm as if it is *always loaded*. Every time you pick up any firearm you should check to make sure that it is empty of any ammunition.

Focus your attention.

Use your head. Whenever you're handling any firearm, you must concentrate and *focus* on what you are doing. You must not let yourself become distracted. Whenever you carry a firearm on your person, you must always remain mindful of its security.

Environmental awareness and security.

You must securely store all of your firearms when you are not carrying, cleaning or using them to prevent them from getting unsolicited exposure. Always be aware of who is around you in your *immediate environment* when you are handling your firearm. Remember that you cannot take back a mistake.

Sure of your target and what is behind it.

Always be sure that what you are shooting at is in fact what you intend to shoot! Never practice shooting in areas not designated for shooting. Bullets can hit something you don't want to hit that is behind and beyond your target. Fired bullets may even pass through many types of walls, and can travel hundreds of feet. The implication is obvious.

Trigger guard.

Keep your trigger finger off the trigger and outside of the trigger guard until you are ready to shoot. The gun cannot discharge unless the trigger is depressed.

Take the time **to read, understand, memorize and follow all 6 of the safety steps.**

By doing so, you will enjoy shooting, prevent accidents, and survive.

This responsibility must be continually taken very seriously. There is no room for error. There is no such thing as a foolproof gun; only fools would try to delude themselves into believing that there is or can be. There is no substitute for your personal responsibility and common sense in the handling, use, and storage of firearms.

The survival equation is:

Personal Responsibility
+ Knowledge
+ Safe Gun Handling
= Gun Safety and Survival

Accidents are the result of human error resulting from neglect of the basic rules of firearms safety. Therefore, it is your responsibility to prevent accidents. You cannot afford to have a firearms-related accident!

▶ **Are there any exceptions to these rules?**

The answer is unequivocally **NONE**. No exceptions!

▶ **What type of handgun is right for me?**

Different situations demand different levels of protection. Manufacturers therefore design specific types of handguns to meet the specific needs of different situations (i.e., law enforcement, military, plainclothes undercover, and civilian). We will endeavor to make you aware of quality handguns that are currently available and that range from sub-compact through compact pistols into intermediate and full-size service sidearms.

With varying climactic situations, weight, clothing and concealability are considerations that must be taken into account in deciding what type of handgun is right for you. For example, winter months lend themselves, due to the heavy layers of clothing worn, to carrying the larger handguns. However, weight and comfort are still considerations. On the other hand, summer months lend themselves, due to the minimal clothing worn, to carrying small, reliable, sub-compacts.

No one specific firearm can possibly cover all of your defensive needs in every situation. In order to best guide you through the myriad of firearms on the current market, our recommendations are based on professional and practical evaluations, and on circumstances you may encounter. It is also important to take into account your particular body size and hand size, as well as the types of clothes you typically wear, the settings in which you work and that you inhabit, and your physical abilities and disabilities.

▶ **Should I purchase a subcompact handgun?**

Subcompact pistols present a non-intrusive way of carrying a concealed firearm given their minimal weight and size. However, when relying on a sub-compact pistol, quality has to be the primary consideration in making your choice. With size reduction, often comes bullet caliber reduction. As such, you want the most dependable handgun you can depend on in meeting and prevailing against any unsolicited threat or attack.

There is an ongoing debate in the field of firearms self-defense and even in law enforcement about what is the minimal caliber suitable for self-defense. The bottom line is that in a tactical situation, you are going to bank on the element of surprise so that you can escape. A well-concealed subcompact, until it is needed, gives you that opportunity. It's much more effective to reach for a .32 caliber subcompact than a pocketful of air.

If you are in law enforcement, and you wisely choose to carry a defensive backup gun, it is essential that you also choose a subcompact that is of the highest quality. Sound decisions based on bad quality are self-defeating. So, open your eyes and smell the roses. Don't die in the line of duty, survive it.

Gun Dealers: Weapon Manufacturers

L.W. Seecamp *(Milford, CT. Tel: 203-877-7926; Fax: 203-877-3429).* In our personal experience with superior quality, highly concealable subcompact handguns through training and use in actual survival incidents, one product line jumps to the pinnacle—Seecamp. The L.W. Seecamp .32 caliber double action only, blow-back operated, sub-compact pistol is a very high quality handmade pocket pistol that is given so much professional attention at the factory, you would swear it was custom jewelry designed for Tiffany's or Bailey, Banks and Biddle. See Figure 6.2. The Seecamp .32 ACP pistol is pictured at the left of the line-up. The other two from left to right are the North American Arms .32 caliber "Guardian" and the Beretta .32 caliber "Tomcat."

There are many professionals, politicians, and entertainers who, due to their public exposure, are potentially high profile targets. Many such individuals feel the need for a highly discreet and reliable carry firearm to increase their comfort level in different situations, from the board room to the golf course, or from Hollywood to New York or Washington, D.C. You owe yourself that same level of prudent protection you gain with the quality exhibited by a Mercedes or a Hummer. L.W. Seecamp's .32 caliber subcompact semi-automatic pistols provide that same level of distinguished, discreet protection and reliability.

Figure 6.2

The Seecamp has no sights to get snagged in your pocket. It is meant to be pointed at the target and shot one-handed instinctively ("point shooting" is discussed in detail later). It is a gun for close-quarters tactical defense. It's an "in-your-face" gun or "belly gun." However, given its precision construction, it is an accurate shooter and can be **accurately** shot to point of aim with practice at up to 7 yards. Please note that, as with any firearm, to be able to shoot the Seecamp effectively and "instinctively," requires lots of practice.

North American Arms. N.A.A. of Provo, Utah *(800-821-5783 www.naaminis.com)* produces a variety of subcompact firearms that include highly concealable revolvers and semi-automatic pistols. Built to quality specifications, N.A.A.'s product line reflects a well thought-out process of engineering for maximum reliability of operation and concealability.

N.A.A.'s semi-automatic, double action only blow-back operated, sub-compact pistol, the Guardian, is produced in two caliber sizes, .32 and .380 (See Figure 6.2). This gives any user a viable alternative in effective defensive concealed carry preparation. Like the Seecamp, the Guardian pistols are designed to be pointed at the target and shot one-handed. They are guns for close-quarters tactical defense. However, they do have rudimentary front and rear sights that come standard, and custom sights (e.g., Novak low profile night sights and Express 24/7 big dot front night sights) can be added by the factory after purchase. These pistols are a little bigger than the Seecamp, and as such, they can also be shot with a two-handed grip using the front sight to aim.

N.A.A.'s line of mini-revolvers, most commonly in our experience, lend themselves to concealed carry in a vest, jacket, pants or skirt pocket, or on a keychain, belt buckle or necklace. These mini-revolvers are a highly concealable, reliable, and safe form of self-defense with single action operation. They are only meant for close-up work and are true "belly" or "in-your-face" self-defense guns. Mini-revolver calibers are confined to .22 (short, long, long rifle, and magnum). The .22 magnum distinguishes itself from the pack of other .22 calibers in performance. The N.A.A. Black Widow .22 magnum will give the bad guy true arachnophobia.

N.A.A.'s defensive products are affordable, non-intrusive and reliable to every tactical defense consumer who doesn't need or want to become "Dirty Harry." All professionals will appreciate the ease of carry, ease of presentation, and ease of operation of these weapons should the need arise. N.A.A. is the "Britney Spears" of the gun world—great lines, shape, size, looks, achievement, and performance.

Beretta U.S.A. *(301-283-2191; www.berettausa.com).* Within the numerous feline products manufactured by Beretta U.S.A. Corporation, the Beretta Tomcat .32 caliber ACP sub-compact pistol must be considered for several innovative and practical considerations. This kitten certainly hisses at criminal aggression or attack! See Figure 6.2.

For the inexperienced firearm shooter, it is the easiest and safest firearm in determining its loaded cartridge status with the manual barrel release and pop-up feature that exposes a live or empty chamber. The experienced professional or the novice can determine quickly if the firearm is loaded or not. In addition, with that system of operation, one can place a fully-loaded magazine in the magazine well, expose the barrel chamber to the manually open position, load the top off round, close the barrel and be ready for engagement without having to cycle the slide.

This firearm is accurate, reliable, and effective in close quarters. It also comes in four finishes—stainless steel, black matte, high gloss blue, or titanium (with stainless steel slide and barrel). Beretta also produces a limited production model especially worthy of mention and consideration. Formerly designated the "Alleycat" and now called the "Tomcat Tritium," this pistol has eyes that glow in the dark with its XS Express Sights Systems Big Dot tritium front nightsight. This feature makes it notably easier to point and shoot.

Like the Seecamp and Guardian pistols, the Tomcat is designed to be pointed at the target and shot one-handed. It is for close-quarters tactical defense. However, the Tomcat's slightly large size and width and its front and rear sights make it easy to shoot with a two-handed grip using the front sight to aim. Additionally, while the Seecamp and Guardians are *double action only* (DAO), the Beretta Tomcat is *double action* on the first shot and *single action* on all subsequent shots. This provides for greater accuracy and longer distances. **Note:** It is recommended that, since the Tomcat has an inertia type firing pin, it be carried with **the manual mechanical safety on** and the hammer in the half-cocked position. This assures the greatest degree of safety with a loaded chamber because it places the hammer in an intermediate "drop catch" position. The weapon does not have a drop safety. So, the manual safety must always be engaged, and with the hammer half-cocked in the drop catch position, this adds an extra measure of safety should the pistol be dropped or there be a sharp blow to the hammer spur.

The Beretta name has been world renowned since the 16th century in Italy, and is recognized for its products' quality in design and function as well as its reliable worldwide customer service policies and attentiveness. The Tomcat is a fine edition to the Beretta litter and to the sub-compact category of highly concealable self-defense handguns. Cathy Williams, Beretta U.S.A.'s Advertising and Communications Manager, professionally assisted our efforts in presenting to you updated and accurate information relating to the Beretta product line.

Kel-Tec *(321-631-0068; www.kel-tec.com)*. Kel-Tec CNC Industries Inc, founded in 1991 in Cocoa, Florida, initially as a machine shop, started to manufacture firearms in 1995. The company specializes in handguns for concealed carry by law enforcement personnel and licensed civilians. Kel-Tec is also gradually diversifying into home defense rifles with the production of their Sub-2000 carbine which comes in both 9mm and .40 S&W caliber versions.

The Kel-Tec "P-32" is a semi-automatic, locked breech double action only pistol, chambered for the .32 ACP cartridge. The magazine has a 7 round capacity, but Kel-Tec now makes and sells a high capacity 10 round magazine. The P-32 is definitely the lightest and thinnest .32 auto pistol ever made, coming in at just over 9.4 ounces with a fully loaded magazine and a round in the chamber. This makes it ideal for concealed pocket carry. High Noon Holsters and Stellar Rigs make excellent pocket holsters with a spare magazine pouch for this gun, and Kel-Tec makes an easy to install waist band carry clip that makes use of a holster unnecessary.

This little pistol is ergonomic, accurate, and has minimal perceived recoil. The small grip size and light but long trigger pull make the P-32 ideal for female shooters.

The P-32 is a very affordably priced gun that is made of quality materials; a high carbon steel slide and barrel, a rectangular frame machined from solid 7075-T6 aluminum, and a grip made of ultra high impact polymer. A hammer block safely holds the hammer away from the firing pin in the decocked position. It can be easily shot two-handed or one-handed and like the other pocket pistols discussed, it is definitely a "point and shoot," deep concealment carry gun.

Summary. Please note that each of the four pocket pistols recommended is very unique. You really need to handle and try them out if possible to help you evaluate which one is best for you. They all shoot differently. The Beretta Tomcat is the only double action/single action of the four. The other three are double action only.

The Tomcat is the beefiest. For some people, this makes it easier to shoot, and it certainly is more suitable than the rest for shooting with a two-handed grip. It has a steel slide and a high strength aluminum alloy frame. It is an excellent weapon.

The Seecamp is the smallest of the group, the second lightest in weight and the most concealable weapon. It is all stainless steel. Of the group, the Seecamp is most suited for point shooting, and it purposely has no sights. It has a heavier trigger pull than do the Beretta Tomcat and the Kel-Tec P-32. However, the trigger pull is not as heavy as that of the Guardian .32 or .380. The Seecamp is a handmade work of art and really is in a class all by itself. It is a gun you may want to hand down to your children or put in your will. It is very reliable and accurate.

The N.A.A. Guardian .32 is slightly bigger than the Seecamp, all stainless steel, and it does come with rudimentary sights. The Guardian .380, which fires the larger and more powerful .380 ACP round (9mm short) is bigger yet. The Guardians are nice guns and reliable.

The Kel-Tec P-32 is the most lightweight and the thinnest little pocket pistol. It is also the most affordable. Another advantage it offers is that Kel-Tec makes 10-round magazines for it. Imagine carrying a lightweight super thin pocket pistol weighing under 10 ounces loaded with 11 rounds and with a spare 10-round magazine! That's 21 rounds in your pocket! And you can do this when you carry your Kel-Tec P-32 in a Stellar Rigs kydex pocket holster.

In sum, the four sub-compact pocket pistol products discussed above are the most prominent in excellence and deserving of recommendation for their quality, reliability of operation, and ease of concealed carry. They are absolutely the industry's leaders and unaffected by seasonal changes. You can carry them any time of year, any place, in any mode of dress, and in any climactic environment feeling confident that you will survive from the Amazon to the Antarctic. Of course, they are especially welcome in hot or tropical climates where stripping down your clothing layers also strips down your defensive weapon concealment options.

▶ Why do we recommend certain product lines?

At this juncture, it is probably important to understand why we recommend certain product lines. Our judgments are based in several objective, factual criteria. These are: quality, sound operation, and accessibility of corporate staff for questions and repair issues. In our experiences, both practical and in writing this text, we have found that the manufacturers listed have been readily accessible, friendly, and a wealth of information on all topics pertinent to their product line.

The most important value of any product line is being able to discuss life-important issues relative to your firearm or related product with the people who design and produce that product. These manufacturers have been open and willing at every opportunity to assist us, and we're sure that they will be just as responsive to you, the purchasing public. Additionally, we base our evaluations on field-testing and operation of the items listed for their practical concealability, ease of operation, functionality, reliability, and ease of maintenance.

Too many of our students or colleagues have reported that, at one time or another, they were misled into purchasing a poor quality firearm. They were surprised to discover that they had purchased a "rock" as opposed to a "protective element"; meaning a firearm of little value that was inaccurate, unreliable, hard to upgrade, hard to maintain, hard to repair, and hard to unload.

Our purpose is to save you the personal and financial expense of being stuck with a "lemon" or "rock," erroneously believing that your life can be protected by a faulty or sub-standard product. That is a false sense of confidence and security which can lead to your demise and thus, is dangerous. There is no substitute for quality. The few dollars more you spend purchasing quality products exponentially can facilitate your practical training experiences, your development as a safe shooter, your shooting enjoyment, and in the bargain, increase your life span.

▶ Should I purchase a compact handgun?

A recommendable compact handgun provides a high measure of concealability, reliability, accuracy, and functionality as do all the other categories listed. A quality compact handgun is an easily concealable firearm that you are comfortable carrying in a quality holster on your hip, or if it is small enough, in your pocket. Some of the manufacturers that meet the aforementioned criteria for semi-automatic pistols, in our opinion, are: Heckler & Koch, SIGARMS, Glock, Kahr Arms, Beretta USA, and Smith and Wesson. Manufacturers who, in our opinion, meet the aforementioned criteria for revolvers are of course, Smith and Wesson, who present a very wide product array, and Sturm, Ruger & Company.

Heckler & Koch *(703-450-1900; www.hecklerkoch-usa.com).* As a practical measure, for dignitary protection, law enforcement operations and civilian concealed carry, Heckler & Koch (HK) jumps to the top of our list as a world-class operation. The intelligent thought process behind the design, functionality, reliability and safety of HK's high quality line of **U**niversal **S**elf-loading **P**istols (USP's) has been proven world-wide to be unchallenged. They are made both in compact and full-size versions; with the compact USPs having a shorter barrel length and shorter grip. The USP compacts come in the following calibers: 9mm, 40 S&W, .357 SIG, and .45 ACP. They are based on the full-size USPs.

The HK USP compacts are built with ergonomic, narrow grips and polymer frames that are supported with steel inserts at high stress points. The slides are high carbon or stainless steel. The hammers are bobbed so that they won't snag.

The USPs have a frame-mounted decocker and mechanical manual safety lever that allow for carry in two modes; (1) hammer fully down, safety on or off; double action mode wherein the first shot is traditional double action and subsequent shots are single action; and (2) "cocked and locked"; hammer fully cocked and safety "on." The safety/decocker allows you to fully decock the hammer from its fully cocked position and then put the gun into safe mode. The USPs also come in Double Action Only (DAO) Law Enforcement Models (LEMs) without the decocker/safety lever.

From Navy Seal teams to government agents, to the stay-at-home mom, HK has consistently provided that extra measure of reliability and security that professionals as well as defense-oriented civilians depend on routinely in a firearm. Often quoted as being the Rolls Royce of manufacturers, HK has an unsurpassed product line. Their web site depicts all of their models.

You cannot go wrong giving serious attention to considering HK's compact product line of double action semi-auto pistols. From the extremely compact 9mm P7M8 to the USP compact series, quality and reliability greet you with each and every model.

Please note that the size and ergonomics of the HK USP compacts make it possible to point shoot them one-handed if you have to in a pinch, although they are best shot with a two-handed grip using the sights.

SIGARMS *(603-772-2302; www.sigarms.com).* SIGARMS of Exeter, New Hampshire, is a prominent supplier of military and law enforcement sidearms throughout the world. The precision, ease of operation, and functionality of their double-action, semi-automatic pistols make them a favorite of many defensive shooters. Throughout SIG's long history, quality has always been their most prized code of conduct. SIGARMS manufactures accurate and reliable, compact sidearms constructed to the highest European (a.k.a., the world's) standards. They fit the needs of professionals and civilians.

Several compact SIGARMS "SIG Sauer" double-action models which we recommend highly based on both our personal ownership and tactical use, are the .380 caliber SIG-Sauer P-232, the 9mm P-

228, the P-229 and P-239 which come in 9 mm, .40 caliber and .357 SIG, and the P-245, a superior, compact .45 caliber entry. SIG is the "BMW" of the firearms world. Their web site depicts all of their models.

Like the HKs, the size and ergonomics of the compact SIG Sauers make it possible to point shoot them one-handed if you have to in a pinch, although they, too, are best shot with a two-handed grip using the sights.

We love our compact .45 caliber SIG Sauer P245's for their accuracy, shootability, power, portability and concealability. As the P245 is built and operates on the same principles as its older, full-size cousin, the .45 caliber P220, we shall explain the construction and operation of the amazing SIG P220 sub-sequently.

The SIG Sauer P239 is a great concealed carry weapon. It comes in 9mm, .40 S & W, and .357 SIG firepower in either a rust-resistant Nitron finished package or Two-Tone. Its compact, slim profile, given its 8-round capacity single stack magazine (in 9mm) or 7-round capacity single stack magazine (in .357 SIG or .40 S & W), provides excellent ergonomics and handling characteristics for shooters with small or large hands. While magazines are caliber specific, the .357 SIG and .40 S & W barrels can be interchanged in the P239. This is a gun to take just about anywhere it is legal to carry in all four seasons.

Glock *(770-432-1202; www.glock.com).* A personal favorite in our stable of thoroughbreds is the Glock semi-automatic pistol line. Having kept Steve personally secure during tactical, police, dignitary protection and investigative activities, his Glock sidearm has always provided him with an unsurpassed level of comfort. Being one of the first law enforcement officers in the country to purchase and carry one on active duty, his personal G-17 has over 175,000 rounds through it without a single mal-function. Glock, with its sheer simplicity, durability, reliability, accuracy, longevity, and affordability leads us to think of it as the Chevrolet of the firearms market. It is affordable for every-one, and therefore every self-defense minded civilian and law enforcement professional should have one on their person, in their residence, and in their garage.

Having an ever improving and expanding caliber line of pistols since its inception in the 1980's, Glock has taken over as the standard police duty sidearm and backup gun of choice. Glock models that well fit the compact model category are the Glock 26 in 9 mm, Glock 27 in .40 caliber, Glock 19 in 9 mm,

Glock 23 in .40 caliber, Glock 30 and the newer Glock 36 in .45 ACP, Glock 32 and 33 in .357 SIG, and the Glock 29 in 10 mm.

Baby Glocks. Actually the Glock 26, 27, and 33 are sub-compacts and are affectionately termed, "baby Glocks" or mini-Glocks. They do lend themselves with training and practice to one-handed point shoulder shooting, although they are best shot with a two-handed grip.

Compact Glocks. The *compact* Glocks 19, 23, 29, 30, and 32 are best shot with a two-handed grip, but again in a pinch can be handled one-handed.

No matter which Glock model you choose, all calibers and sizes are as accurate and reliable, and fun to shoot, as the original 9 mm Glock 17. You'll never see a Glock rust or fail to operate in any climactic conditions. Also, through Glock's Sport Shooting Foundation (GSSF), Glock genuinely supports shooters and their interests through regularly scheduled sporting competition shooting events, a quarterly news publication, and making available at an affordable price, their firearms and accessories. This sets an industry wide example of excellence and customer satisfaction.

We would never hesitate to carry a Glock pistol for personal defense into any situation. We feel that we can rely on our Glocks never to let us down.

The simplicity of the Glock's design and their ease of maintenance provide any firearms instructor with an excellent tool for opening a student's wide eyes to the virtues of ease and simplicity in a handgun. A Glock 23 compact pistol makes an excellent first semi-automatic pistol, and second, and third, and... It provides a gentle and manageable introduction to the world of semi-autos given its ease of operation and maintenance. Miraculously that first Glock does seem to have a tendency to give birth to a whole town of Glocks (Glock 27, 26, 19, 17, 30, 36, and so on).

Kahr Arms *(845-353-7770; www.kahr.com).* A significant entry on the playing field of quality sub-compact and compact semiautomatic pistols is Kahr Arm's series of reliable, double action only models. True to the statement that great things come in small packages, a Kahr should be placed high on your consideration list of compact alternatives.

All law enforcement officers and defense-minded citizens should consider a Kahr a viable primary and back-up firearm choice. Kahr produces a number of sub-compact and compact models to choose from. Our personal selections and preferences are the "MK" series, the K9 and the PM9, of which we both share first-hand knowledge and positive experience. The MK9 is a sub-compact 9mm that comes either in all stainless steel or with a stainless steel slide and a polymer frame (the PM9). The MK40 is the same gun chambered for the .40 caliber round. The K9 is a half-inch higher and longer version of the MK9.

All of these models are small enough for easy concealment and can be worn in a pants pocket holster or a belt slide or inside the waistband holster. They can be accurately shot (with practice) one-handed or two-handed. The MK9, MK40, and PM9 are especially suitable for pocket carry. The K9 is a pleasure to carry concealed in a good belt scabbard or inside the waistband (IWB) holster, given its thinness and compactness.

With Kahr's recent purchase of Auto Ordnance, you can rest assured that they are also expanding into the large caliber handgun market. Visit Kahr's web site where you can obtain detailed consumer information on all of their models.

Walther America *(800-372-6454; www.waltheramerica.com).* Smith and Wesson's contribution to the truly compact line of semi-automatic pistols is found in its collaboration with one of Europe's quality gun manufacturers, Walther. The Smith/Walther product line in compact pistols, the Walther America's PPK and PPK/S line, often referred to as the "James Bond 007 sidearm," offers the fruits of a productive collaboration between two world-class firearms manufacturers.

The Smith/Walther PPK comes in a 7 + 1 round capacity .32 ACP caliber as well as in a 6 + 1 round capacity .380 ACP. The PPK/S comes in a 8 + 1 round capacity .32 caliber as well as in a 7 + 1 round capacity .380 ACP caliber. Both models are blow-back, traditional double action on the first shot, semi-automatic pocket pistols. These handguns are easy for comfortable concealed carry in a pocket or inside the waistband holster. They also are equipped with a manual safety/decocker and a loaded chamber indicator. Finishes come in either stainless steel or blue steel. This has always been a well-constructed and easy-to-carry firearm. Carl Walther's designs have always been classic and are respected as such.

Smith & Wesson *(800-331-0852 www.smith-wesson.com).* Smith and Wesson's world-renowned series of compact, defensive 2-inch snub nose J-frame revolvers are offered in several configurations: enclosed internal hammer, shrouded hammer and exposed hammer. Construction materials to reduce weight in their "Airweight" and "Airlite" series include aluminum, titanium or scandium alloys as compared to their heavier stainless or blued steel brothers in their more traditional format.

These models come in the following calibers: .38 special, .357 magnum, and .32 H & R magnum. The cylinders for all of these models are chambered for 5 rounds (except the .32 magnum which is chambered for 6 rounds) and share the same quality construction and operation. Smith's attention to detail, responsiveness to the consumer, and warrantee and customer service are unparalleled. These small handguns lend themselves beautifully to concealed carry in a pocket holster, purse, or other concealed places where space is of the essence. These "wheel guns" meet the needs and perform admirably for individuals who may feel uncomfortable or overwhelmed by semi-automatic pistols and their operation. Smith and Wesson's catalog of revolvers and semi-automatic pistols is so extensive, you really owe it to yourself to visit their web site and/or secure and study their catalogue to get a full perspective of their large product line.

In compact semi-autos, we recommend Smith's remarkable Model 3913 9mm either in the LadySmith(LS) model or the Tactical S & W (TSW) model. It holds an 8-round single stack magazine. Ergonomics are excellent making the gun a pleasure to shoot for most shooters with small or large hands. It comes in a stainless finish and shoots well enough to drive tacks. We also recommend, in .45 ACP caliber, the Model 457 in the Smith "Value" line. This is a compact single stack .45 caliber pistol holding 7 + 1 rounds. It comes in a blackened finish. Both weapons are extremely reliable, durable, accurate semi-autos that have received high grades in the industry.

What is also unique about these S & W autos and all of their other autos, is their excellent safety features: they have manual mechanical slide-mounted safety decocker and they have magazine disconnects. This means that even with a loaded chamber, the gun will not fire with the magazine out. These features have saved numerous police officers' and civilians' lives in scuffles with criminals who stole their guns and tried to shoot them with their own guns—they couldn't when the criminal did not know how to disengage the safety or the defender had time to release the magazine. This bought valuable time!

In compact revolvers, we look to the S & W J-Frame series. Originally introduced in 1952, the S & W "Airweight" series of lightweight small-frame .38 S & W Special revolvers with aluminum frames and steel cylinders and barrels offer exceptional value and performance. The blackened double action only (DAO) "Centennial" Model 442 with internal hammer, is a perfect pocket carry weapon, allowing you to pack five chambered rounds of your favorite defensive .38 special or .38 special + P ammunition. It weighs in at 15 ounces.

More recently, Smith & Wesson introduced their Airlite Series of J-Frames, and larger, medium-sized K and L frames. The Airlites frames are built of an aluminum/scandium alloy and the cylinders are made of titanium. These elements make the Airlites remarkably lightweight even in .357 magnum caliber! We select the blackened double action only (DAO) "Centennial" frame Model 340 PD with internal hammer that weighs in at a remarkable 12 ounces! This sub-compact pocket cannon holds five rounds of .357 magnum ammunition or .38 special + Ps.

In a medium-framed, Airlite, the 18-ounce Model 386 "Mountain Lite" packs 7 rounds of .357 magnum power into its titanium cylinder, providing you with a formidable, but portable home defense weapon.

Moving up in large bore caliber power, the 18-ounce Model 396 "Mountain Lite" packs 5 rounds of .44 S & W Special power into its titanium cylinder on the same frame as the Model 386.

If you prefer all stainless steel snubbies in the J-Frame series, we recommend Smith's DAO "Centennial" Model 640 with internal hammer. You can carry this 23-ounce weapon in your pocket loaded with five rounds of .357 magnum ammunition or .38 special +P ammunition. This weapon is built to last generations and to hand down to your grandchildren. If you prefer the same gun with an external, spurred hammer, you can get it in the 23-ounce Model 60.

Sturm, Ruger & Company *(www.ruger-firearms.com)*. Sturm, Ruger & Company is a quality manufacturer that has been producing affordable and functional firearms for many years. Their market offerings range from 2-inch spurless-hammer, undercover, double action only revolvers to full-size service revolvers and semi-automatic pistols. Their products demonstrate good quality, finish and reliability. The innovations of the company's founder, William Ruger, in the firearms field are legendary. Ruger's manufacturing procedures, employing precision molded investment castings, are world-renowned.

You can learn about the numerous service-sized semi-automatic pistols and the lines of revolvers that the company produces by perusing their web site. Especially popular are Ruger's SP-101 concealed carry .357 magnum revolvers, their P-series full-size service pistols in 9mm, 40 S&W and .45 ACP calibers, and their offerings in .22 caliber target pistols and single and double action revolvers.

Beretta U.S.A. *(800-636-3420 www.berettausa.com).* In a departure from Beretta's conventional product design line, the newly released 9000S Types F (single/double action) and D (double action only) are two strays you can rely on if you are confronted by criminal aggression. They are great strays with a champion pedigree.

The sleek design and innovative features of these models provide a good comfort level with low weight and superior caliber performance when they hiss a 9 mm or .40 caliber growl. In either law enforcement operations or civilian defense, the 9000S Type F's and D's stealthy postures present a clear advantage in your tactical defense. Like any cat, she's calming to her owner and frightening to aggressors.

We also strongly recommend Beretta's compact version of their longstanding and proven 9mm Beretta 92 series, as well as their 8000 series "Cougar" models chambered for either 9mm, 40 S&W, or .45 ACP calibers. These babies really growl. The .45 ACP Beretta 8045F with manual safety/decocker lever is also an extremely accurate, reliable, sturdy, and truly beautiful weapon.

Single-Action .45 ACP. If your needs and preferences run to a classic "1911 style," single-action semi-automatic pistol, Colt (www.colt.com), Kimber (800-880-2418; www.kimber america.com), Para-Ordnance (416-297-7855; www.para ord.com), and Springfield Armory (800-680-6866; www. springfield-armory.com) all offer compact (4-inch barrel length with a shorter grip) and subcompact models (3- to 3.5-inch barrel lengths).

We had the opportunity to evaluate several from Kimber's line and we discovered that they spell P-E-R-F-E-C-T-I-O-N! Chambered for the powerful .45 ACP cartridge, Kimber's "CDP II" (Custom Defense Package) Series II 1911's are beautiful as well as being top performers. They feature a lightweight aluminum frame machined from a solid 7075-T7 aluminum block and a stainless steel slide. A carry bevel treatment rounds and blends corners and edges so the pistol cannot grab or snag on clothing and holsters.

Frames include 30 LPI front strap checkering for a positive grip regardless of the conditions. Flat, checkered mainspring housing and hand-checkered double diamond rosewood grips aid in control. Mepro-Light Tritium three dot (green) night sights, extended ambidextrous thumb safety, match grade Premium Aluminum Trigger, beveled magazine well, stainless steel small parts, high ride beavertail grip safety and beveled slide serrations are all standard. Built for long-term concealed carry, these beautiful CDP II .45 ACP 1911 pistols weigh between 25 and 31 ounces.

The *"Ultra CDP II"* is based on the Stainless Ultra Carry II and includes all of the Kimber CDP features. Barrel length is 3 inches and weight is only 25 ounces. It shoots very accurately with surprisingly manageable recoil for good second and third shot recovery. It has all of the accuracy of a full-size single-action 1911 pistol with none of the weight and size giving it excellent carryability. It is the smallest .45 caliber 1911 package that we are aware of, and has unsurpassed quality in every aspect.

The *"Compact CDP II"* is based on the Compact Aluminum Stainless and has all the features of the Ultra CDP II, including stainless steel small parts on the frame. Barrel length is 4 inches and weight is only 28 ounces. As is the case with the Ultra CDP II, the Compact's grip length is shorter than that of the full-size Kimber 1911s. The *"Pro CDP II"* has all the features of the "Compact CDP II," including a 4-inch bushingless bull barrel. It also has an aluminum frame, but it has a full-length grip.

In sum, the "Compact" and "Pro" CDP II pistols are great choices for those shooters who desire a high quality 1911 that is in between the full-size 1911s and the "Ultra CDP" 1911 pistols in size and weight. They shoot exceptionally well and are great concealed carry guns. In our book, they are the best in their class.

▶ **Should I purchase a full-size handgun?**

In revolvers, a full-size handgun is usually called a "service sidearm" when its barrel length is 4 inches or greater. In semi-automatics, service use can range from 4 inches to 6 inches (mostly 4 to 5 inches).

Usually larger and more weighty, some full-size service handguns are not as easy to carry concealed. This does not present a problem for uniformed police and military use, or for competitive shooting. Mechanically identical to their smaller relatives, three variables physically distinguish these larger guns from their smaller relatives—their weight, barrel length and magazine capacity (at least prior to the Brady Bill).

Full-size handguns do offer very viable home and store/business defense capabilities to assure your survival. It is important to recognize that the longer the barrel and the greater a handgun's weight, the greater the gun's accuracy and the less the gun's recoil, hence, greater manageability. Therefore, it is worthwhile to consider owning at least one full-size revolver or semi-automatic handgun (for some of us maybe at least 10!) for those times when you don't need to carry concealed, or if you get a great purchase deal on a good quality, full-size handgun.

With a few exceptions, the above-mentioned revolver and semi-auto manufacturers have extensive lines and calibers of full-size handguns to perform the duties of service sidearm carry, military combat responsibilities, home defense, and target and competitive applications. Because of the numerically overwhelming varieties of excellent, quality offerings, please take some time to study the web sites given. Focus on what you want, what meets your needs and pocketbook or wallet.

We highly recommend the following full-size models for the reliability, shootability, ease of maintenance, ergonomics, good value, and given the quality and reliability of the manufacturers that support these products. We cannot recommend any one of these over any other. You just have to try them out; feel them in your hand, shoot them, study their features, their types of actions, etc., in order to evaluate which one is best suited to your individual needs.

However, you really cannot go wrong with any of these excellent, full-size handguns.

Beretta 92 and 96 Series. The Beretta 92FS in 9mm and the 96FS in 40 S&W have been tested and proven accurate and extremely reliable by numerous law enforcement and military organizations world-wide. These semi-automatics operate on a short recoil, delayed locking block system which yields a fast cycle time and delivers exceptional accuracy and reliability. The guns' frames are forged from a lightweight, aircraft-quality aluminum alloy.

The FS Models are double action for the first shot and single action for all subsequent shots. They have an external ambidextrous manual safety (easily accessible by the thumb of a right- or left-handed shooter) that also functions as a decocking lever, a trigger bar disconnect, rotating firing pin striker, and a firing pin block device that secures the firing pin. They also feature a chamber-loaded indicator which is both visible and tactual.

These pistols feature an open top slide design that diminishes jamming or stovepiping. It allows the user to load the chamber one cartridge at a time should the magazine be lost or damaged. They are made with Beretta's "Bruniton non-reflective matte black finish," which is a functional corrosion-resistant coating.

These pistols feel excellent in the hand offering a sure, firm grip and good pointability and control. The disassembly latch is conveniently located to simplify field-stripping and maintenance.

These pistols also come in the Model 92D which is a double action-only version of the standard 92FS, with no external safety levers and the hammer spur removed. "D" models are simple to operate with the exact same smooth trigger pull for each shot. The "Type M" variants of the "92 Compact L" and "96 Compact L" hold a single stack 8-round magazine. This creates a notably slimmer profile that's ideal for individuals with smaller hands or for those who do not like the thicker grip of the standard issue 92 and 96 pistols.

Glock Models 17, 21, and 22. A full-size double action/ safe-action Glock will serve you well as your "always carry" sidearm, as well as for home defense. The grip is big enough to fit even the largest of hands. The gun is ergonomic and fits many people's hands in a two-handed grip very well. The extra size and weight helps to dampen recoil. You just have to decide which caliber is right for you if you want a full-size Glock.

Note that the full-size models in 9mm and .40 S&W will fit in the same holster. The full-size .45 caliber has a slightly wider, beefier slide and grip to accommodate the larger .45 ACP round.

If you like 9mm parabellum (NATO's official round), your gun is the full-size Glock 17. This gun may be one of the most shootable and pointable big, serious caliber guns on the planet! Another nice feature with this gun is that pre-Clinton ban (pre-Brady Bill) high capacity (read "full capacity" as originally designed) magazines are available where legal, for non-law enforcement civilians. However, it is imperative that you check your local and state laws. These original magazines hold 17 rounds. That's a total of 18 rounds with one in the chamber!

If you like the 40 S&W round, your gun is the full-size Glock 22. Full capacity magazines for the 22 hold 15 rounds of powerful 40 S&W ammunition. If you like the classic .45 ACP caliber round, then your full-size Glock model is the Glock 21. The Glock 30 has a slightly shorter grip and barrel length to make it more concealable, and thus, falls into the "compact" size class.

HK USP Series in 9mm, 40 S&W, and .45 ACP. The HK full-size **U**niversal **S**elf-loading **P**istol (USP) series, which include 9mm, .40 S&W, and .45 caliber models, are top of the line. They are similar in design and operation to their compact cousins, described previously, and are the smaller compact pistols' progenitors.

SIG Sauer P220. The remarkable full-size SIG Sauer P220 is a perfect combat and self-defense pistol. It works well for concealed carry with the right holster rig (as made by companies such as Bianchi International, Blade-Tech, DeSantis, Don Hume, Galco International, Gould & Goodrich, High Noon Holsters, Kramer Handgun Leather, Lou Alessi, Matt Del Fatti, Michaels of Oregon, Milt Sparks and Mitch Rosen). It is also a superior choice for a self-defense and home defense handgun.

This classic gun is an ergonomic masterpiece that feels natural in your hand. It is a double action/single action .45 caliber semi-automatic pistol that has been around for years with only minor changes (evolutionary improvements) for one good reason—it works, and works very well! Thus, the P220 has formed the basis for all of the other "Classic P Series" SIG Sauer handguns which include the P225, P226, P228, P229, and P245. This line of superior double action semi-autos makes up a big percentage of the sporting, personal defense, military and law enforcement sidearms in the world market.

The SIG Sauer line is made both in Europe and the United States. In the USA, it is manufactured in Exeter, New Hampshire at the headquarters of the American company, SIGARMS.

The SIG Sauer P220 has a steel slide, a steel breech block, a steel feed ramp, a solid guide rod, a heavy-duty woven recoil spring, a target grade steel barrel and an aluminum alloy frame. The breech block contains the firing pin and is a separate steel piece secured to the slide with a roll pin. The aluminum alloy frame has a heavy steel cross bar that the barrel cams up against to move up and down for locking and unlocking. There is a steel insert in the frame that makes up the feed ramp, so that rounds do not slam into aluminum during the feed cycle.

All of the SIG Sauer pistols, of which the SIG P220 is the progenitor, are very strong, reliable and durable. As with all of the other pistols in the SIG Sauer line (e.g., the P245, 226, 239), the P220 incorporates SIG Sauer's unique, patented, 4-point safety system. This system includes (1) an automatic firing-pin lock, (2) a frame-mounted decocking lever, (3) a safety intercept notch and (4) a trigger bar disconnector.

This double action/single action pistol is made to be carried hammer down with a round in the chamber. The SIG's first shot is double action with a long, smooth, reasonably heavy but manageable, trigger pull. All subsequent shots are single action. The gun has a decocking lever but no mechanical manual safety. So, if you've fired your first double action shot, and your weapon's hammer is now fully cocked and ready for the second single action shot, and you don't need to take a second shot, you can fully and safely decock the hammer, and return the pistol to its safe mode.

When the pistol is decocked, the hammer does not drop to a full rest position against the firing pin but instead falls to a safe, intermediate position. The other integral safety features listed above prevent an accidental discharge should the pistol be dropped, even when the pistol is cocked! To be fired, the trigger must be fully engaged and pressed through its entire arc of motion.

The P220 magazines hold 8 rounds of powerful .45 ACP ammunition. Today, some 27 years since its introduction, the SIG Sauer P220 still retains its well earned status as one of the finest "out of the box" big-bore pistols produced. It sets the standard for quality DA .45 caliber pistols, as does its much younger, more compact cousin, the SIG Sauer P245.

The P220 comes standard from the factory with high contrast bar dot low profile combat sights, 3 dot combat sights, or with the optional SIG Sight "Tritium" Night Sights. It also comes with the standard black plastic stippled stocks and the standard SIG blued finish, or with an optional two-tone or stainless steel finish with accessory light rails.

Because of its aluminum alloy frame, this big-bore P220 is lighter than many other full-size pistols. However, although it is light in weight, it is a heavyweight when it comes to giving and taking punches! After 10,000 rounds, a SIG Sauer is just beginning to be broken in. Just like a Volvo after 100,000 miles, the SIG wants to be driven and driven and driven.

In sum, you can rely on the SIG Sauer line of pistols, and count on the big bore SIG Sauer P220 .45 ACP to give any bad guy a reason to beat feet. It is one gun you should want to keep at home and at your side. If you have never tried one, you owe it to yourself to do so. After you do, you may never leave home without it, or let your home go unprotected without it.

Smith & Wesson's 5900 series of full-sized tactical 9mm pistols are winners. The 5903TSW holds 10 + 1 rounds of 9mm ammunition and has a full-sized aluminum alloy frame and stainless steel slide with Novak low mount sights.

It is an ergonomic, lightweight and accurate pistol. It can be had as the 5906 TSW in all stainless which makes it 10 ounces heavier. Smith also makes the full-sized .40 caliber 4000 series and the .45 caliber 4500 series in both all stainless and aluminum alloy frame models with stainless steel slides. We encourage you to peruse their extensive catalog.

Para-Ordnance LDA Series .45 ACP Pistols *(980 Tapscott Road, Scarborough, Ontario M1X1C3. Tel: 416-297-7855. Fax: 416-297-1289. www.paraord.com).*

Para-Ordnance, manufacturers of high magazine capacity, 1911 style, single action .45 caliber pistols originated a highly successful line of high-magazine capacity, 1911 style, double action .45 caliber pistols called the "Light Double Action" or "LDA" series. What is unique about these pistols, is that they provide the look, feel, and performance of the traditional John Browning style, 1911 single action pistol, but they are designed to be carried hammer down on a loaded chamber with the safety on. This eliminates the issue of having to carry the .45 caliber 1911 pistol "cocked and locked," that is, with a loaded chamber, the hammer cocked, and the safety on.

All Para LDAs incorporate three vital safety features: (1) a thumb safety that disengages the trigger; (2) a grip safety that locks the hammer assembly; and (3) an internal firing-pin-block to prevent an accidental discharge if the hammer is struck or the pistol is dropped.

Para-Ordnance's newest entry in this innovative line is their "Para Tac-Four 13.45 LDA." This pistol powerhouse has a 4.25-inch barrel and accommodates a magazine that holds 13 rounds of potent .45 ACP firepower, where legal. It's LDA trigger system is light and smooth and this counters flinching. Given its solid, stainless steel construction, it is good at absorbing felt recoil. In conjunction, its double column magazine and wider grip frame, as compared to those of its LDA single stack cousins, spread out and diffuse perceived recoil a bit more also. This quality pistol's flush (bobbed) hammer and bobbed beavertail make for an attractive, functional, concealable, snag-free, and easy-drawing pistol.

Para's high capacity, double-stack LDA models are also available in 9mm and .40 S&W. The 9mm models offer the greatest round capacity (for law enforcement only) followed by the .40 S&W models (where legal pre-ban full capacity magazines are available).

For ease of concealed carry, ergonomic shootability by people with different size hands, and true to the original, John Browning style single stack 1911s, Para-Ordnance offers their single stack line of LDA .45 ACP caliber pistols. We were shipped two to evaluate.

The Para Companion Carry Option pistol, Model CC745SN, is a compact, single stack LDA .45 ACP double-action semiautomatic pistol that is suitable for concealed carry. When you know how to operate it safely and are well-trained, you can take it with you wherever it is legal, and you'll know you are well protected. This attractive pistol features a 3.5" barrel, 7-round single-column magazine, stainless steel finish, and double-diamond checkered cocobolo stocks. Like the micro-sized Para Carry, the Para Companion Carry Option has a spurless hammer, a low-profile thumb safety and a rounded-off grip safety that projects further from the mainspring housing for more positive action. Green 3-dot Tritium night sights are standard on the Para Companion Carry Option.

The Para-Ordnance proprietary Light Double Action trigger system is unique in the industry. It can accurately be described as sweet and smooth. This minimizes flinching. Integrated into a well thought out total shooting platform, this provides an exemplary combination of pistol controllability, shootability, and concealability.

All Para LDA pistols are accompanied by an owner's manual instructional video that serves as a supplement to the highly detailed printed instruction manual. Both the manual and the 11-minute video, narrated by Triple Crown IPSC Champion Todd Jarrett, explain pistol operations, functions, parts, takedown, reassembly, cleaning and maintenance procedures, built-in safety features and basic rules of firearm safety.

All new Para pistols come with the company's Millennium Lifetime Service Policy that went into effect on January 1, 2001. This no-nonsense service policy is simple. If you are the original retail purchaser of a Para pistol, and adjustment or repair is required because of any defect in materials or workmanship, they will provide you with all necessary service, free of charge, for as long as you own that pistol.

For the many shooters, both civilian and law enforcement, who prefer the feel of the traditional John Browning style M1911A1 with the single-column 7-round magazine, Para-Ordnance offers the full-size 7.45 LDA model. This is a single stack, all stainless steel version of their 14.45 LDA Pistol. It's balance and feel are similar to that of a traditional 1911, but it's trigger pull is "light double action" (i.e., LDA). Thus, like all of the Para LDA models, it can be carried hammer down on a loaded chamber with the safety on.

Checkered double diamond rosewood grips are standard. Black grips are optional. The full-size 7.45 LDA features a 5" barrel and a 7 plus 1 round capacity. Its overall length is 8.5" and its height with the magazine is 5.75 inches. The 7.45 LDA was acclaimed by *Guns & Ammo Magazine* as one of their "Handguns of the Year." This full-size .45 ACP 1911 style, double-action semi-auto combines the instant readiness of double-action with the smooth, crisp trigger of a fine-tuned single-action with no transition from first to second shot and excellent shot-to-shot consistency. This translates into superior second and third shot recovery.

The magazines that shipped with the Para Companion Carry Option Model CC745SN came with black plastic followers—unusual for 1911 style pistols. We tested six of these magazines and fired over 300 rounds of assorted jacket hollow point (JHP) and full metal jacket (FMJ) ammunition (200 grain Winchester Personal Protection JHPs and 185 grain Winchester Ranger Law Enforcement + P JHPs) and 230 grain Winchester FMJs). One of the magazines when empty, failed to enable the slide to lock back, but it nevertheless fed. Overall, we experienced about 8 malfunctions. Several were double feeds, several were failures to feed, and one was an ejection failure. The magazines with these plastic followers work, but we do not have the utmost of confidence in them—not enough to stake our lives and survival on. However, the gun itself is great. So, we went to several other, after-market magazine manufacturers.

Chip McCormick Corporation Magazines *(512-280-4280; P.O. Box 1560, Manchaca, TX 78652; Fax: 521-280-4282; www. chipmccormickcorp.com).* We found that Chip McCormick's "Shooting Star" 7 round M1911 Officer's Model magazines worked great in this gun. The McCormicks are reasonably priced and have excellent fit and finish.

McCormick's 8-round "PowerMags" with the optional officers/compact base pad conversion also work great and offer an extra round. These "PowerMags" have extra heavy-duty springs which reduce wear and spring fatigue, thus, providing greater tolerance for keeping fully-loaded magazines for longer periods before rotating them to release spring tension and material compression fatigue.

MEC-GAR USA, INC. *(Hurley Farms Industrial Park, 115 Hurley Road #6G, Oxford, CT 06478; 203-262-1525, 800-632-4271; Fax: 203-262-1719; www.mec-gar.com)*

We tested MEC-GAR's 1911 Officer's model .45 7-round magazine with spring leaf follower (Item #: MGCO4507) and found it to work perfectly well as expected. These magazines come in blued or nickel plated, and with or without rubber bumper pads attached to the magazine base plate.

Mec-Gar is the original equipment manufacturer of magazines to some of the world's most prominent firearm manufacturers (e.g., SIGARMS and Beretta). Mec-Gar is known worldwide as the largest producer of fine quality rifle and pistol magazines. Their products are produced in Italy in their state-of-the-art stamping facility and tool shop, and the company is 100% dedicated to the manufacturing of consistently superior quality magazines that conform to, or exceed, customer (i.e., firearm manufacturers) tolerance specifications.

Mec-Gar magazines demonstrate superior functional reliability. They have earned the trust in their product and company. As a result, Mec-Gar has been awarded numerous law enforcement, military and government contracts. They are the official supplier of Beretta M9/92F 15-round magazines for the U.S. Army and of the SIG P220 7-round magazines for U.S. Government Federal law enforcement agencies.

We had the opportunity to test Mec-Gar's 10-round capacity and high capacity (15- and 17-round) magazines for the 9mm Beretta 92FS and the 9mm SIG Sauer P226 and P228. They worked flawlessly and were truly 100% reliable.

The bottom line is that Mec-Gar magazines can be counted on to get the job done—that is, to assure your survival. The company works very closely with each gun manufacturer to optimize the design of the magazine, keeping in mind that the consistent and reliable operation of semi-automatic pistols depends largely on how well the magazine feeds and ramps the bullets.

Mec-Gar magazines are made from certified Carbon Steel AISI 1010 or from superior 17-7 PH aircraft-grade stainless steel and they are precision formed to meet the most severe specifications and tolerances. Their magazine followers are made of either injected plastic or micro-die-cast metal alloy, or are stamped from hard steel. They are designed to ensure the absolute reliability of loading ammunition and their positive feeding.

All of the Mec-Gar magazine followers that we have tested demonstrate that they travel smoothly in the magazine tube. They correctly activate the pistol's slide-stop lever, when the pistol has one, to reliably lock back the slide after the last round is fired. The magazine springs are fabricated from high tensile strength spring wire and are provided with reinforced coils that have stiffening folds to increase their thrust force.

Some models of Mec-Gar magazines feature a patented design which uses a unique spring and follower design allowing for additional rounds to be introduced into a compact space in their new standard 10-round magazines. This patent also allows two additional rounds to be introduced over the standard capacity in their standard tube size, flush-fitting, high-capacity law enforcement magazines, without overstraining and fatiguing the magazine spring.

You can purchase after-market Mec-Gar magazines for the following manufacturers' firearms: AMT, Armscor, Astra, Beretta, Bernadelli, FN Browning, Charles Daly, Colt, CZ, Kel-Tec, Kimber, Llama, North American Arms, Remington, SIG-ARMS, Smith and Wesson, Springfield Armory, STI, Standard Arms, Star, Steyr, Tanfoglio, Taurus, and Walther.

Best Handguns for Beginners

Beginners are best served learning on compact to full-size double action (DA) or double action only (DAO) pistols. The pistols that meet these criteria the best in our opinion are the double action only line of Glocks, SIG Sauer's high quality line of double action pistols with their single-stage decockers, and the high quality, double action pistols with the two-stage decocker/manual safeties made by Heckler & Koch (HK), Smith & Wesson (S&W) and Beretta.

In revolvers, we stand by Smith and Wesson, as the unbeatable standard for both beginners and advanced shooters.

SIG Sauer's personal size, double action Model P232 in the very recoil manageable .380 ACP caliber, and their compact size, double action Model P239 in the recoil manageable 9mm caliber, or slightly snappier .40 S&W caliber are great pistols for beginners, and they will last and be treasured for a lifetime. In addition, the double action SIG Sauer Models P228 in 9mm, and the P229 and P226 in either 9mm or .40 S&W, also offer viable options for the beginner. The shooter will never outgrow these great, safe guns. These guns are very easy to maintain (disassemble, clean and reassemble).

Heckler & Koch's USP Compact pistol in either 9mm or .40 S&W caliber is also a great double action handgun with many built-in safety features that can serve a beginner well. Furthermore, it is also a gun of the highest quality that the beginner will never outgrow. As mentioned earlier, the HK USPs come in a number of variants—DAO and DA (with either a single-stage manual decocker or a two-stage decocker/manual safety). These guns are also very easy to maintain (disassemble, clean and reassemble).

Smith & Wesson's line of double action 9mm pistols with two-stage decocker/manual safeties offer reliable function, accuracy, durability, pleasant shootability, simplicity, functionality, ease of maintenance (disassembly, cleaning and reassembly), and ease of carry to satisfy most shooters' needs regardless of level of experience. We especially recommend Smith's compact, single stack Lady Smith 3913, their compact, tactical 3913 TSW, and their third generation, full-size 5900 TSW series 9mm pistols.

Beretta makes the double action 9mm 92 series both in full-size and compact versions, as well as the more compact 9mm Cougar line of pistols. We definitely recommend them as well. They also are easily maintained.

Finally, Glocks are affordable, reliable, durable, accurate, shootable, ergonomic, and as well, easy to learn to take care of (i.e., field-strip, clean and maintain). They are double action only and have their patented safe action triggers which minimize the chances of an accidental discharge unless one violates cardinal safety rules numbers 1 and 6 (Finger *off* the trigger until ready to shoot AND Finger *off* the trigger until ready to shoot).

Glocks have no manual/mechanical safeties or decockers for beginners to get confused with. Beginning shooters have a lot to pay attention to. Most beginners do well with the 9mm Glocks, either in the compact Glock 19 or full-sized Glock 17 models, or in the subcompact ("baby Glock") Glock 26 configuration.

Learning to shoot and operate a pistol requires total concentration on following the basic safety rules among other things. Thus, the simpler the pistol's controls the better.

It is our opinion that 1911 single action pistols, as well as the Para LDAs, demand that the shooter think about too many things simultaneously. There is just too much for the beginner to hold in mind. The safe operation of these pistols demands considerably more than an elementary, basic knowledge of pistols and shooting.

A Carbine for Home Defense. Kel-Tec manufactures and sells a great folding fighting carbine that makes a great home defense gun; the Sub Rifle 2000. It is a small, self-loading carbine that comes in versions for either 9mm or .40 S&W pistol cartridges. The "Sub" is much more portable and concealable than most legal shotguns (and a lot easier on your strong side shoulder!). It weighs only 4 pounds unloaded. Unfolded in its operable position, it extends to a length of 30 inches. Folded up it extends only 16 inches, which is its barrel length.

Different versions of the Sub-2000 will also accept different modern handgun magazines—a real plus! For example, there is a Glock version that accepts Glock high capacity magazines (Glock 17 magazines in the 9mm version and Glock 22 magazines in the .40 S&W version), a Smith & Wesson version, and reportedly a Beretta version. The factory standard magazine holds 10 rounds. Apparently, the standard Sub-2000 version in addition to accepting the standard Sub magazines, will accept magazines for a S&W 9mm Model 59 pistol.

Being a small rifle, the Sub-2000 has a greatly extended range compared to a handgun (practically up to 150 yards according to Renee Goldman of Kel-Tec). Its superior precision is also very useful against small or partially covered targets at shorter ranges. Of course, for home defense, we are only talking about ranges of less than 7 yards!

As stated by Kel-Tec, the Sub-2000 requires less training to master than a handgun. Emphasis has been placed on user safety in the design of this practical, easy-to-use, compact defensive weapon.

The Sub is made of mostly polymer, and our personal testing indicates that this does not affect durability or accuracy, only price. This quality firearm, like all of Kel-Tec's innovative, functional products, is affordable.

We found this arm to be a pleasure to shoot and to be X-ring accurate at up to 75 feet. It is easy on the shoulder and comfortable to hold and aim. We found perceived recoil to be negligible. The rifle ate, without one malfunction or stoppage, every 9mm round we fed it; Winchester Silvertips, Fiocchi full metal jackets (FMJs) and lead-nosed semi-jacketed hollow points (SJHP), Zero FMJs, Speer Gold Dot jacketed hollow points (JHPs), Federal Hydra-Shoks, and MagSafe frangibles, as well as some others. After 3000 rounds, this Sub was still firing accurately and reliably. Everyone who handled and fired it at our range facility liked it.

Factory Specifications. The Kel-Tec Sub has six main component parts: the barrel, bolt, frame, firing mechanism, stock, and magazine. The barrel is made of SAE 4130 Ordnance steel and attaches permanently to the front sight and hinge assembly. The bolt head is casehardened steel, and contains the firing pin and extractor. The bolt extends backwards and houses the recoil spring assembly and operating handle.

The frame is injection-molded in two halves, the left side holding the ejector and serial number. The frame houses the firing mechanism, forms the grip and encloses the barrel hinge and stock tube. The trigger connects via a transfer bar to the sear. The hammer is driven by a double torsion spring. A recessed, manual push button safety disconnects the trigger bar and blocks the sear, locking it into the hammer. The butt stock and tube also form the housing for the reciprocating bolt assembly. More details can be found on Kel-Tec's web site (www.kel-tec.com) and in the Sub's operator's manual.

Operation. The bolt can be locked in the rear position by the operating handle. The main safety is a protected push-bolt type that when engaged, disconnects the trigger bar and interlocks the hammer and sear. By rotating the barrel upwards and back, this Sub can be reduced to a compact 16" x 7" package which facilitates secure storage in a small space. Then all that is required, if trouble presents itself, is to unfold the gun, lock the barrel in place, and charge the weapon, as long as a loaded magazine was already in place in the magazine well.

The rifle's rear sight is of the aperture type and the fluorescent front sight can be adjusted for both windage and elevation. The Sub can easily be disassembled without tools for cleaning and maintenance.

We highly recommend this gun for all that it gives you for a very reasonable price. The fact that versions are made to take high capacity Glock or S&W or Beretta magazines is also a real plus. It is a great little rifle at a price that will also leave you money for a Glock, Beretta, Smith & Wesson, or yes, even a Kel-Tec pistol.

This carbine is really portable. We know a dedicated physician, a real healer, who still makes house calls in inner city, dangerous neighborhoods. He carries his folded Sub-2000 carbine with two extra magazines in his doctor's bag. He also carries a Kel-Tec P-32 in his pocket with an extra high capacity, 10-round magazine, and a Smith & Wesson Airlite snubbie in his jacket or coat pocket. No, his name is not Doc Holliday, but he is smart.

▶ **Where should I go to buy a handgun?**

Firearms can be purchased either at a gun shop or at a shooting range that has a gun shop. Firearms can also be purchased at gun shows. Gun shows you'll have to remember are just dealers that get together at a specific location to sell their products and then they are out of town! You are very often left with little or no recourse with your purchase should you have a problem.

Our direct experiences with the firearm manufacturers we have talked with have been extremely positive and gratifying. The industry leaders have proven themselves to be positive and honest and helpful. All of the manufacturers we have mentioned and recommended in this book have directly and thoroughly answered all of our questions without hesitation.

Find a gun dealer that you trust. You do this through research and personal interaction. Everyone is not honest or knowledgeable. Don't be hustled. Take your time. It **will** be worth it.

The industry itself, in terms of the firearms manufacturers and manufacturers of necessary accessories (such as holsters, safes, ammunition, speed loaders, etc.), is very respectable and honorable. It sets a standard that we wish other industries would emulate. We have no hesitation in unconditionally recommending any product mentioned in this text. Contact information on the companies mentioned in the text is given in the back of this book. Our goal is to establish a template that both novice and professional alike can rely on for quality information and material products. However, we cannot possibly mention every quality product out there, although we have strived to mention what we like best.

Our suggestion is that when shopping for a firearm, you find a range facility that will let you rent or that offers formal classes taught by qualified and certified instructors. In such an environment, you can best determine which type of firearm will best suit your particular needs because you can try out different weapons and accessories. It is always best to try before you buy.

A true professional will not seek profit over professionalism. The definition of a professional is a person who is qualified by virtue of training and experience to offer specialized services and who strives to maintain excellent ethics and accountability in the delivery of service. Any true professional's main goal is to serve and help his or her clientele, and in the firearms field, not to hide in the shadow of "your" tombstone. The authentic firearms sales or training professional will seek to help you determine your actual defensive needs.

After all, an ethical gun salesman or firearms instructor wants to see you on a regular basis and to keep you as a client as he or she obtains satisfaction from observing you develop your performance skills with your chosen weapon(s). Ethical professionals will never push you into buying a particular product. They will help you make an informed choice which involves assessing the type of firearm you are most comfortable shooting, carrying and safely storing.

You may find yourself nervous, confused, or "out of your element" when you go to purchase a firearm. If this is what you experience, know that this is where the value of a truly concerned and dedicated professional can shine through. His or her role is to explain to you in terms you can comprehend, with no condescension, the varieties of firearms available, how they operate, and the importance of not being seduced into believing that "cute" or "sleek" or "shiny" are better.

Three key rules of thumb are:

1. *Form should follow function.*

2. *Function follows from a quality product* that is chosen wisely by an educated, well-advised consumer, and

3. *Function follows when you purchase a quality handgun from a knowledgeable and reputable firearms salesper-son* who cares about your needs and takes the time to competently explain the gun to you and how to use it.

A young lady came into our range with a .380 caliber semi-automatic pistol that she needed help operating. She did not know how to release the magazine to reload, and she had no idea how to field-strip the gun for cleaning. She said she purchased the gun at another range and took "lessons" but she could not demonstrate a functional grip or aiming position with the pistol. This was disturbing as her reason for pur-chasing a gun was that she was being stalked by an old flame who was a dangerous felon recently released from prison! We convinced her of her ineptness and vulnerability with the gun by conducting with her the "21 feet across the room test." Role-playing, we staged an attacker coming across the room to get her with a non-existent knife in hand, while she attempted to release the empty magazine and replace it with another empty magazine that we pretended was loaded. She couldn't release the magazine and would have been "dead meat." In fact, the gun shop salesman who sold the pistol to her had not taken the time to show her how to field-strip the weapon when she bought it. When she brought it back to him after purchase for him to show her how, he tried to disassemble it but he could not!

In this case, none of these three rules of thumb were applied. Form did not follow function. The gun was designed with an awkward magazine release and the disassembly was difficult. The pistol was a poorly designed, inexpensive "junk gun" that this uninformed lady was guided to choose by a salesman who just wanted to make another sale.

This lady was helped by showing her how to grip the gun and fire it, as well as helping her adapt a functional stance. We went over these skills with her until she got them down cold. They included how to release the empty magazine and how to reload. We explained to her the limitations of her low caliber pistol; what it could be expected to do and what it couldn't. Then, we showed her how to field-strip the gun for cleaning and maintenance using a special procedure we developed to make cleaning a pistol easy and enjoyable when you would rather not take the pistol apart.

This lady came back to practice regularly at the range and also took our basic and advanced NRA approved personal defense firearms courses. She eventually purchased a Glock 26 9mm semi-automatic pistol.

▶ How do I select a handgun from all of the choices given?

As you examine the manufacturer's web sites and brochures and visit local gun shops, pay particular attention to all of the mechanical, internal and hand-operated external safeties provided on each model by each manufacturer. Educate yourself and compile a list of your objectives as well as your personal attributes and needs so that you can make the most appropriate and informed selection of model and manufacturer for you. No one handgun is perfect for everyone or every situation or for that matter, everyone's pocketbook. We cover criteria for choosing the "right" handgun for you below.

▶ How should I go about choosing a handgun?

Some questions to think about and answer when you are choosing the best handgun for you include:

1. Which type of firearm do you shoot most accurately with? This includes determining which handgun allows you to have your best second and third shot recovery should you need to take those subsequent shots in a tactical defense situation.

2. You really are much better off if you can take a class to develop and determine your basic safe gun handling and shooting skills before you buy. Purchasing a quality defensive firearm is an expensive proposition that you should treat as such. You really need to experience what feels right for you before you can make a truly informed choice.

3. Don't rush your choice. Don't allow yourself to be pressured. Never rely on a salesman behind a gun store counter to make that pressing choice for you because he may operate strictly on a profit motive basis. If this is the case, then he or she is capable of selling you a door knob for your self defense if you are willing to buy one.

Remember that there is no one right model of handgun for everyone. This bears repeating: *one size does not fit all.* When you shop for a defensive handgun you must assess **how you intend to use the weapon**. Here are some questions to ask:

1. Are you going to obtain a concealed carry permit and if so, how, when and where and how often are you going to carry? Obviously the size and configuration of the firearm will set limits on this. Also factor in your body size and the clothes you typically wear.

2. How are you going to safely store your firearm at home? We will cover safe storage options later on. You cannot store a full-size service sidearm in some of the smaller

pistol safes on the market that are made for subcompact or compact pistols or revolvers.

3. Another *important* consideration is *ease of maintenance.* We will refer to this later on.

4. How are you best able to transport the weapon to pistol matches and ranges if you should choose competition shooting as one of your outlets?

5. What caliber should you use? You need to choose a caliber that can do the job but that you can train yourself to handle for effective performance.

If you choose to ignore everything we have mentioned, then at the very least, do not make your purchase a one shop shot (we mean stop!). Get a feel for the prices of handguns in your area because prices can actually vary as much as 100 to 200 dollars for the same exact model! So, be a wise consumer. Your purchase might make the difference between your survival or demise.

Also keep in mind that if you are new to firearms, you are probably entering an environment not common to most people and new to you. Therefore, learn the jargon and not be taken advantage of. This equally applies to those who are experienced with firearms as well. Whomever you are, do not allow yourself to be intimidated or bullied. Leave if you feel that way. You want to seek out level-headed, helpful dealers and a comfortable, safe and clean environment in which to shop and shoot.

Choosing a pistol is a highly personal decision. However, employing a number of practical, sensible criteria can make choosing easier and more effective.

Another Important Consideration to Keep in Mind About Pistol Size. Often, the full-size version of a particular semi-automatic pistol accommodates magazines with greater ammunition capacity than does the compact version of the same model. Think about this in deciding on what gun to buy. You should try both full-size and compact versions of a gun, if possible, in the holster in which you intend to carry the gun. This is because very often, the full-size version is no more difficult to carry comfortably concealed than the compact version!

The full-size version of a semi-automatic pistol has a longer barrel and usually a longer grip than does the compact version (usually a 4½-inch to 5-inch barrel as opposed to a 3- to 4-inch barrel). However, in many cases, the same holster is used to carry both versions. So, the only difference you feel when the gun is worn on your hip (especially with a quality belt slide or scabbard holster) is the size and length of the grip. Therefore, you have to test out how much this makes a difference for you when you are standing and sitting. You may very well be capable of carrying the full-size gun just as easily as the compact.

Many quality leather belt scabbard holster manufacturers such as DeSantis, Don Hume, Galco, Gould and Goodrich, offer models with three belt slots (one in the rear and two in the front). This allows you to choose either a forward canted or a high, upright ride. These holsters can accommodate different barrel and grip lengths.

In addition, a good leather belt holster hugs your weapon close in to your body. This keeps your weapon well-concealed and gives your weapon a stable ride. So, you have to try things out to get the best fit of gun and holster for you. Remember that this is an individual decision based on what you are comfortable with and your particular body type and size.

Backup or Main Weapon?

You must decide whether the pistol you are considering is going to be your backup gun or your main weapon. To paraphrase Larry Seecamp of L.W. Seecamp Company:

> *In a defensive confrontation, your first choice of weapon ought not to be a nuclear bomb.*

So, it makes sense for some people, who need to carry, to carry two handguns. As a "backup gun" which can serve tactically as the first line of defense, any of the following small pocket handguns in a pocket holster can serve you well: the Seecamp .32 caliber sub-compact pistol; the North American Arms .32 or .380 caliber Guardian sub-compact pistol; the Beretta .32 Tomcat sub-compact pistol; or a small and light Smith & Wesson J-Frame snub-nose Air Lite or Airweight revolver.

Your "primary weapon" can serve tactically as your second line of defense if something bigger is needed. In other words, it may make the most tactical sense to save the most powerful weapon as your last resort. You can carry your bigger and higher caliber second firearm (e.g., 9mm, 40 S&W, .45 ACP) in a quality inside the waist band (IWB), belt slide, belt scabbard, or paddle holster. We will discuss how to choose a good holster for your weapon.

"Pocket Pistols"

Your circumstances may require you to carry a "pocket pistol" instead of a larger model. There are a number of factors to consider in your choice of a pocket handgun: configuration, reliability, size, weight, features, caliber and cost.

Just like the larger sized guns, pocket handguns come as both revolvers and semi-automatics. These pocket handguns operate similarly as their big brothers. What you may also find are Derringer-style pistols. These handguns have twin barrels and an internal mechanism which fires a round in one barrel and than a round in the other. We generally recommend AGAINST carrying Derringer-style pistols as they have limited application and some characteristics we just do not like.

For obvious reasons, you will need a pocket handgun that is reliable. Consider models from only manufacturers with reputations of producing quality. Although you probably won't be running thousands of rounds through it, you will want a weapon that you know will work when you need it.

Pocket handguns are obviously supposed to be small enough to fit into your pocket. Well, pockets come in different sizes because people come in different sizes. A pocket handgun should be small enough so that its outline is not imprinted on the pockets of the clothes you'll wear when you are carrying it.

There are pocket guns small enough to slip into a shirt pocket. What you have to be careful of, though, is purchasing a handgun that is too small. A gun that disappears into your hand will be more difficult to hold and therefore more difficult to shoot well. So you'll want small, but not too small.

The weight of a pocket handgun affects your personal comfort. You don't want a brick in your pocket that will make you walk funny and that you are going to want to fidget with all day long. Adjusting your handgun is NOT the same as adjusting your car keys.

To design a pocket handgun requires more of a manufacturer than merely scaling-down a large handgun. Actions, safeties, sights, triggers, and frames have to be re-engineered to accommodate the same size. Consequently, the smaller handguns have features and characteristics not typically found on larger handguns. For instance, some traditional double action semi-automatics require you to carry them half-cocked and locked because they do not have drop safeties. Some micro-revolvers are single action only and do not have drop safeties, which requires you to carry them with the hammer down between charge holes in the cylinder. Other small handguns are ammunition sensitive. So not only is it important for you to discover these characteristics before you buy such a gun, you must adapt your defensive response accordingly.

Smaller handguns are generally made for smaller caliber ammunition. In general, light bullets are not as destructive to tissue as heavy bullets. So shot placement with a pocket handgun becomes more critical. Pocket handguns also have short barrels, and therefore have shortened effective ranges. Therefore, you should rely on a pocket handgun to defend yourself against close encounter only. You must shoot a critical area of your assailant when he/she is very close to you.

That being said, pocket handguns come in caliber's from .22 to .40. In general, the larger the caliber, then the larger and heavier the firearm will be. So be aware of the trade-offs. We also recommend that you avoid .25 ACP caliber handguns. In our opinions, this caliber does not penetrate sufficiently to be relied upon for self-defense.

Quality pocket handguns can range in cost anywhere from around $200 to over $600. Remember that the price you will pay is often not only a function of the handgun, but the dealer. So paying more may not always be an indicator of your getting a better handgun. Your patience and research will be a valuable investment.

Evaluating a Handgun for Purchase

Eventually you will commit to the purchase of some handgun. We have already presented to you some of the factors that should go into your decision-making process. However, it will be YOUR decision. Remember, it is a decision that you want to LIVE with ultimately.

Remember, using a handgun to survive an encounter requires two main ingredients. First, you must have a quality handgun that has been properly maintained so that you are absolutely confident that it will function when you need it most. Second, you must be able to place the shots you make. We have already discussed a great deal about the first ingredient. Let's touch upon the second.

In order to be able to place the shots you make, you must be able to shoot properly and safely. So before you commit yourself to the purchase of a handgun, we STRONGLY encourage you to learn how to shoot. This is not a catch 22. We have dedicated a good portion of our book to the safe handling and proper shooting of handguns. So we urge you to read and learn. However, reading how to shoot and actually shooting are two entirely different exercises. Since there are many gun ranges that offer you the opportunity to shoot a variety of rental firearms, we recommend you apply the lessons found in this book to actually shooting on the firing line. Find a range that stresses safety and education. What may be even better is finding a range that offers NRA pistol courses. Participating in such courses will give you the chance to shoot a variety of handguns under supervised conditions. The bottom line is to "learn to drive before you buy your first car."

The first-hand experience you gain from handling and shooting a firearm has a great deal of influence on what handgun you eventually choose. If you don't know how to stand properly and how to hold the gun properly and how to use the sights properly and how to squeeze the trigger properly, then how can you possibly evaluate whether a gun is good for you or not? The truth of the matter is that without the first-hand experience you will only be guessing.

So at this point you do not have all you need to make an informed purchase of a handgun. There is still much of the book remaining for you to read, many exercises for you to perform, and many experiences for you to encounter. Relax! Your handgun will still be out there when you ARE ready.

Commonly, most shooters, as they practice, will often forget the cardinal rule of shooting, and ignore that which surrounds the target they are firing at. Mistakenly shooting an innocent person or object is unforgivable. Only practice and being aware of your surroundings matter! Take the guesswork out! Practice, practice.

▶ **Why use training rounds (i.e. inert rounds or snap caps) for dry firing?**

Firing pins, or spring released strikers, come through the firing pin or striker channel hole to strike and ignite a round of ammunition. The firing pin or striker is designed to stop at primer contact. If the chamber is empty, the firing pin or striker will microscopically stretch past its defined terminal position. Excessive dry firing in this manner may, over time, result in material fatigue. Eventually, this can lead to malfunctioning due to chipping, bending, or shearing of the firing pin or striker. Since this potential condition cannot be predicted, you would be risking whether or not your firearm will operate when you need it to.

Snap caps, or commercially available "dummy rounds" are recommended for dry fire practice. Spent shells may also be used.

CAUTION. Just the same as when cleaning your firearm, DO NOT have any live ammunition present during a dry fire exercise. If using spent cases, paint the bottom with a marker. Leave the other end open for quick identification. You are the ultimate safety for any firearm you handle. Never rely on anyone else verifying inert rounds.

▶ **What are my options for safely storing my handgun in my home?**

Consider some of the factors of firearms security and storage. You want to prevent unauthorized persons from accessing the firearms, while still permitting yourself and other authorized persons to be able to access and use them. You want to use storage devices that inhibit thieves from stealing your guns, that prevent corrosion by the environment, and that reduce the chances of being destroyed by a disaster.

All security devices or storage containers are not substitutes to your acting responsibly and behaving safely. They are only supplements. Also keep in mind that children are naturally curious and quite often clever enough to defeat the plans of well-intentioned adults.

You should store those firearms that you do not regularly carry and are not part of your home defense plan. You'll place these firearms into what we'll refer to as *cold storage. Cold* has nothing to do with temperature (duh!). *Cold* is referring to the fact that you are not using these guns regularly, that you will store them unloaded, and that you will keep them locked up. Since you will not need quick access to them, you should consider using a locked cabinet, safe or vault.

But what about those guns that you do carry regularly and/or are a part of your home defense strategy? We'll refer to those as *hot* weapons. Like *cold* weapons, these too must also be secured properly in your home. *Hot storage* is a bit more complicated. You may want to keep your hot weapons loaded. You may need to be able to access these firearms quickly and easily to defend your lives during a criminal home intrusion. Of course, it is imperative that you still prevent children and unauthorized persons from accessing these guns since you are going to be keeping ammunition in or near them. Yes, this is quite the balancing act.

Transporting a firearm from your home to a range (or elsewhere) and back is yet another matter. You must comply with the laws of the jurisdictions in which you live, your ultimate destination and all those through which you transport. In many cases the firearms must be unloaded and placed within a locked, ammunition-free container. So it is most likely that you will also need portable gun storage.

You do not want to be sleeping with a handgun under your pillow. There is really no good reason to do so. Many gun shops have bins with used holsters that they will sell at reduced prices. Take advantage of this. If you nail or screw one of these holsters to a bedpost or the rear of a headboard, you will still have ready access to your handgun. Of course, there is a downside! The easy access that the holster offers to you is the same easy access it offers to children or anyone else. So DO NOT use this method for storing a handgun if you have children in your home.

Trigger locks are common and inexpensive firearm safety devices. The lock's body is mostly made of metal and is composed of two halves. Each half is slightly larger than the trigger guard of most handguns. One of the halves has a post sticking out of it. The post fits through the trigger guard. The second half has a hole that accepts the post from the first piece. When installed properly, the two halves lock snugly to the trigger guard and prevent the trigger from being pulled. You can prove this to yourself using an unloaded gun. With practice (using an unloaded gun) you can learn to remove a trigger lock very quickly and smoothly.

Trigger locks have limitations, even when installed properly. They do not prevent somebody from loading or unloading the gun. They still permit somebody from cycling the slide on a semi-auto. On a revolver, when the post is positioned in front of the trigger, a person can still cock the hammer. This would indeed be very dangerous if the revolver was loaded. Why, you ask? With most revolvers when the hammer is cocked, the cylinder is locked closed and the gun cannot be immediately unloaded. In order to de-cock the hammer, you will have to remove the trigger lock first. Well, when a revolver's hammer is cocked, it takes only a few pounds of pressure to discharge it. So you absolutely, positively do not want to be in your home while removing the trigger lock from a cocked and loaded revolver. It would be better to do so on the firing line of a local shooting range. AVOID THIS SITUATION.

With this or any other device that you may use for hot storage, you will need to practice unlocking and preparing a weapon. PRACTICE WITH AN UNLOADED WEAPON. Consider the circumstances under which you will need it. It may be dark. You may have been sleeping. You will probably be scared over the prospect that some scumbags are in your home. This would NOT be the time for you to read the instructions that came with your locking device. OOOOPS. You want the process of accessing and safely readying your weapon to be committed to your muscle memory well BEFORE you need it to fend off some bad guys. So you need to practice and use your common sense: PRACTICE WITH AN UNLOADED WEAPON.

Cable locks are popular as well. As you might expect, a cable lock is a cable with a lock on it. To install one onto a semi-auto, you would open the slide, and then run the cable through the ejection port, down the magazine well, and out the butt of the grip. To install on a revolver, you would run the cable through a few charge holes in the cylinder. When in place, a cable lock does prevent you from loading the gun, working its action, and firing it. Like everything else, through practice you will learn to remove it surely and swiftly.

The Life Jacket Gun Guard system (www.life-jacket.com) is a very favorable firearm safety device. Like a clamshell, it envelops the action of a handgun. When it is installed, it prevents somebody from playing with the trigger and action of both semi-autos and revolvers. The Life Jacket is closed and opened with a built-in key lock. Since the lock is OUTSIDE the trigger guard, you are much less likely to discharge the weapon unintentionally. The Life Jacket comes in either a shell of polycarbonate (around $20) or steel (around $40), and is lined with foam. It keeps your handgun snugly safe. A Life Jacket is appropriate for transporting your handgun to the range and securing your handgun someplace in your house (like within a nightstand drawer). You even have the option to bolt it to a wall or other fixed surface. With some practice (using an unloaded gun) you can learn to open a Life Jacket and ready your weapon very confidently and efficiently.

You can make an inexpensive yet effective gun box by modifying a military ammunition can. You should be able to purchase a standard military ammo can at a local military surplus store or mail order house. A can is made of steel and has a lid with a rubber moisture seal. Line the interior with some egg crate foam or carpet remnants. After you attach a hasp and add a good lock, you will have created a secure moisture-resistant firearms container. You can use it to transport your weapon to and from the range. Or transform it into a safe by bolting it to your bedroom or cabinet floor. We are confident that if you apply your creativity, you will find other appropriate solutions.

There are a wide variety of cases on the market designed for storing or transporting guns. Models come in all shapes and sizes. Some can hold a single gun, while others may hold more than four. Many have exteriors made of plastic or metal with an interior padded with foam. Usually those that do not have built-in locks can still be secured with small padlocks.

A lock box is another alternative for your hot storage needs. You can keep the box in the night-stand drawer. A box usually has a pushbutton combination lock. When you know the combination, its design allows you to enter it quickly. When you don't know the combination, you can spend all day trying to guess it. Prices for lock boxes start at around $50. They may be an attractive option for those of you with children.

When you have more than a few guns to store, you will probably want to consider purchasing a gun safe to address your cold storage needs. Like almost everything else, gun safes come in different sizes and have a variety of characteristics. Some are designed for handguns alone while many accommodate both long guns and handguns. Often it is a question of capacity. You can find small models that hold just a few handguns to huge walk-in vaults that hold dozens of long guns.

You will also discover that some gun safes are made much heavier and sturdier than others. Many safes use simple but effective locking mechanisms: others have expensive electronic access systems. You will even find some with sophisticated environmental controls. You can usually spend as little as $75 on a decent gun safe. As you can imagine, you can spend thousands. You can really go overboard if you allow yourself.

Two companies that are worthy of a good look are American Security Products Company (AMSEC; 800-421-6142; www.amsecusa.com) and DAC Technologies (800-920-0098; www.dactec.com). AMSEC makes safes ranging in size from those that hold one to two pistols to major league storage safes. AMSEC's "Pistol Packer" model is an affordable and portable storage box with a mechanical pushbutton combination lock. This heavy duty container can hold a full-size service sidearm with a spare magazine, or several compact handguns. The "Pistol Packer" is small enough to fit in many desk drawers. It is equipped with a handle, so it can be used to transport your firearms.

DAC Technologies makes an inexpensive electronic push-button digital safe. It is battery powered, but has a mechanical key back-up just in case the battery power source fails. It can hold as many as four pistols with spare magazines on its two shelves.

These products are good. However, don't limit yourself to them just because we mention them here. Check Home Depot, Wal-mart and other department stores. Many of them have viable products appropriate to your needs.

Keep it simple! You should deliberately avoid placing loaded weapons or ammunition in your cold-storage containers. Yes, you always want to treat any weapon as though it is loaded when you pick it up, even from cold-storage. So keep it simple. Keep cold-storage *cold!*

Devise your home defense plan. Decide on what techniques, tactics and tools you will use to ensure your survival and that of your family. Don't adopt the concept that when the stuff hits the fan, you'll enter your gun vault and ponder to yourself, "Hmmmm, what gun is the flavor of the day?" Keep it simple! Keep it real!

▶ Storage: Loaded vs. Unloaded?

At some point you are going to ask yourself the question, "Am I going to store my home defense handgun loaded or unloaded?" Only you can answer it. But we can give you some food for thought.

Just so there aren't any misunderstandings, for purposes of this discussion we will consider a handgun to be loaded when it contains live ammunition, and to be unloaded when it is does not contain any live ammunition.

Keeping your handgun unloaded but locked-up in a hot storage device is a viable option. You will want to keep nearby a full magazine or speedloader as the case warrants. You will want to practice accessing your weapon, getting to the ammunition, and loading. (Practice with dummy ammunition!) Some may say, "When I have to get my weapon I don't want to be slowed down by having to load it." Slowed down? After you have access to your weapon, it will take a practiced person only a few seconds to load it. Think about it. In the case of a pistol, all you have to do is insert a magazine and rack the slide. For a revolver all you do is open the cylinder, insert and release the speedloader, and then close and index the cylinder. We're talking only seconds.

If you are deliberately unloading your weapons before you secure them, then you have taken a big step in preventing an accident. A gun cannot fire, intentionally or otherwise, if it is not loaded.

You must take to heart that even if you store your handgun in an unloaded condition but you keep its ammunition nearby, then you or anybody else who can access your handgun can readily load it. So you must still prevent unauthorized hands from accessing these firearms. Innocent lives depend on your preparedness.

Now let's consider the case where you are keeping your home defense gun in a loaded condition. Since you are intentionally keeping it loaded, you must choose a storage device that not only prevents unauthorized access, but will minimize the possibility of unintentionally discharging the weapon through incidental handling. You will also be relying on the gun to be actually loaded when you need it. So you must develop habits that ensure the gun is indeed loaded, but without increasing the risk of accidentally firing it.

Here is a hypothetical story we created to illustrate a point:

Husband and Wife are sleeping. They went to bed about an hour ago. Wife wakes up for a reason she cannot immediately explain, that is, until she hears an unfamiliar voice and some noises coming from downstairs. She notices that the light she and Husband intentionally leave on at night is now off. It occurs to Wife that somebody is in her house. After giving Husband a few not so dainty shakes while urging him to get up, Wife moves to her nightstand drawer to ready her handgun. Wife unlocks her storage device and picks up her weapon. Wife, who normally stores her weapon loaded, notices that her handgun doesn't feel quite right. Now some thoughts run through her mind, "Damn, did I forget to load this? Did Husband borrow it again and forget to load it?"

At this point, let us pause for some questions to you, our reader: "Is Wife's gun loaded or unloaded?", "What are the causes of Wife's doubts?". Fear? Adrenaline? Husband being a dufus again? Remember that it is dark, Wife may be momentarily disoriented, and Husband is wearing his lucky green pajamas. Well, determining the exact causes of Wife's concerns is a futile exercise. The fact that she has doubts about the condition of her weapon compromises her ability to defend herself well. Wife will now have to determine if her weapon is indeed loaded or not. Do you think fear, adrenaline and darkness will help her do so efficiently?

The story demonstrates a reasonable argument that could be made against your keeping home defense firearms loaded. Instead consider storing these weapons unloaded and locked in their hot storage devices. Keep a full magazine with the pistol, or a full speedloader with the revolver. Before retiring for the night, do a visual spot check of the handgun and magazine (or speedloader). Update your gun-readying procedure to include steps that deliberately clear the gun, and then load it. These two steps, when practiced, will take only a few seconds to execute and will reassure you that the firearm is ready to help you in your defense. Plus you will reap any additional benefits that may come from storing your weapons unloaded. Keep it simple!

Yes, there's that "p" word again, "practice." Practice is crucial. We're not trying to beat you over the head (well, not too much, anyway) but you must remember that to learn these new physical and intellectual skills does require some effort and dedication on your part. You need to incorporate into your mental and muscle memories good and safe habits while avoiding bad habits that you will have to break later. Your patience, persistence, and practice will maximize your proficiency and performance. You will prevail. (Enough alliteration for now.)

When practicing the process of loading a weapon at home, then for goodness' sake, DON'T USE LIVE AMMUNITION. Use common sense. Purchase or borrow some plastic orange training rounds for filling your magazines or speedloaders during your practice sessions. Practice these exercises with live ammo at the range.

The decision to keep those weapons that are a part of your home defense plan either loaded or unloaded usually comes down to your comfort and that of other adults in the household. We showed that speed isn't really an issue. Trust in your equipment, and confidence in yourself and your habits, are paramount.

7

Ammunition

▶ **What is a "bullet"?**

A bullet is a projectile made of lead, aluminum, copper-jacketed lead, or a shot shell that is dispensed from a round of ammunition that is fired from a handgun, shotgun or rifle. The bullet makes up the head of the round and is the part of the round that is projected out of the gun and strikes the target (hopefully) when the gun is fired.

Bullet head types have certain physical characteristics which name them:

1. **Target rounds** or **wadcutters** are projectiles that are flat-faced, seated flush with the case (usually lead) contained mostly within the case, and punch a clear scorable hole in a particular target.

2. A **semi-wadcutter** is a truncated cone-shaped lead or copper-jacketed projectile that extends somewhat out of the casing.

3. **Round nose** or **conical-shaped** lead or copper-jacketed lead bullets are most commonly called "ball ammunition" because of their circular head.

4. **Jacketed soft points** are lead projectiles that are three quarters enclosed in a copper jacket which allows for greater expansion of the bullet head once the lead tip strikes its target.

5. **Frangible** bullets are aluminum or soft metal projectiles that break into numerous pieces upon contact when striking the target. They *fragment.*

6. **Hollow points** indicate just that. There is a hole or cavity in the bullet head through the center of its circumference. They are designed to produce expansion approximately 2 to 3 times the bullet's original diameter. They very often don't perform that way. Their unpredictable performance is due to the wide variation in bullet composition, ballistics, and the medium into which they are fired.

7. A handgun **shot shell** contains a number of pellets contained within a plastic case mounted at the projectile section of a round of ammunition. Upon firing, the numerous pellets release in a circular pattern with a diameter that is determined by the amount of pellets and the velocity with which they are propelled. In a handgun, they are most usually used for snake or rodent control. We do not recommend this ammunition as a defensive round.

▶ **What are the components of a live cartridge or round?**

All rounds of ammunition are comprised of 4 component parts: (1) the bullet (or projectile); (2) the case or casing made up of either aluminum, steel or brass; (3) the propellent which is the smokeless gun powder that is ignited and that generates the expansive high pressure gases that propel the bullet out of the gun toward its target; and last but not least, (4) the primer which is the ignition source that ignites the smokeless gunpowder with a contained explosion when struck by the firing pin. See Figure 7.1.

Figure 7.1

▶ **What are the different types of handgun ammunition?**

Handgun ammunition is defined in terms of either "caliber" or "millimeter" (mm). Both of these terms describe the diameter of the circular base of the projectile or bullet. Caliber is measured in either hundredths of an inch or in terms of millimeters. Inch measurements are most common to the United States. The metric system of millimeters is used by the rest of the world.

Lands and Grooves
Contained within the bore of a barrel is the rifling. The rifling consists of lands and grooves. As their names imply, the lands are the high spots and the grooves are the low spots. They give the bullet spin, trajectory and accuracy as it goes out to its target. The diameter of the barrel's bore (i.e., internal area) is measured in terms of the distance between the lands from one side of the bore to opposite side 180 degrees.

Ammunition or caliber must match the caliber of your firearm. That is, the diameter of the bullet (the projectile) must correspond to the diameter of the barrel's bore. If you fire the wrong caliber you may cause damage or malfunction to your gun. It will not be more bang for your buck, it'll just cost you a few bucks more in repairs or replacement. Hopefully, it won't cost you an eye or worse.

Ammunition Calibers
The most common caliber in the world used for target shooting and small game hunting as well as by beginners has consistently been the .22 caliber short, long and long rifle. These differ in terms of case length and powder charge.

Powder charge is measured in terms of actual number of grains of powder or volume taken up. A good visual comparison would be grains of pepper. The more grains there are, the more volume of pepper there is, the greater the sneeze. The more grains of gunpowder there is, the more explosively the bullet leaves the gun. Powder grains are not given by the manufacturer on boxes of ammunition sold. It is proprietary information.

Bullet weight is also measured in grains, but so that you are not confused, it is grains of physical weight. Boxes of ammunition do report bullet weight in grains (e.g., 185 grains).

.22 Caliber. The .22 caliber round was the first totally self-contained round of ammunition produced for modern day revolvers. It was formulated by Smith and Wesson. It is probably the least expensive round you can buy. Its primer is contained in the external rim at the base of the casing, hence it is called "rimfire." Few other calibers fire from the external rim. Most everything else is "centerfire," ergo the primer is contained in the center of the base of the casing.

It is important to remember that even with the .22 caliber's relatively small sting, the .22 projectile will travel to a distance of 1 mile, as will most other calibers, if unobstructed.

.25 and .32 ACP. Within the shooting community today are a wide variety of handgun ammunition calibers. Starting with the lower calibers and moving up from the .22, they include the .25 ACP (Automatic Colt Pistol) and the .32 ACP which is a popular round for today's ultra-concealable pocket pistols.

.38 Special. The .38 special is perhaps the most common and popular round for revolvers, or "wheel guns" as they are called. This round has been most common to police and military revolver use. However, because of its ballistic limitations in terms of speed and penetration, numerous law enforcement agencies approached ammunition manufacturers to provide a higher velocity, more powerful round to combat the organized criminal problems that were so frequent in the 1920's and 1930's.

Magnum Calibers. A collaboration between Philip Sharpe (the inventor of the Sharpe's rifle) and Major Douglas Wesson of Smith & Wesson resulted in the formulation of a service round to meet law enforcement's needs for greater firepower than was provided by the .38 special revolver cartridge. Thus was born the .357 magnum revolver cartridge. The name "Magnum" was the brainchild of Douglas Wesson who was an avid champagne connoisseur, and in the vintner's world, the term "magnum" refers to a slightly longer than standard bottle. As Wesson always drank from magnum bottles; ergo the term .357 magnum for the slightly longer cartridge case length and more powerful powder charge.

Later additions to the more powerful magnum line were the .41 and .44 magnum series for law enforcement and hunting. As with the relation between the .38 special and its longer and more powerful cousin the .357 magnum, the powerful and popular .44 special gave rise to the popular .44 magnum for revolvers.

9mm. The 9mm Parabellum (i.e., meaning "for war") or "Luger" is also known as the 9mm NATO and 9x19. It is a popular semi-automatic round that was originally introduced for the German Navy Luger model 1902 military pistol. It is the oldest of all of the current mainstream auto loads. The .380 ACP, a common cartridge for pocket pistols that is slightly more powerful than the .32 ACP is an offshoot of the 9mm Luger. In Europe, the .380 ACP is also known as the 9mm Kurtz or 9mm Browning Short.

.40 S&W. The .40 Smith & Wesson (S&W) caliber semi-automatic cartridge, also known as the 10mm short, was developed in the late 1980's by Smith & Wesson because of control problems a lot of shooters had with full power 10mm cartridges. The .40 S&W has proven itself to be accurate, controllable and reliable in all situations.

Several additional calibers within the marketplace and pushed by sales people are the .357 SIG and the 10mm. These rounds introduce severe recoil and consequently hamper second and third shot recovery. For these reasons, we do not recommend these calibers for novices. Each of these rounds does have their following and does have advantages when used in conjunction with extensive training. However, they are hard to find and cost prohibitive. For revolver shooters who enjoy large caliber ammunition, the .44 special and .44 magnum provide viable alternatives. However, the .44 special, while a relatively manageable power load (with practice), is also hard to find and expensive. The .44 magnum generates major recoil, but is much more available.

.45 ACP. Finally, we come to the .45 ACP ("Automatic Colt Pistol"). It was developed originally for the U.S. Military by John Browning who also developed the Colt .45 pistol and the Browning High Power 9mm. The 1911 Colt .45 pistol had been the mainstay of our military since its inception in 1911 until 1985 when it was replaced by NATO 9mm powered ammunition. The 1911 series pistols have been the most aesthetically pleasing and hence popular handguns since their inception. The .45 ACP cartridge is one of the most used cartridges on the planet and still remains highly effective in terminating a criminal threat.

There are other configurations of ammunition available within the current market place that meet situations head-on and probably just as many on various drawing boards.

▶ **What is the difference between personal defense and target or range ammunition?**

When we are talking about defensive uses of handgun ammunition, there is absolutely no difference save for some important variables. To stop or "neutralize" a human being who has the means and ability to take your life, certain criteria must be addressed. The first one is bullet weight which affects depth of penetration.

Criminal adversaries, like any other human beings, have very resilient physical bodies. Therefore, to permanently damage and destroy major organs and stop the aggression, you need adequate depth of penetration. The minimum bullet grain weight that we recommend for 9mm, .38 special and higher calibers is 124 grains to accomplish adequate depth of penetration and permanent cavitation, which means a permanent gaping hole.

The Myth of the "One Shot Stop." There is no handgun on the planet with which one shot can be relied upon to neutralize a criminal adversary. We must rely on multiple hits which leads to our second consideration. The bullet must have low enough velocity or speed so we can get off a good (meaning *accurate*) second or third shot. This translates into *good second and third shot recovery* which means getting back on target as soon as possible. You will find that most exotic rounds produced in the market place are exactly the opposite with high speeds and low grain weight. They tend to produce more recoil which can hamper second and third shot recovery. In addition, they tend to be cost prohibitive and thus, not readily usable for practice because of their premium expense.

Our suggestion is to find a good quality, clean burning source of ammunition that provides at least the minimum grain weight we have recommended, that is not outrageously expensive, and with which you can practice on a regular basis to enhance and maintain your shooting skills.

It doesn't matter if you are shooting an elephant gun. You must have the skills for your first one or two shots to be accurate, or you might as well forget it. What we mean is that shot placement is the most effective and valuable criterion for practical defensive shooting.

Body Structure. If you look around at an average roomful of people, you will see how body structures vary. Body structures affect depth of bullet penetration and likelihood of getting permanent cavitation and incapacitation. From the extremely thin person you could poke your finger through, to the heavy-set person you have to drive a bulldozer through, to the weightlifter whose muscle mass is such that you need a harpoon to go through, fat and muscle density produce obstacles that only bullet grain weight can overcome and defeat. Therefore, the most effective defensive round is a slow-moving and heavy projectile such as the .45 ACP at 230 grains moving at around 850 feet per second (fps).

It is just common sense if you think about this for a second. A bow and arrow produces considerably less velocity and foot-pounds of energy than any handgun or rifle round produces, but many an African elephant or Kodiak grizzly bear have been dropped with one arrow shot in the right place. Exotic rounds lead to empty pockets and may not always perform the way they are intended in a clutch. We can't change the wind, but we can adjust the sails.

It is a fact that within any given caliber starting with .38 specials and 9mm, there is a balance or compromise that one has to make between bullet weight, powder charge, and projectile speed. It's basic physics that ammunition of lesser bullet grain weight has higher velocities and less impact capabilities than do heavier slower moving rounds. This means that within any given caliber, a lighter bullet with greater speed is more likely to go through your target endangering those behind it than heavier rounds that are more likely to stop within the target and create a permanent wound cavity.

+P and +P+ Ammunition. This difference is compounded by the fact that some manufacturers produce "hot rounds" that are labeled as +P and +P+ ammunition. These are rounds that have increased powder charge. In a heavier bullet, this is a good thing because it delivers less recoil than the magnum velocities of the same cartridge and promotes better depth of penetration and cavitation. However, in the lighter rounds that deliver greater speeds, the result is often that there is not enough surface contact, expansion and tissue destruction to neutralize the adversary. Human physiology is the other dependent variable that must be factored in to ballistics decision making. The factors that have to be considered are: muscle mass and tone, depth and mass of body structure, insulating fatty tissue, clothing, and sheer adrenaline in the attacker.

It is a little-known fact that some newer high caliber (.44 special and .45 long Colt) very light weight, alloy revolvers being produced (e.g., Taurus's titanium models) act like kinetic bullet pullers following the recoil generated by the first shot. That is, the gun slightly dislodges the projectile from the subsequent rounds in the cylinder causing the revolver to jam and lock up. So, if you purchase a large caliber, light weight revolver, you should purchase double crimped ammunition. Double crimped ammunition means that instead of a single crimp at the top of the casing bullet connection, there are two crimps on the casing to doubly secure the projectile and eliminate projectile slippage.

▶ **How do I choose the right ammunition for my handgun and for the purpose for which I use it?**

Given the two caveats above (i.e., grain weight and velocity), hollow point ammunition from a reliable manufacturer that expands well beyond its original diameter would be an optimum choice for defensive purposes.

Recommended Reliable Hollow Points

One brand that comes to mind immediately is Federal Cartridge Company's Hydra Shok. From Steve's personal experience both in police work and in the private sector with dignitary protection and the like, Federal Hydra Shoks have been his primary choice each and every time he feels he might find himself in a dangerous situation. His personal experience from numerous years of usage reveals that Federal Hydra Shoks are durable, reliable, accurate, clean shooting, and highly effective rounds.

Several other quality manufacturers that immediately come to mind without thinking twice when considering defensive ammunition are Remington and Winchester. Remington's Golden Saber jacketed hollow points (JHPs), Winchester's SXT hollow points and Winchester's Silvertips hollow points are excellent choices. These three products along with Federal's Hydra Shoks have proven track records for providing reliable accuracy, optimum penetration depending on bullet grain weight, and effective expansion and cavitation on impact. Federal Cartridge Company recently acquired Speer Ammunition. We also highly recommend Speer Gold Dot hollow-points.

Two examples of frangible or fragmenting rounds are Glazer Safety Slugs and CCI Speer shot shells. Frangibles are most notable for producing large impact, surface cavitation which isn't always permanent but is supposed to effect quick neutralization of the target. However, you need depth of penetration to cause organ damage and neutralize the target. These rounds don't accomplish the depth of penetration needed to effectively stop a perpetrator.

Human beings are very resilient having elastic tissue which seals a surface wound to the skin back up almost immediately to the skin's original condition. So, to effectively stop an assailant, you need to cause large and deep, permanent cavitation. An example would be running a sharp-pointed stick through a human body—it displaces and destroys tissue and causes permanent wounds.

Zero Ammunition Company also is a leader. They make a highly recommendable, clean firing series of calibers which Steve has put to practical use in his range training exercises for over 8 years. Having fired several hundred thousand rounds in personal and student use collectively, Zero has proven itself to be a clean burning, effective, accurate, reliable and inexpensive product.

With all that said, keep in mind that it's impossible to maintain a continual baseline of effective bullet configurations without keeping an ongoing updated data file. This is because any of the ammunition manufacturers can change their bullet composition and powder charges without public notice. So, you as the shooter must continually read available product information and use the products regularly to sort it all out and update what meets your personal criteria and defensive needs.

In other words, start your own data base. As you regularly practice at the range shooting the defensive ammunition of your choice, you will develop your proficiency with that ammunition and also your confidence that it will work well for you when you really need it.

In some states, hollow point ammunition is illegal to all but law enforcement. However, the good news is that you can rely on the fact that jacketed "hardball" (round nose), soft point, or truncated cone ammunition can be just as effective and valuable for your personal defense and survival as long as you keep within the bullet grain weight limitations and specifications described earlier.

Lead ammunition in whatever configuration gives reliable expansion but often fouls the working components of your firearm. However, in a tactical situation, when lead is all you have, it is the best bullet on the Planet Earth and it just means that you will be cleaning your weapon with a little bit more diligence than with jacketed ammunition. There are numerous ammunition companies continually seeking your ammo dollar. So, be selective in your evaluation and diligent with your purchasing choices.

Whatever your ammunition manufacturer choice, always store your ammunition in a secure box placed in a secure, cool and dry area so that your ammunition will be resistant to corrosion and will work for you as designed when needed.

▶ What does "stopping power" really mean?

The term is readily misused in motion pictures, in advertisements, in magazines, in many visual depictions, in the television community, and by some nondescript authors. The term itself implies that one shot will neutralize an adversary. Statistically that is unfounded when you are talking about someone who has the means and motivation to take your life! Many aggressors just do not know that they are supposed to fall down dead because they were shot. On the other hand, some people will faint when stuck in the ass with a pin, let alone being shot. This example is cited in the professional literature as "psychogenic reaction."

> *The more positive side of the psychogenic reaction concept is that if you believe that you are going to survive you will survive! And that is our goal, that YOU will survive.*

As previously stated, you should never rely on the idea of getting a one shot stop. You can neutralize or deter an explosive, violent confrontation only with good shot placement and adequate caliber weight in grains as described earlier. Don't be misled by nonsensical and non-sensible terms such as "stopping power," "shocking power" and the like. They are all hollow and meaningless terms when describing what actually happens in a real violent confrontation.

As an example, numerous people have described in the professional literature how individuals have survived .44 magnum shots to the head at extremely close range and lived to get up and walk back to their car, blocks away, before dropping. Had they had the means and equipment to return fire, they could have readily done so. Avoid being taken in by slogans and misquoted and misleading explanations by alleged "experts" on the effects of being shot. The fact is that human beings are extremely resilient when it comes to surviving severe physical insults and injuries. It has been often described how, in combat, soldiers have had their arms or legs severed from their body and still survived to fight on until relieved.

A drug crazed, adrenaline pumped maniac intent on doing you harm may not know at that moment that he is supposed to fall down and play dead just because you've shot him in the chest with your .38 caliber weapon. However, this is surely not the time to rely on pepper spray so that the offender will cease and desist! This is also surely not the time to discover that you cannot pull the trigger on another "human being" or that you left your gun at home! Carrying a firearm is a conscious, mature, deliberate, thought out decision.

You have to believe within yourself that you will survive a confrontation and indeed you will! The words "stopping power" imply that with one shot all aggression will cease. The anatomical truth is that it is a rare occasion when that occurs. Usually if it does, it is purely by luck, good or bad. If your luck is like ours, maintain your proficiency and don't depend on one shot stops or, for that matter, on rabbits' feet.

8

Revolvers

▶ Is a revolver the right firearm for me?

The revolver offers simplicity of operation that many shooters prefer. You just load your rounds of ammunition in the chamber's cylinders, close the cylinder, and you are ready. Most untrained and many novice persons feel ill at ease with semi-automatic pistols with their more complex operating mechanisms. Thus, revolvers provide a more comfortable and manageable alternative.

The only tactical difference between quality revolvers and semi-automatic pistols for personal carry and protection is the amount of ammunition they can contain. This leads us back to informed training and testing. All decisions of this nature should be made from an informed standpoint. Our job as authors is to inform you about the essential criteria that should go into making this selection.

Revolvers come in varying frame sizes (small, medium and large) and barrel lengths (commonly ranging from snub-nosed 1⅞ inch to 8⅞ inch on large frames). They also vary in terms of weight given differences in material composition. The heavier revolvers are made of all stainless or high carbon steel. The lighter ones are made of aluminum alloy frames, and the lightest (e.g., S & W "Airlites") are made of titanium or scandium alloys. Revolvers also come in different calibers ranging from .22s all the way up to .45 ACP, .44 magnums and specials and greater. Additionally, revolvers come with different round capacities ranging from 5-shot revolvers up to some 9-shot .22 caliber revolvers.

Your choice of revolver will depend on such factors as how you intend to employ it and the size, weight and caliber that you can effectively handle. What is functional for you? Once again, we urge you to make an informed choice referencing an *experienced shooter* whom you definitely trust.

Through the generosity of Smith and Wesson and its dedication to consumer and shooter education, we had the opportunity to test and evaluate several weapons in their outstanding revolver product line. Smith and Wesson is the summit of revolver quality on the planet. Steve holds a personal loyalty to S&W after personally carrying S & W revolvers in Vietnam, on the job in the Philadelphia Police Department, and in pistol team competition for over 30 years.

S&W manufactures a wide variety of revolvers so that there are at least one or more models to meet the carry and home defense needs of virtually anyone. We both treasure our S&W revolvers. They are works of art.

The Model 442 .38 caliber snub-nose Centennial Airweight with the internal hammer provides good pocket carry with its light weight and small J-Frame size. It is an extremely accurate double action only (DAO) revolver that is very controllable in that it has great second and third shot recoil recovery, an essential attribute in a defensive weapon. In a nutshell, it is a pleasure to shoot. This firearm is unbelievably comfortable to carry and conceal, easy to handle, and is low maintenance. The Model 442 is the nicest Airweight we've shot!

Beware of facsimile copies of this S&W in the marketplace. They don't have the same standards of quality control, accuracy or reliability. They very well might spend a large percentage of time being repaired on the South American continent—ergo not meeting your personal defensive needs and safety requirements in your land.

The Model 640 stainless steel snub-nose Centennial J-Frame shares the same internal hammer design of the 442 which means DAO, not binding in your clothing, and ease of concealment in holstered carry. To this point, twenty-five shooters of varying skill levels at our range have been involved in the testing of these firearms. All of them have shown a similar degree of fondness for the gun, and accuracy with it, to boot. What's remarkable is that their shooting performance was almost identical in accuracy irrespective of the wide variation in their levels of experience.

These firearms, to say the least, have changed a number of minds relative to revolver concealment and carry. Their quick delivery from the holster and outstanding controllability, minimal recoil, and accuracy lay a foundation for secure self-defense and protection. The results are predictable no matter whose hands these guns are in. Lights out for the "bad guy."

We found that the straight out of the box Smith and Wesson Model 640 we tested with either .38 special or .357 magnum ammunition lent itself to quick smooth transition from holster to target. Both of the above guns provide clean, crisp DAO actions that both men and women can appreciate and find a comfort level with. The quality name of S&W speaks for itself.

The S&W .44 Special "Mountain Lite" Model 396. For larger framed shooters, who like more punch in their packet, the Model 396 Mountain Lite 5-shot .44 special is an elegantly designed and manufactured aluminum alloy, medium K-Frame double action/single action (DA/SA) revolver with an exposed hammer, titanium cylinder and steel barrel that delivers an accurately placed shot time after time due to its HIVIZ front sight and adjustable rear V-notch sight. The 396 is an outstanding law enforcement backup, undercover carry piece, and a handgun hunter's or home defender's dream for big caliber response. Its light weight and beauty are both unbelievable and are matched by its performance.

We did notice one specific problem that can be readily addressed however; that is, the open back strap grip provided out of the box. The recoil generated to the v-notch of the shooter's hand is quite strong. However, this is easily corrected with a pair of Pachmayr backstrap covered grips (Lyman Products Corporation). While we are on the topic, Lyman manufactures an outstanding line of after-market Pachmayr grips for almost every revolver and pistol made and sold on the marketplace. With this single and simple after-market refinement, the 396 .44 special delivers superior performance and reliability. It is one hand cannon that we hope you are never lucky enough to be forced to fire when a criminal finds himself looking down its cavernous barrel.

If you are fortunate to purchase one of these, it comes in a robust, well designed case that any collector will be proud to own. This .44's double action is butter smooth and you can drive tacks given its accuracy as long as you tame the recoil. It's definitely carryable in the right holster. We had the opportunity to evaluate the #77 "Tortilla" (with thumb break) and the #88 "Street Combat" (open top) fine leather, belt slide "pancake" holsters made by El Paso Saddlery *(915-544-2233; www.ep saddlery.com)*. They fit like a glove and make a great, safe, mobile home for this heavy duty, fight-stopper revolver! We heartily recommend them. DeSantis also makes their excellent leather speed scabbard to fit this model.

▶ **Selecting the right caliber revolver.**

As we pointed out earlier in the book, caliber considerations should be begin with a bullet weight minimum of 124 grains and heavier. The variable is what second and third shot recovery you have as an individual with that particular caliber in that particular firearm. This is only discovered by getting practical experience in shooting. This is why getting training with several different calibers is an important part of making an informed decision regarding which caliber is right for you. For depth of penetration, anything under 124 grains is not likely to consistently meet your needs for terminating a criminal assault. You might find lighter calibers to be more pleasurable to shoot in terms of less recoil. However, they might also be a day late and a dollar short when it comes to survival.

The Lighter the Gun and Shorter the Barrel, the Greater the Recoil. Keep in mind that the lighter the revolver and the shorter the barrel, the more the gun will tend to recoil. This is just basic physics, but it is nothing that you cannot control. In sum, there is an interaction between bullet weight, powder charge, firearm weight, and barrel length that has to be balanced, and each individual has to discover what the optimum balance is for their individual defensive needs. Sheer determination has been known to overcome all those variables.

▶ **How do I maintain my revolver?**

No matter what type of firearm you own, be it revolver, semi-auto pistol, rifle or shotgun, you must maintain its cleanliness of both operation and function to make sure that the money you spent will not have been in vain because you mistreated or neglected your firearm. How often should you take care of and clean your carry firearm? Each and every time you fire it, you should clean it because the time that you do not, could be the time that it could fail you. Personally we do not like living with failure. In this area of self-defense, you cannot afford to fail because failure could mean your premature demise.

Our survival is based on fact not fiction. As such, we treat our weapons, ammunition and holsters equally well because they are all equal parts of our survival equation. Leaving one part out makes the other several points moot and this is unacceptable. You must develop each and every part of your personal survival equation equally.

Your firearm is a costly investment. You owe it to yourself to give it the respect, maintenance and care that it deserves especially since it could save your life one day. How much time is your life worth?

Care and cleaning. You must clean your firearms regularly to keep them functional and to maintain their value. After all, at some point, you might decide to upgrade for whatever reason, and you don't want to diminish the value of your investment through improper or negligent care.

▶ **What materials will I need to maintain and clean my handgun?**

We are now going to compile a list of the items you will need to maintain any firearm in today's marketplace to its highest standards. It's not rocket science; just common sense. We advocate creating your own cleaning kit as opposed to purchasing any of the ready made pre-packaged ones which are sold in most sporting goods, gun shops, and mail order. This is because you can personally select and design each component of your kit. This makes the most effective kit you can put together.

Your first stop is going to be at a dollar store to purchase a cheap welcome mat. The dimensions of these are usually 12 by 24 inches which gives you a good working area as you remove and clean parts. Secondly, you need a roll of paper towels to place over the cleaning mat so that any debris coming off of the firearm accumulates on the paper, and is easily disposed of, once you have completed cleaning your firearms. Plus, it helps you spot small parts.

Next, you'll need a good quality cleaning agent. Recommended by all quality gun manufacturers is a cleaning product called "Break Free" which is a cleaner, lubricant and protectant all in one product. Break Free comes in a plastic opaque container. It is a binary liquid compound which means that if viewed in a clear container, there is a visible line of separation in the compound. To be totally effective, the product therefore must be shaken well prior to application.

Then, you'll need a quality cleaning rod. Now, as you investigate various gun-cleaning rods and kits available, you will find that the majority are made of aluminum with articulating handles. This means that the handle of the rod spins like a windmill. That's NOT what you want. For minimum, let alone optimum functionality, you want a rod with a solid handle that is part of the rod. For maximum rod longevity, you want a rod that is made of brass and that is accepting of all brush manufacturers. Remember, most ammunition casings are brass.

Your cleaning rod should be approximately 12 inches in length. This length will clean barrel lengths ranging between 2 inches and 8⅞ inches. The big loop at the solid handle end of your brass rod ensures that you will be turning your cleaning brush (which is attached to the insertion end) clockwise through both chambers and barrel to complete the most effective debris release possible.

Next is a bore-cleaning brush. We recommend stainless steel bore brushes because they maintain their integrity 10 to 15 times longer than the common brass brushes one will see in the commercial cleaning kits. Holding the bore brush between your fingers, you'll notice that the bristles spiral like the threads of a screw from bottom to top. This should tell you that it has to be turned to be maximally effective. (Stainless steel bore brushes can be used safely in either stainless steel or blued firearms.)

The reason we turn clockwise is simple: If you turn counter clockwise the brush comes off the rod. A simple example is if you were to turn a screw into wood work with a screwdriver, wood chips would fall at your feet. A cleaning brush is designed to work exactly the same way. It cleans debris from the barrel and chamber in the same way that wood chips fall out as you turn the screwdriver clockwise.

Brushes should also never be dipped in lubricant or cleaner. They work best as a friction device to strip debris from metal, and if coated with a lubricant, adequate friction cannot be generated or maintained. You also do not want to use the bore brush like a bottle brush, scrubbing back and forth because that will prematurely collapse the bristles. To be most effective, the bore brush should be turned totally through either the barrel or the chambers and then all the way back through to point of origin in a clockwise motion. This frees the hot baked-on carbon material that spent ammunition produces.

Added to your cleaning kit should be a stainless steel, a brass, and a nylon toothbrush. It's important to understand the differences. A stainless steel toothbrush can only be used on a stainless steel firearm. The reason is that like materials will not hurt one another. The brass and the nylon brushes can be used either on stainless steel, high carbon steel, or blued firearms. Blueing is a chemical compound that retards and inhibits rust on carbon steel.

NOTE: A stainless steel toothbrush cannot be used on a blued firearm because it removes the blueing.

Be extremely conscious of the previous sentence because, removing the blueing from your firearm is extremely detrimental to it and unacceptable to the professional you are learning to be. Only a brass, bronze, or nylon toothbrush can be used safely on a blued steel or polymer frame, chamber and barrel.

Additional Items You Will Need

1. A **quality screwdriver** which won't bugger or strip the slot on your firearm's screws because in most cases, these screws cost 6 to 8 dollars apiece and you cannot find them at the local Sears or True Value hardware store. However, you can find quality screwdrivers at Sears—"Craftsman" brand only because they are guaranteed for life should you accidentally chip or break the blade. To find the proper screwdriver size, measure the screw's slot length at home! Don't go whipping your gun out in Sears fitting screwdrivers to it. You are liable not to make it home and your legal fees will be substantially higher than your firearm's investment!

2. **Medical length Q-Tips** which have long wooden dowel shafts that reach deeply into any cavity.

3. A **clean mascara brush** or a computer cleaning brush designed to get into very, very tight spaces.

4. **Teflon tape** should be included in case you have a problematic screw that continues to loosen up repeatedly. Most people have partially used rolls of Teflon tape (or plumbing tape) in their cupboards. Because it takes an extremely small piece of this to wrap threads on any firearm, a roll of Teflon tape will last you around 3000 years relative to firearm maintenance.

5. **2-inch, lint-free cleaning patches** (commercially available). They run about $2.00 for a package of 100. If you are really frugal, you can cut up old tee shirts into 2 inch squares.

Warning! Be conscious of the fact that some cleaning products on the market are carcinogenic and may also act like glue inside of your firearm, deteriorating the metal and retarding

the action. Investigate on your own and request product information checklists as well as checking web sites on the Internet
before you actually expose your investment to the lubricating
cleaning solvent in question. Beware of products brewed in some
guy's basement and sold at a gun show by a guy with a large,
baseball-size goiter on his neck.

Seriously consider using **rubber or plastic gloves** when you
clean your guns. We realize that this can dampen your dexterity
a bit but if you are concerned about exposure to lead residues
and to cancer-causing solvents, this is a good preventative
measure. Also, make sure you have adequate ventilation where
you clean. Stay away from "Frankencleaners."

▶ **How do I clean my revolver?**

1. Lay out your cleaning mat and paper towels Set up your
   equipment to your strong side which means your dominant
   hand. Center the firearm on the mat and open the action
   (cylinder). **Make sure the revolver is unloaded**. Too many
   people have been shot while cleaning allegedly "unloaded"
   revolvers!

2. Dry brush each of the cylinder's chambers from the loading
   end one by one with the bore brush until you feel little to no
   resistance.

3. Invert the firearm so that the business end (or the muzzle)
   faces you and dry brush the barrel bore where you will have
   more resistance because of the lands and grooves.

4. That completed, hold your muzzle end at a 90-degree upright, insert your thumbnail inside the frame about one-half
   inch below the forcing cone end of the barrel (the forcing
   cone is the interior end of the barrel opposite the face of the
   cylinder) and using your thumbnail as a light reflector, look
   down the muzzle and inspect the barrel interior for any
   peripheral debris.

5. Now take the appropriate toothbrush (stainless only for
   stainless and nylon for blued) and brush the face of the
   cylinder down to remove excessive carbon deposits or black
   carbon rings on the cylinder face.

6. As you now have the firearm with the cylinder open, clean the top strap (portion of the frame above the cylinder) with a toothbrush. Pay extra attention to the area between the forcing cone (the rear end of the barrel) and the top strap.

7. Still with the cylinder open, clean the recoil plate, which is opposite and to the rear of the cylinder loading area and where the firing pin protrudes. You can proceed to brush this area with the toothbrush to remove the baked-on carbon deposits. As you look at the recoil plate, you will see a rectangular opening or window. That's the window for the "hand." The hand is an internal lever that, when the trigger is pulled in double action or the hammer is cocked in single action, engages a cutout on the star at the rear of the cylinder called the rachets which revolve each of the chambers between the barrel and the firing pin; ergo the terminology *revolver*. Now, take a dry Q-Tip and lightly swab the exterior portion of this window without jamming it into the slot.

8. That being done, take a fresh Q-Tip to the ratchets attached to the top of the star (the star being the device at the rear of the cylinder that removes the empty shell casings when you are unloading). Expose the star by pressing the spring-loaded ejector rod rearward through the cylinder from the front. Once you have accomplished that, you then clean the underside of the ejection star and the inside face of the cylinder below it, which is the star-shaped seat for the ejection star.

Caution. **With the star still open, you are looking to remove unburned grains of smokeless gunpowder. They resemble grains of black pepper for lack of a better description. If they are left unattended, they will raise the star sufficiently high enough so that it will be difficult to open and close the cylinder. This is where some people would foolishly bang on the cylinder to open it. This will cause serious functionality problems for the revolver!**

9. Now we are ready to lubricate. Take one patch and center 2 drops of Break Free on the patch. Fold it in half, like a bandanna, as if you were going to hold up a 7-Eleven store and insert it in the eyelet of the cleaning rod. Swab the chambers first through the loading end of the cylinder in a

clockwise motion all the way through and all the way back. Using the same patch, from the crown (tip end) of the barrel (or muzzle end), swab the barrel clockwise in and out. Then remove the patch.

10. With the same patch, wipe down all of the surfaces that you previously cleaned with your toothbrush (i.e., the cylinder face and rear, the recoil plate, top strap, forcing cone), and then, once that is done, wipe down all the remaining exterior surfaces of the revolver.

As you can probably tell by now, we are not changing oil at the neighborhood Jiffy Lube. So, less is better when using Break Free. It permeates the pores of the steel of your firearm with an active agent to prevent rust and material decay. You don't want to overdo it because excessive lubrication attracts dirt and debris and actually becomes muddy if you leave it unattended too long.

As we approach the final few drops of Break Free in our firearm care and cleaning procedure, I hope that by this time you learn to associate care and cleaning with something that you like doing, such as listening to music or watching your favorite soap opera or ball game, thus insuring that cleaning your firearm never becomes a chore.

11. Looking laterally at your firearm laying on its side, notice that directly below the muzzle end of the barrel there is what is called the front bolt which secures the ejection rod into the revolver once it is closed. The front bolt is a spring-loaded device that requires approximately half a drop of lubricant twice annually. Holding the muzzle down to the mat with the gun vertical and the back strap facing up, put a half drop on the front bolt and depress it several times letting gravity do its work.

    CAUTION. **Never use anything made of hardened steel which can cause scratches or digs such as a screwdriver! Use something softer than the metal, such as a plastic handle of a toothbrush.**

12. With the cylinder open, looking at the ratchets on the star, directly in the center of the ratchets is the center pin. The center pin which is also spring-loaded secures the cylinder into the recoil plate when the cylinder is closed. Twice

annually put a half a drop on the center pin and depress it manually several times to accomplish its proper lubrication.

13. **For the following 5 steps (13 -17), prepare yourself with a good flathead magnetic screwdriver and an ashtray so that you can remove and keep track of the expensive screws.** These steps apply to most models of Smith & Wesson revolvers and to some non-S&W models. These steps (13-17) should only be employed when you feel an inhibited spin of the cylinder which is due to binding from dirt and debris. With repeated usage, any revolver's cylinder can either become retarded or totally bound up from the gunpowder that attaches itself to the interior of the crane or yoke. To correct this problem and free the cylinder from hindered movement, use a flathead screwdriver to remove the screw directly over the top of the trigger. Place the screw in a secure spot where you can find it again (e.g., an old tuna fish can or ashtray). Once removed, the crane/yoke and cylinder can be pulled freely from the frame; just pull the yoke/crane assembly forward and out of the revolver in the direction of the muzzle. In some revolvers such as the Smith and Wesson revolvers, the cylinder can be removed from the crane or yoke assembly. In other manu- facturer's revolvers, such as Colts, those two components cannot be separated without a specialized tool.

14. Now, with a nylon toothbrush (as opposed to a stainless brush which can scratch and damage anything softer than stainless steel such as alloy revolvers and blued or black matte finish guns), brush the dirt off the full circumference of the crane's top barrel. If you see any dirt or debris on the bottom barrel, clean it off also.

15. Put two drops of Break Free on the top barrel of the crane and reassemble the crane and the cylinder. Now, treat the combination of the two components as a centrifuge machine. Spin the cylinder clockwise letting gravity dispense and propel the Break Free to the interior walls of the cylinder cleaning the interior walls with the agitating action of the spinning. Remove the crane which is blackened by the dirt inside the cylinder and wipe the crane off with a rag or paper towel. Now put the two components back together again without adding additional Break Free and spin it some more. Take the crane out again and wipe it off again. Continue this process until the Break Free runs clearly onto your paper

towel when you wipe the crane's top barrel with it, or when the cylinder runs extremely freely and unbound on its spinning axis; the crane. This repetitive procedure should take about 6 runs to thoroughly clean the cylinder interior.

16. Make sure to use some Break Free on the outer surface of the cylinder also to remove the exterior dirt or at least your body salts from handling if you have not already done so.

17. Reassemble the crane and cylinder. Do this by holding the bottom barrel of the crane at the 3 o'clock position adjacent to the cylinder and then gently place it back into the revolver's frame. Close the cylinder. Now find your screw. Newer revolvers have a spring-loaded screw which requires you to place a small drop on it. Reinstall the appropriate screw that you removed earlier.

18. Finally, if you have an exposed as opposed to internal hammer on your revolver, with the cylinder open to make sure that the gun is unloaded and remains so, cock the hammer. That is accomplished by pushing the cylinder release latch rearward on the revolver (this is the same procedure for most revolvers with the exception of Rugers) and simultaneously cocking the hammer. This enables you to complete the following procedure without a tragic accident: With the hammer cocked, drop three drops of Break Free randomly down inside the action. While you hold the cylinder release lever rearward, manually dry fire the gun double action approximately 25 times. If equipped with a hammer nose, place one-half drop on it and its slot, then wiggle it a bit.

With the springs and levers system internal to all revolvers, by pulling the trigger double action, it acts as if it were a washing machine agitator cleaning and scrubbing all the interior portions of the gun. Any dirt removed will come out in droplets through the window of the trigger. They won't be of sufficient quantity to cause any damage to your purse or holster—it's just 3 drops. If your revolver is dirty internally, these droplets will most usually be black. Should that be true, you may want to continue to dry fire until you see a clear droplet of Break Free at the top of your trigger.

We've reached the revolver finale. You now have a safe, reliable and protected firearm to carry and depend on. Congratulations! It wasn't as difficult as you thought, was it? Once you have gone through these steps several times following our procedures, it will become automatic and second nature for you. You will be able to more readily enjoy that ball game, soap opera or piece of music while you are maintaining your equipment.

▶ **What types of safety mechanisms do revolvers have?**

The main safety of most revolvers produced today is the "rebound slide." This, in conjunction with the "hammer block" (which most closely resembles the shape of a musical note), prevents accidental discharge of a revolver should it accidentally be dropped or banged from an external source. The rebound slide additionally prevents firing should the hammer be cocked and dropped as long as your finger is NOT depressing the trigger. If your finger does depress the trigger rearward, this would then complete the trigger's rearward travel and at the same time move the rebound slide to its furthest rearward extension thus releasing the hammer to the firing position. We know that this sounds a bit complicated, however the rebound slide is really just a metal block attached to the pin of the trigger which unless pushed to its most rearward extension by the trigger actually serves to prevent the hammer from being unintentionally lowered to its firing position.

We often demonstrate this in our classes on the shooting range by having a hammer lowered and striking it forward on its spur *with the gun facing downrange*. The firing pin will not protrude through the recoil plate to fire a round of ammunition. We further demonstrate with the gun facing downrange that even when the hammer is cocked, and struck with a real hammer on the spur, as long as your finger is not on the trigger, even when the hammer falls, it will not fire a live round of ammunition.

For those of you who are antique gun collectors or history buffs, the old western type single action Colt .45 revolvers and the like had no rebound slide or hammer block. Thus, the chamber under the firing pin or hammer nose was always kept empty to insure against accidental discharge. If the hammer were struck from an external source, had there been a round below the hammer it would have fired. In order to fire the gun, the shooter would cock the hammer, the next loaded chamber would be aligned with the firing pin, and then the weapon would be fired by pressing the trigger.

▶ **What are my safe carry options for my revolver if I have the right to carry?**

As we have already discussed, holsters come in many shapes and sizes and are produced by a variety of manufacturers giving you numerous choices. Our best suggestion is to experiment with the products of several different reputable manufacturers. Make sure that you maintain strong side usage, which means your shooting hand side.

Remember that the shortest distance to any target is a straight line, and you want to avoid the 180-degree mistake. That is, you should never sweep your body from your opposite side with a loaded firearm. During a criminal confrontation or law enforcement activity, adrenaline is pumping and you might, no matter how well-trained you are, gravitate inadvertently to the trigger. That could lead to an accidental discharge into your own body as you are sweeping from a position that we don't recommend, and if you think about it, you probably won't use.

We know that many quality and reputable manufacturers produce and sell cross draw and shoulder holsters. We certainly do not mean to impugn their integrity. There is definitely a market for these products because people do want them, and they do serve some people's needs very well. However, with that being said, it is our experience and opinion that shoulder holsters and cross draw holsters are typically slow to draw from and potentially dangerous. A competent strong side shooter can put 3 shots in your head before you even clear your belt buckle.

Strong side carry lends itself to a straight line sweep between your holster and your adversary. A straight line is the shortest and quickest distance between two points—the muzzle of your weapon and your adversary. During a criminal attack, time is of the essence. You are not holding the bad guy up. He is holding you at bay, and chances are he already has produced some type of weapon. You barely have enough time to respond, let alone to go into some exotic Bruce Lee or "Miami Vice" type of move. Strong side carry enables you to respond most effectively.

You need to feel comfortable with your selection of holsters whether it is an inside the pants holster, a pocket holster, or a strong side belt or paddle carry rig. You have to practice with your equipment no matter what it is in order to maintain your level of proficiency. Plinking with the kids on a Saturday afternoon is light years from protecting yourself and them during a criminal attack. Each does require mental preparation, but the latter requires more than the former given the fact that it is more dramatic and life threatening. Recognize that the *"3 T's"* of firearm responsibility and survival are *Train, Train, and Train.*

A quality pocket holster provides a viable and convenient concealed carry option for small frame revolvers, and also for small, sub-compact semi-automatic pistols which we will cover later. If you wish to consider a pocket holster for your small snubbie revolver, keep in mind that the key to a successful draw from a pocket holster is for the gun to come out, and for the holster to stay in place in your pocket. All quality pocket holsters will be constructed to accomplish this.

Be aware that a defensive firearm is only as good as the holster in which it travels and the manufacturer that supports it. If you cannot get to your weapon in time, or if it drops out of your holster, it will not matter if it is a $2000 customized firearm or a clothesline rope. It is useless to you.

▶ **What features in a revolver make it most suitable for concealed carry?**

Any revolver on which the hammer is bobbed (which means that the hammer spur has been removed) or internal to the frame makes it simpler and quicker to produce during a critical situation because the hammer can't bind or catch on your clothing or holster.

Caliber choice is up to you because by this juncture, you should have considered, with professional advisement, which caliber is most functional and effective for your personal defensive needs. However, in a revolver, the most common caliber and the minimum to get the job done in most applications is the .38 special. All .357 magnum revolvers will handle .38 special rounds.

Two-inch barrel lengths or less (the snubbie) are the appropriate size for pocket or jacket concealment purposes. The revolver manufacturer we rate highest for sheer quality, reliability, durability, accuracy, service and number of choices is Smith and Wesson.

Keep in mind that light weight also facilitates ease of carry and concealment as well as not being distracting. If you are going to carry your gun all day (especially in your pocket), the weight can wear you down. However, also keep in mind that there is a tradeoff between weight, barrel length and a revolver's shootability and accuracy. The lighter the weight and shorter the barrel the more recoil there is likely to be and the harder the gun will be to manage especially with heavier ammunition loads.

When a revolver is your main choice of weapon for concealed carry usage, a speed loader or Bianchi speed strip is a necessary addition to increase your ammunition capacity and your comfort level.

▶ **How do I prevent an "accidental discharge"?**

An "accidental discharge," or "AD," means that the weapon has fired or gone off without a deliberate physical action taking place on your part to fire your weapon. That means you pulled the trigger without checking the action to make sure that it was empty, or that you manually lowered the hammer with your finger on the trigger negating or overriding the rebound slide and hammer block on your revolver.

Another way that an "AD" can occur is if you have purchased a weapon that you are totally unfamiliar with or that has not been explained to you properly. A little knowledge can be worse than having none. ADs frequently happen when an irresponsible person is not paying attention and ignores cardinal safety rule Number 2 which states that *all firearms are always loaded.*

If an irresponsible adult leaves a weapon within close proximity and within the reach of children or those otherwise of limited capacity to understand the functions or dangers involved with firearms, this too can lead to an AD.

Any time a finger is placed within the trigger guard and the gun is not pointed downrange or at a criminal adversary, the imminent danger of an AD is a clear and present danger and a catastrophe waiting to occur. This unfortunately happens more often than it should (which is NEVER) and results in unnecessary deaths or severe injuries.

9

Semi-Automatic Pistols

▶ **Is a semi-automatic pistol the right defensive carry firearm for me?**

Semi-automatic pistols offer flat carry as compared to the relative bulkiness of revolvers. This means that they do not print as noticeably in your pocket or on your belt through your covering clothing as do revolvers. They offer, at minimum, more ammunition capacity than any defensive revolver. More rounds translate into better protection.

Compact concealable semi-autos are more accurate at greater distances than revolvers of comparable size and weight when we are talking about short barrel carry guns. Semi-autos have less complicated action mechanisms which translates into ease of maintenance and care. The internal mechanisms are stronger than those of revolvers so this translates into greater physical longevity of the pistol for practice.

The bottom line is that semi-autos give you the ability to have more rounds on hand in the weapon if you need it, and for most shooters, semi-autos allow greater accuracy in a flatter and equally sized package.

Put side by side it would be an easy choice once you visualize the differences, and your training begins. Two-inch revolvers lend themselves more to expert carry than to carry by novices for defensive purposes. Sure, there are a select few who can draw and shoot a revolver accurately and faster than some experienced shooters can even draw their semi-auto, but such prodigies are few and far between.

The ultimate decision rests in your being educated and gaining practical experience with both semi-autos and revolvers. That way you can make an informed decision rather than going solely on the recommendation of someone you haven't met, who doesn't know your needs, and who probably won't accept a collect phone call from you.

You cannot make the choice of your carry or home defense gun and your survival based solely on reading this book or any other text. You need to get out to a range and try out the different firearm options to experience for yourself what is comfortable for you, financially viable, and practical for carry and/or home defense. Do not base your information on emotional, second-hand war stories or truly unenlightened sales people.

▶ **What type of semi-automatic pistol should I get?**

With the wide variety of quality semi-automatic pistols on the market today, there are a number of determining factors that will lead to your personal choice. One is the capacity of the magazine (i.e., the number of rounds of ammunition that the magazine holds in the gun). Even in the aftermath of the Brady Bill, numerous manufacturers have after market, legal, pre-Ban, high capacity magazines available for purchase. Although over-inflated in price, these high capacity magazines still offer a viable application as an alternative to carrying multiple magazines. In other words, a 17-round magazine is better than two 10 rounders in terms of less bulk for carry purposes.

A second consideration is caliber and that is only determined through practical training at your local pistol range to determine which caliber you can handle and best suits your needs and your budget. You will find that if you stay away from over-priced exotic ammunition, your practice sessions will go a lot further and your proficiency will increase dramatically.

The third determining factor is ease of carry. No matter what quality firearm you purchase, if it is too large and heavy, it will be uncomfortable to carry. You are most likely to leave it in the dresser drawer for the burglar where it will do you more harm. Put it this way: A rock in your pocket is better than a catapult or slingshot left in the castle. Only by experiencing different fire-arms at shooting facilities that offer firearm rentals of various manufacturers can you determine which type of handgun best meets your needs for optimal carry, concealment, second and third shot recovery, as well as affordability.

Be careful to stay away from foolish purchases of inexpensive pistols that some gun store salesmen might lead you towards because he is making 300 percent profit. If it's chrome and shiny, the salesman may be looking at you like a monkey at the zoo. On the other hand, you have survived up to this point in life or else you would not be reading this book. You have done so by being intelligent, discriminating and seeking to be informed.

So, your homework assignment is to go out and look around and put the knowledge we're giving you to work for you. If you save for a few months, you probably will be able to afford a quality semi-automatic pistol that will last you several lifetimes. That is extremely important when you consider all of the other financial obligations you probably have incurred. We think you'll find this homework assignment fun, enjoyable and enlightening.

▶ **What manufacturers' products best suit defensive needs in a semi-automatic pistol?**

Irrespective of calibers (which is a personal choice), several manufacturers' products jump to the top of our professional list.

Our Compact Choices. We use the following compact, high quality semi-automatics regularly in potentially combative situations. They are our choice of compact, concealed carry defensive weapons:

- The compact SIG Sauer line: P245 in .45 ACP, P239 in 9mm and .40 S&W, P228 in 9mm, and P229 in .40 S&W.
- The Heckler & Koch (HK) USP Compact .45 ACP as well as the .40 S&W.
- The Beretta "Cougar" 8045F Compact in .45 ACP.
- The subcompact Kahr Arms MK9 and PM9 in 9mm, MK40 in 40 S&W, and the compact K9 and P9 in 9mm.

In the Glock firearms line, we favor the following models:

- The subcompact, "Baby Glock" 27 in 40 S&W and the 26 in 9mm.
- The compact Glock 23 in 40 S&W and Glock 19 in 9mm.
- The compact Glock 30 and the "slimline" Glock 36 in .45 ACP.

Our Full-Size Choices. We regularly carry and rely on the following full-size semi-automatics. They are our choice of full-size, concealed carry defensive weapons. Yes. They conceal very well as we discussed earlier.

- The classic, full-size SIG Sauer P220 in .45 caliber ACP, and the SIG Sauer P226 in 9mm.
- The Beretta 92FS in 9mm.

- The full-size Glock 17 in 9mm.
- The Glock 22 (same size as the Glock 17) in .40 caliber.

Believe it or not, with a good belt slide or IWB holster, the full-size Glock 17 or 22 carries just as easily concealed as does a compact Glock 23 or subcompact Glock 26!

- In .45 caliber, we love our full-size Glock 21s.

For Pocket Backup. For pocket backup, in case the situation deteriorates quickly, the sub-compact pocket pistols we have chosen selectively for protection of our own lives are the:

- L.W. Seecamp .32 semi-automatic
- Beretta Tomcat .32
- North American Arms .380 and .32 Guardians
- Kel-Tec .32 ACP and .380 Model 3AT

These pistols have repeatedly proven themselves to be accurate, reliable and dependable in any tactical situation. We feel confident in these models. These products are all practical for street use as well as home defense. Many "top shelf" professionals we know own and use at least one or more of the models previously listed.

If we are "in the mood" to carry a snub-nosed revolver, we both feel that nothing can beat the lightness and performance of the small, compact Smith & Wesson "AirLite" J-frame revolvers such as the Models 337PD and 340PD ("PD" stands for personal defense), their Models 442 and 642 "Air Weights."

▶ **What types of safety mechanisms do pistols have?**

On semi-automatic pistols, physical or mechanical manual safeties are engaged to prevent accidental discharges or "ADs." A manual safety is best described as a steel mechanism that blocks or retards the hammer drop travel to the firing pin and thus prevents the firearm from discharging.

The Colt 1911-A1 pistol provides a fine example of mechanical physical safeties. It has three. First, it has a grip safety on the back strap so that if the grip safety is not depressed, the weapon will not fire. Second, it has a mechanical manual locking safety on the frame that when engaged, prevents the hammer from falling. That means if the trigger is pulled when the safety is engaged (assuming this safety is in fully functional condition!), the weapon won't fire. Safeties should only be tested with live ammunition at a pistol range with the weapon facing safely downrange, and not in your kitchen where we know all firearms are loaded.

Last but not least, the 1911 style pistol has a half-cocked position of the hammer. Should the mechanical safety fail or not be engaged and one's finger is not on the trigger, this half-cocked resting position is intended to prevent an AD should the weapon be dropped or struck. Mechanically it is a secondary ledge that is cut into the hammer's interior surface. This secondary ledge is designed to be caught by the sear. This prevents hammer free-fall and discharge should the single action notch on the hammer which rests on the sear suffer material fatigue and failure. However, this feature does not work 100% of the time. Should it fail, you have a full auto sub-machine gun.

Most commonly today, safeties are interior to the firearm and not readily visible. Collectively they consist of the following mechanisms: 1. The *drop safety* which blocks the firing pin's forward movement should the weapon be dropped or struck by an external source. 2. The *firing pin safety* which prevents discharge of the weapon until the trigger is pulled to its most rearward position which disconnects this safety. 3. In the case of the Glock specifically, there is a *trigger safety* which actually looks like a secondary trigger inside the center of the main trigger. The weapon will not fire unless the two (which together are called the "safe action trigger") are depressed straight back simultaneously.

Actually, the Glock has three internal safeties that operate in sequence:

1. The trigger cannot be fully depressed unless the Glock *"Safe Action" trigger safety* (a trigger within the trigger) is pulled straight rearward thus disconnecting the trigger safety.

2. Once the trigger is fully pressed rearward, a vertical extension on the internal trigger bar pushes the internal spring-loaded *firing pin safety block* inside the slide upward, which unblocks the striker or firing pin. How-

ever, the firing pin cannot move all the way forward to strike the chambered round until,

3. the *third* safety, which is the *drop safety,* is disengaged. This drop safety is an internal notch that is part of the trigger housing mechanism in the rear of the receiver or frame. The rear portion of the trigger bar assembly, called the *"cruciform"* rests in this notch and the trigger bar cannot fully disengage from the firing pin and firing pin safety. The sequential safety mechanisms allow the cruciform to drop down and rearward which fully completes the trigger bar's disengagement from the firing pin.

Common to a wide variety of semi-automatics with exposed hammers is a manual decocking lever. It is either attached to the slide or the frame. It works in one of two ways. It either rolls a block of steel (termed the firing pin block) in front of the firing pin while lowering the hammer to its resting position, or through spring tension release, lowers the hammer to the half-cock position, thus preventing accidental discharge.

Finally, one additional safety used by several manufacturers, is the "magazine disconnect." Once the magazine has been removed, pistols so equipped will not fire and their internal mechanisms will not engage until the magazine has been reinserted in the magazine well.

▶ **How "safe" are mechanical manual safeties? The human error factor.**

In Steve's 35-plus years of experience using and teaching firearms, he has probably seen two mechanical failures of safeties. Usually any failure of a firearm can be attributed to the nut behind the gun who neither understands nor has taken the time to learn the proper sequence of operations relating to a specific firearm.

Safeties do not make people more safe. Knowledge and practical experience taught by someone who is knowledgeable in the field (and available on a regular basis to answer questions in a *non-condescending manner)* dramatically reduces the number of potential firearms accidents. It is necessary for the shooter to understand, apply and practice using the information that is specific to each firearm he or she picks up.

Never permit yourself to be distracted at any time when you are handling a firearm! That is our safety rule which mandates that you *focus,* and then focus again. Knowledge is power. Apply it.

▶ **How should I evaluate my "comfort level" with a pistol?**

"A defensive handgun should be **comforting** *not* **comfortable***.* The message is that like an American Express card, "Don't leave home without it."

▶ **How do I maintain my pistol?**

With the varying breakdown or field-stripping procedures for different pistols, it is extremely important that you read the manual accompanying your weapon, and if necessary, consult with a firearms professional to learn the right method of disassembly.

You should know that if you have lost your manual or bought a used firearm and did not receive one, all quality manufacturers will readily supply one at no cost. In addition, many manufacturers have their manuals available for free download from their web sites.

Once your confidence level has risen to the point where you can feel at ease and confident disassembling your particular firearm, then welcome back to our world of cleaning procedures!

Most newly designed pistols have four main component parts:

1. the frame;

2. the guide rod spring assembly;

3. the barrel; and

4. the slide.

An additional component part to be considered separately is the magazine, which is the heart of the semi-automatic pistol. The magazine holds the rounds of ammunition.

The magazine also has four component parts:

1. the magazine tube which contains all of the other components;

2. the internal spring which supports the rounds of ammunition;

3. the follower which is the base plate for the rounds being loaded, and

4. the base plate at the floor or bottom of the magazine that functionally secures all of the other components within the magazine tube.

Note that an additional function of the follower on a quality semi-automatic pistol is to lock the weapon in the out of battery position (which means that the slide is locked totally rearward) once the last round has been fired.

The front of any magazine from any manufacturer can be distinguished from the rear in that the tube's front edges are always rounded and the tube's rear edges are always a sharp 90 degrees. This is a very handy item to know in the darkness. Should you forget, ammunition always follows the same distinctive pattern: rounded in the front and flat in the back.

Rotating Your Magazines

Just like you rotate your automobile's tires on a regular basis, or should be doing so, you need to rotate your magazines regularly. The reason to make it a habit to do this simple maintenance procedure once a month is to save your magazine's springs. Keeping a fully loaded set of rounds in a magazine obviously compresses the magazine spring. Unrelieved, the tension on the spring can permanently deform it. Then it will not function properly and may fail you when you need it. So, don't be lazy and don't gamble with your life! Regularly relieve the tension on your magazine springs and conserve them.

If you use your pistol for home defense, you should always have a fully loaded spare magazine and a loaded magazine in your charged pistol. In addition, you ought to keep at least 2 unloaded or partially loaded spare magazines near your pistol.

Every month, you can unload your loaded magazines and load up your spares.

For example, if the magazine has a 10-round capacity, you keep one of your spares partially loaded with 5 rounds, another spare empty, and a third spare fully loaded. Every month, on the date of your birth, rotate magazine capacities to prevent spring fatigue.

▶ **How do I clean my pistol?**

Irrespective of the amount of rounds you've fired during practice, similar to the revolvers, you should clean your weapon every time you've been to the range perfecting your skills. The more diligent you are in maintaining your firearm and keeping it clean, the more reliable it will remain.

With your cleaning mat, paper towels, and tools, disassemble your pistol into its four main component parts.

> *Caution!* **Always make sure your firearm is unloaded before you begin cleaning!**

Specific to Glock Semi-Automatics: It is vital to your own safety and that of others that you make sure of two things before commencing to field-strip the gun: (1) that the magazine has been removed and (2) that the chamber is clear. This is necessary because the Glock pistol has to be dry-fired in order to initiate disassembly.

After you've visually and physically checked the chamber area to make sure it is empty, you still point the firearm in a safe direction, away from any person or objects of value (S-A-F-E-S-T safety rule #1) as you press the trigger to its most rearward position.

Familiarity tends to breed contempt. This means that "ADs" are *never* acceptable! No matter how experienced you may be, always take a second and third look to make sure that the firearm you are working with is totally empty before proceeding! Doing so makes you a professional as opposed to a reckless cowboy. Now let's begin the cleaning procedure.

1. Start with the barrel. Using the brass rod and an appropriately sized stainless steel bore brush, brush clockwise through the barrel from its loading end. This is unlike a

revolver, where you must brush from the crown end. When you can, always clean from the loading chamber end to avoid unnecessary damage to the crown (the crown being the last point of bullet engagement for accuracy as the projectile leaves the barrel). Brushing in a clockwise motion from rear to front, all the way through and all the way back avoids premature collapse of the brush's bristles. Continue with this procedure until you see no more burnt carbon remnants ("grains of pepper") falling onto your paper towel surface.

2. Then take the nylon toothbrush, sweep the feed ramp (the lower downward angled ramp where ammunition is fed from the magazine follower into the barrel's breech) clean of any carbon material. Directly above the feed ramp is the barrel's hood prominently jutting out rearward from the top of the barrel's breech. This, in conjunction with the feed ramp, directs the ammunition rounds into the barrel's breech. Sweep this hood in the same manner. You don't want to leave any carbon in the hood. When you have completed sweeping the barrel, its feed ramp and hood, lay the barrel off to the side of your cleaning mat.

3. With the slide in the inverted position (sights facing downward on the cleaning mat), use the nylon toothbrush to sweep the slide rails which are the guides for slide to frame attachment (also affectionately referred to as the "choo-choo tracks").

4. Next, clean the interior sections of the slide by sweeping towards the center where the ejection port lies. That completed, at the rear of the ejection port, and by the firing pin window, sweep downward under the ammunition case extractor. This extractor is the hook that grabs the most rearward edge of the shell casing and removes it from the breech of the barrel whether or not the round has been fired.

5. In the center of the underside (or interior) of the slide, is the center rail. The center rail's function is as follows: as the slide moves forward under spring tension or pressure, it strips a round from the top of the magazine and propels it forward into the barrel's breech or chamber. Make sure to clean this towards the ejection port.

Glock Commentary: Within the slide rails of a newly purchased Glock pistol, and around some of the firing pin release components is a copper-colored lubricant lapping compound. The factory puts it there to assure good fit and moving function between the slide and the frame. It usually disperses naturally after several thousand rounds of live fire.

DO NOT CLEAN THIS LAPPING COMPOUND OUT! LET IT WEAR AWAY NATURALLY.

6. The third component is the frame. The only tool you need within the frame is the nylon toothbrush. Sweep away unburned grains of gunpowder and baked-on carbon residue. That completed, we are now going to lubricate.

7. Take a fresh cleaning patch, drip 3 drops of Break Free (shake well to mix the binary compound) in the center. Folding the patch into a "bandit's triangle," insert the folded patch through the eyelet of your brass rod. In a circular motion clockwise from the breech end of the barrel, run the patch all the way through and all the way back. Do this several times to assure that you remove all the debris freed by your bore brush.

8. Remove the patch and wipe down all the exterior surfaces of the barrel, paying particular attention to the feed ramp and hood. With the same patch and no additional Break Free, wipe the interior sections of the slide where the barrel normally rests. When completed, wipe the rear interior sections of the slide including the recoil plate, the areas around the extractor and the areas around the center rail.

Glock Tip: You don't have to lubricate the center rail of the Glock's slide because it is so highly polished that it does not require lubricant to function well.

9. Take the Break Free in hand and, with its straw inserted, drag one drop down each one of the slide rails. On all pistols, (with the exception of a Glock) put a drop on the center rail and move it fully through its entire length with the patch. Now put your slide off to the side and go to the frame with your same patch.

10. Any metal parts you've cleaned with your nylon brush are now to be wiped clean with the patch with no additional lubricant added. This should include the magazine well. You may stick the patch with your finger up the magazine well and clean out any residual debris.

11. The spring and guide rod assembly need simply be wiped with the patch to assure the spring's longevity and rust prevention.

12. Reassembly is your next and final step. Insert the barrel into the appropriate cavity within the slide and then insert the guide rod spring assembly as you are looking at it on top of the barrel. Make sure that you align the direction of the guide rod spring assembly as per the manual's instructions. Now invert the slide to its normal firing position to make sure that the components do not dislodge.

13. Now, consider the frame as the "choo-choo train" and the slide rails as the tracks. Engage the contact points of the frame into the slide rails pulling the slide rearward to its most rearward position or "out of battery." Depending upon the manufacturer's design of your particular pistol, lock or secure the slide and barrel in place by whatever method and lever (e.g., slide release lever) completes that task as indicated in the manufacturer's instructions. Then check for function by racking the slide fully rearward and releasing it several times to make sure that there is no component separation. And then, you are done!

You can safely say that you've accomplished your mission. It was an easier experience than you thought it would be. After you've done this several times, you can enjoy cleaning your weapon and turn up the music.

Specific Field-Stripping/Disassembly/Takedown Steps for Popular Quality Pistols

We are now going to outline the specific disassembly steps that are *unique* to each of the quality concealed carry, double action and double action only, semi-automatic pistols we have recommended. We give them here for your convenience, for clarification and review. This text, however, is no substitute for carefully reading the manufacturer's manual. This is essential for safe operation of your pistol and maintaining a long life for your gun and you.

◆ **Glock Models**

Glock pistols are mechanically locked, recoil operated, "semi-double-action," semi-automatic pistols that have automatic firing pin and trigger safeties. They are "semi-double-action" in that the weapon is half-cocked when a round is chambered. The first half of the gun's trigger press completes the cocking of the gun, and the second half of the trigger press allows the gun to fire. In the first half of the trigger press, the shooter "takes up the slack" in the trigger. The Glock has a "single-action trigger" in that it has only one type of trigger pull (or press) as compared to traditional double-action pistols that have an initial long double-action trigger pull on the first shot while the remaining shots are single-action (hammer or firing pin is cocked by the slide) and have a shorter trigger press. Also, the trigger is "single-action" in that when it is fully pressed beyond its arc of travel that is considered slack, it fires the already cocked gun. The Glock has no external manual safeties, but instead has

Figure 9.1

three built-in automatic mechanical safeties: 1) the trigger safety, 2) the firing pin safety, and 3) the drop safety.

Figure 9.1 shows a field-stripped Glock ready for cleaning.

Disassembly

1.   Make sure the pistol is unloaded. Remove the magazine, and then rack the slide to eject a round from the chamber if the chamber is loaded. With no magazine in the magazine well, double check the chamber visually and with your finger to make sure it is indeed empty.

2.   After you have made sure that the chamber is empty, rack the slide to return the slide into battery and close the action. Then, pointing the pistol in a safe direction, press the trigger rearward. You'll hear the click of the firing pin moving forward. The trigger must be in its rearward position to remove the slide.

3.   Hold the pistol in your shooting hand as follows: With your palm up against the right side of the receiver and slide, bring your index, middle, ring and little fingers up over the slide and your opposing thumb in the notch of the backstrap pointing towards the muzzle under the slide. The tips of your 4 fingers should meet the side of your thumb.

4.   Now pull the slide rearward about ⅛ to ¼ of an inch by pushing forward with your thumb and rearward on the slide with your 4 fingers. Make sure not to pull the slide too far rearward. If you do, it will reset the trigger and you'll have to start the procedure over again.

5.   Pull down all the way on both sides of the slide lock/takedown lever which is located on the receiver above the trigger guard. Use your supporting hand thumb to pull down on the left notch and your supporting hand index finger to simultaneously pull down on the right notch. Simultaneously push the slide all the way forward until it is fully separated from the receiver.

6.   Now, your Glock pistol is disassembled into 2 of its 4 main component parts; receiver and slide assembly. Lay your receiver down and pick up your slide. Remove the recoil spring assembly by doing the following: Push forward on the end where the recoil spring assembly rests with spring tension against the forward facing

portion of the lug of the barrel and lift it up and away from the barrel. Put it down on your cleaning mat.

7. Lastly, lift the barrel up and out of the slide. Do this by lifting it up by the barrel lug and then pushing forward slightly to clear the inside of the slide.

That is the entire disassembly/field-stripping procedure for routine maintenance and cleaning of your Glock.

Reassembly

To reassemble your Glock, reverse the above steps. Note however, that when reinstalling the recoil spring assembly, make sure that the back end (larger end) of the recoil spring assembly rests in the half moon cut in the bottom of the front barrel lug.

After you have reassembled your Glock, rack the slide several times and with the pistol facing in a safe direction, press the trigger rearward. Then rack the slide again to return it into battery and your pistol is ready to be loaded.

◆ Kahr MK9 and MK40 Pocket Pistols

The Kahr pistol is a mechanically locked, recoil operated pistol with a passive striker block and a trigger cocking "double action only" action. After the magazine is empty, the slide is held open in the out of battery position by the slide release lever. As with the Glock, there are no manual safeties. The trigger press is the same for the initial and all subsequent shots. When the weapon is loaded and the chamber charged, the striker is automatically held under partial tension (and also after each round is fired) and it is fully secured by a passive striker block until the trigger is fully pressed to the rear.

Disassembly

1. As with any other weapon, remove the magazine and make doubly sure that the chamber is empty. That is, check the chamber twice, visually and with your finger.

2. Holding the gun in your strong hand, on the left side of the slide and frame, you will see 2 breakdown notches. With your strong thumb on the backstrap, reach over the

top of the slide with your four fingers and pull the slide back until the notches align.

3. With your support hand, reach under the frame and push the slide stop lever on the right side of the frame into the frame and pull its lever on the left side of the frame up and out. Once the lever is removed, depress the trigger once which frees the slide to be moved forward off the frame.

4. Now, move the slide forward off the frame.

5. Laying the slide upside down on a padded mat, you'll see the guide rod spring assembly and barrel on the inside of the slide. With your thumb, push forward on the guide rod spring assembly to release the spring tension, and then move it upwards and out of the slide. Then lift the barrel lug up, push the barrel slightly forward, and then rearward and up and out of the slide. The gun is now field-stripped.

Reassembly
1. Reinstall the barrel into the slide. Reinstall the guide rod onto the barrel in the slide.

2. Reinstall the slide onto the slide rails of the frame.

3. Pull the slide rearward with your strong hand until the small alignment marks match, and then place the slide stop lever pivot arm through the frame until the slide stop lever is flush to the frame.

4. Check for function by racking the slide several times and then reinsert the magazine. You are done.

◆ HK USP Compact Pistols

The HK USP Compact pistol is a traditional double-action semi-auto, self-loading pistol with a recoil operated, modified Browning-type action. The pistol has an external, manual, frame-mounted two-stage decocking/safety lever. When the pistol is "off safe" (i.e., the safety lever is thumbed into its downmost position), the first shot is full double action (longer trigger press) and subsequent shots are single action (the hammer is already cocked and the trigger press is lighter and shorter).

Disassembly

1. As with any other weapon, remove the magazine and make doubly sure that the chamber is empty. That is, check the chamber twice.

2. Make sure the manual safety is "off." Rack the slide so that the hammer is cocked. Now hold the gun in your strong hand and visually note the circular front pin of the slide release lever on the left side of the slide and frame.

3. With your strong thumb on the backstrap, reach over the top of the slide with your four fingers. Then pull the slide back until the axle of the slide release is visible through the recess on the left side of the slide directly above the slide release lever's circular front pin on the left side of the frame.

4. With your support hand, reach under the frame and push the axle of the slide release on the right side of the frame into the frame. The lever will pop up out of the left side of the frame and you can remove it.

5. Now, move the slide forward off the frame.

6. Laying the slide upside down on a padded mat, you'll see the guide rod spring assembly and barrel on the inside of the slide. With your thumb, push forward on the guide rod spring assembly to release the spring tension, and then move it upwards and out of the slide. Then lift the barrel lug up, push the barrel slightly forward, and then rearward and up and out of the slide. The gun is now field-stripped and ready for cleaning.

Reassembly

1. Reinstall the barrel into the slide. Reinstall the guide rod onto the barrel in the slide. Make sure to align the opposing angled locking surfaces on the rear end of the recoil spring guide rod with those located on the bottom of the barrel lug.

2. Reinstall the slide onto the slide rails of the frame.

3. Pull the slide rearward with your strong hand to the point where the recess in the left side of the slide is positioned over the hole where the axle of the slide release will go. Hold the slide in that position.

4. Insert the slide release lever from left to right into the frame until the slide release is flush with the left side of the frame. Reassembly is now complete.

5. Check for function by racking the slide several times. Use the decocking lever to decock the hammer, and then reinsert the magazine. You are done.

◆ SIG-Sauer Pistols (Compacts and Full-Size Models)

The SIG-Sauer pistol is a mechanically locked, short recoil operated, semi-auto self-loading pistol featuring an automatic firing pin safety lock, double action/single action trigger (i.e., first shot double action and subsequent shots single action), single stage decocking lever, and an external slide catch lever. It does not have a manual, external safety. The decocking lever allows the shooter to lower a cocked hammer safely into the safety intercept notch without the shooter having to touch the trigger or hammer. The firing pin stays locked automatically when you decock the pistol.

Disassembly

1. As with any other weapon, remove the magazine and make doubly sure that the chamber is empty and the pistol unloaded. Check the chamber twice.

2. Pull back on the slide with your support hand as far rearward as it will go and lock the slide open by pushing up on the slide catch lever with your strong thumb.

3. Turn the takedown lever on the left side of the frame from its horizontal 3 o'clock position down to a vertical 6 o'clock position.

4. Gripping the stock of the pistol with your strong hand, with your support hand, pull back on the serrations of

the slide slightly to disengage the slide catch lever. Then hold the slide firmly as you glide it all the way forward gently until it slides off the frame.

5. Laying the slide upside down on a padded mat, you'll see the guide rod spring assembly and barrel on the inside of the slide. With your thumb, push forward on the guide rod spring assembly to release the spring tension, and then move it upwards and out of the slide. Then lift the barrel lug up, push the barrel slightly forward, and then rearward and up and out of the slide. The gun is now field-stripped and ready for cleaning.

Reassembly

1. Reinstall the barrel into the slide. Reinstall the guide rod onto the barrel in the slide.

2. Reinstall the slide onto the slide rails of the frame and with your support hand push it all the way rearward. Then lock the slide out of battery by pushing up on the slide catch lever.

3. Push the takedown lever back up to its horizontal 3 o'clock position.

4. Now bring the slide back into battery by pulling all the way rearward with your support hand on the serrations and letting the slide go back into battery. Work the slide several times to make sure that it is on properly.

5. Lastly, decock the cocked hammer by pushing down on the decocking lever with your strong thumb. Then, re-insert the magazine. That's all there is to it.

◆ **Beretta Tomcat .32 ACP Pocket Pistol**

Disassembly

Disassembly procedures for the Beretta are very simple and easy.

1. Make sure your finger is off the trigger and that the manual safety is engaged. Push forward on the barrel

release lever to pop up the barrel and make sure the chamber is empty.

2. Remove the magazine by depressing the magazine release button.

3. Now swing the barrel all the way forward about 110 degrees on its hinge until it stops.

4. Disengage the safety and fully cock the hammer.

5. Grasp firmly with your thumb and index finger around the front section of the slide. Push it rearward about ⅛ inch and then lift the front end of the slide above the frame's barrel hinge. You should hear a click indicating that the recoil spring lever has disengaged from the slide. Then, pull the slide forward until it clears the frame's guide lugs and take it off the gun.

6. *Caution!* **Do NOT release the hammer to its forward position by pressing the trigger when the gun is disassembled with the slide removed.**

Reassembly

Reassembly of the Beretta Tomcat .32 pistol is essentially the reverse of disassembly.

1. With the hammer still fully cocked, elevate the front end of the slide and position its rear end over the frame just in front of the frame's guide lugs in the rear of the frame.

2. Carefully push (or slide) the slide rails back over the frame's rear guide lugs. Then lower the front end of the slide so that the slide gently rests on the frame.

3. Move the slide forward until the front of the slide stops against the frame's barrel hinge ears.

4. Now with your left and right thumbs positioned on both left and right sidewalls at the front of the slide, press down on the slide until you hear and feel the *click* which indicates the slide has re-engaged with the frame. Visu-

ally check to make sure the slide's underside is parallel to the frame.

5. Swing the barrel back to its closed position.

6. Rack the slide by pulling it all the way rearward and then releasing it. Make sure that the pistol goes back into battery. The action of the slide should cycle the hammer and return the hammer to the cocked, single action position.

7. Lower the hammer and reengage the safety.

8. Now to reload, **with the chamber empty** and **the safety on**, insert a loaded magazine. With the **safety engaged** and **the chamber empty**, press the trigger which will cock the hammer into its *half-cocked position*.

9. The last thing you do is tip up the barrel to insert a round in the chamber. Then you lower the barrel.

NOTE. The way to safely carry this gun with a round in the chamber is *with the gun in the half-cocked position with the manual safety on* (i.e., "half-cocked and locked"), as this gun does not have a drop safety.

◆ **North American Arms Guardian .32 and .380 ACP**

The N.A.A. pocket pistol is a double-action-only (DAO) semi-automatic pistol with a simple blowback-operated action. It has no external manual safety levers.

Disassembly steps are the same for both N.A.A. Guardian models (.32 and .380 ACP). The Guardian is disassembled into its 4 main components for cleaning: the frame, slide, magazine, and recoil spring assembly.

The double action only (DAO) Guardians do not have a magazine disconnect to prevent the pistol from being fired with the magazine removed. They also have no external manual safety. Therefore, the first step in field-stripping the Guardian is to point the pistol in a safe direction **with your finger off the trigger**, remove the magazine, and then pull the slide all the way rearward to check the chamber. If there's a round in the chamber, it should be ejected. Then, check the chamber one more time to make sure that it is indeed empty. Then proceed to field-strip the gun:

Disassembly

1. With your trigger finger, depress the slide release button located at the right rear of the frame. Simultaneously with your support hand, pull the slide rearward with the friction grooves and then pull up, releasing the slide from the frame. Then slide it forward and off the frame.

2. Located beneath the fixed barrel is the guide rod spring assembly which is also to be removed from the frame. That's all there is to it. The gun is now disassembled for cleaning.

Reassembly

1. Insert the guide rod spring assembly the way you removed it with the spring guide rod facing forward.

2. Put the slide back on the frame held rearward up at approximately a 45-degree angle and capture the guide rod spring assembly with the front bridge of the slide.

3. Being careful not to pop out the guide rod spring assembly, pull the slide rearward and down simultaneously as you compress the guide rod spring assembly, and then as you are doing so, squeeze the trigger approximately ⅛ inch.

4. Then, with the hammer partially cocked, lower the rear of the slide back onto the frame. Then rack the slide several times to check the action for function. That's it. Simplicity at its best!

◆ Walther PPK and PPK/S .380 ACP Pistol

Disassembly

1. **Apply the manual safety** and remove the magazine. Make sure the chamber is empty. If it isn't, empty it by racking the slide all the way rearward to release the round. Now double-check the chamber to make sure that the chamber is empty and the pistol is safe. Make sure that the manual safety is on.

2. Grip the pistol firmly in your shooting hand pointing away from you and in a safe direction. With your index finger and thumb of your support hand, pull down on the front underside of the trigger guard. When it comes all the way out of the frame, let it rest sideways up against the notch it goes into, on the underside of the frame. Make sure it doesn't spring back up into the notch by keeping it pressed sideways to the support hand side of the frame with the tip of your trigger finger.

3. Now, holding the pistol firmly in your strong hand, with your support hand, reach over from the support hand side of the slide. You want to get a good *firm grip* on the slide so that you can pull it all the way rearward and then lift its rear up and slide it forward off the frame.

    The *easiest* way to do this is if your support hand index, middle, ring and little fingers are reaching over the top of the slide to the other side while your opposing support thumb is *pushed firmly* up against and parallel to the rear of the slide's support hand side.

4. Now pull the slide all the way rearward. Then lift it off the frame from its rear end. Now slide it all the way forward slowly and easily off the frame. **Try NOT to let go of the slide while you feel the spring tension. If possible, you do NOT want the hammer to cock and then drop freely forward while the pistol is partly dismantled!**

5. Pull the recoil spring forward off the barrel.

Your Walther PPK or PPK/S is now disassembled into its four component parts (slide, receiver or frame, recoil spring and magazine) for cleaning.

Reassembly

1. Slide the recoil spring all the way back on the barrel, **narrow end first, the way it came off**.

2. Make sure the hammer is cocked and the trigger guard is down out of the frame as in disassembly.

3. Make sure the manual safety on the slide is still in the "on" position. Also, make sure that the ejector located on

top of the left side of the receiver behind the barrel chamber remains flush with the frame. Now, put the slide back on the barrel with the slide held rearward up at approximately a 40-degree angle while you capture the front of the recoil spring with the front bridge of the slide.

4. Pull the slide fully back (making sure the ejector stays flush and the trigger guard remains down) until it stops. Then push the rear of the slide down over the frame until it lies flat. You'll have to align the rails on the receiver with the slots on the slide. Then ease the slide forward all the way.

5. Now, push the trigger guard back up into the notch in the frame.

6. Finally, rack the slide several times to make sure it's on properly. Push the manual safety lever up into the unengaged position. Now, cock the hammer, and make sure that the decocker works properly. Put the magazine back in the well and you are done.

◆ Seecamp .32 ACP Pocket Pistol

The L.W. Seecamp's personal protection pistol is a fine illustration of precision craftsmanship in the art of pistol-making mainly due to the skills and artistry applied to each and every pistol by Larry Seecamp, an American gun manufacturer of extraordinary ability. Its well thought-out engineering and custom manufacturing process make the Seecamp an extremely accurate pistol.

We field-tested our out of the box Seecamp at our indoor range at target distances ranging between 5 and 21 feet, using the recommended Winchester Silvertip .32 caliber ammunition as well as the recommended Speer Gold Dot jacketed hollow points and Fiocchi's semi-jacketed hollow points in .32 caliber. All of these rounds provided superior performance and accuracy. There were no feed failures or stoppages. Compared to other .32 pistols we've tested, the Seecamp's performance and accuracy were flawless, and the fit and finish of this classic pistol is superior.

Field-Stripping and Cleaning. The field-stripping procedures for this gun are unique and a bit tricky when you first perform them, so they deserve specific attention. Field-stripping and disassembly procedures are well written in the Seecamp manual for seasoned firearms handlers. **It is essential that anyone who wants to operate this pistol read the Seecamp manual!**

We will now summarize the steps for disassembly and reassembly with clarification where necessary. Practice these steps and they will become easy and automatic.

Disassembly

1. First unload the pistol. This is done as follows:
   (A) Pivot the magazine catch located behind the magazine base plate to the rear. The magazine will drop down from the bottom of the magazine well about ⅛ of an inch.
   (B) You can now pull the slide all the way rearward to eject a live round from the chamber.
   (C) Then completely remove the magazine.
   (D) Pull back on the slide to confirm that the chamber is empty, but note that the slide will only retract far enough to permit such visual inspection with the magazine removed. This is a safety feature built into the Seecamp to prevent a round from being loaded into the chamber when the magazine is removed. It also prevents the trigger from being depressed and the pistol from being fired when the magazine is removed.

2. Insert an empty magazine all the way up the well so that you can pull the slide all the way rearward. Hold the pistol's grip with your strong hand. Use your supporting hand to pull the slide far enough rearward so that you can easily insert a live cartridge, bullet end facing down, into the open space between the partially retracted slide and the frame.

3. When you have retracted the slide far enough to create enough of an opening, hold the slide at that spot with your supporting hand thumb and index finger and with your strong hand insert the cartridge, bullet end facing down. Let the slide close onto the vertical upside-down cartridge to trap it in that space.

4. Holding the pistol in your strong hand, use your supporting hand to insert a $^3/_{32}$-inch armorer's punch into the small hole on the friction grooves on the left side of the slide. Insert this punch far in enough to depress a *"spring-loaded slide retainer plunger"* located inside the slide on the left rear of the receiver. You will feel the retainer plunger click and the rear of the slide release slightly. You can then push up the rear of the slide with your strong hand thumb after you remove the cartridge first.

5. Holding the rear of the slide upward, move the slide forward to separate it from the frame. Watch that the double recoil spring assembly below the barrel, which now is becoming uncompressed does not get lost. Pull the recoil spring out and note that the *single* spring end faces the muzzle and the *double* spring end is what compresses into the frame under the barrel.

6. Remove the empty magazine and clean the gun.

Reassembly

Essentially, reassembly is the disassembly process in reverse.

1. Re-insert an empty magazine all the way up into the magazine well.

2. Insert and push the double recoil spring assembly, double end first, until it stops, into the hole at the front of the frame located below the fixed barrel.

3. Cock the hammer ever so slightly so that you can see it engaging the draw bar. You will see the draw bar moving forward ever so slightly.

4. Catching the front of the recoil spring assembly with the inside front bridge of the slide, compress the spring as you push the slide rearward so that the rear end of the slide is above the hammer. The slide should now be positioned pointed to the rear at about a 25-degree angle upward from the front of the slide.

5. Continue to slightly press the trigger so that the hammer remains slightly cocked as you push the rear end of the slide down onto the frame. When the slide contacts the *"spring-loaded slide retainer plunger,"* it will click into place and you can release the trigger. Continue to press downward on the rear of the slide to make sure it is locked in place.

6. Exerting downward pressure on the rear of the slide, wiggle the slide forward and backward to lock it in place. Make sure the slide is locked in place by pulling upward on the rear of the slide. It shouldn't budge!

7. Rack the slide and let it go several times to make sure the weapon is properly reassembled. That's all there is to it!

Cautionary Notes for Reassembly Procedure
1. The trigger should never be fully pressed or applied when the slide is off the frame.

2. Be sure that the *draw bar to trigger connection* is maintained at all times and that when re-installing the slide onto the frame, you give your full attention to each procedural element, *especially keeping the draw bar to trigger connection intact.*

3. If the draw bar should separate from the trigger pin, don't panic! You can put it back onto the trigger pin. You do this gently with the tip of your finger to hold the *"trigger draw bar connector"* down so it catches onto the tiny cylindrical plunger projecting at the top of the trigger (the "trigger pivot pin") as you press the trigger back slightly.

4. Once the trigger draw bar connector is captured by the slide, engaging rearward movement of the trigger about half its travel distance will allow the slide to be re-seated and the pistol to be operational again.

5. When reinstalling the slide assembly, it is imperative that the magazine be fully seated up the magazine well. The magazine will maintain its magazine disconnect spring integrity should you inadvertently squeeze the trigger while the slide is still off.

An Abbreviated Cleaning Procedure

The following procedure is a natural extension of Larry Seecamp's pistol breakdown procedure. It is an abbreviated procedure that is uncomplicated to perform and thus, it makes it easy to clean your Seecamp each and every time you shoot it. This makes practice at the range with your Seecamp more fun given the knowledge that you can easily clean your gun afterwards. You can perform the more thorough disassembly and cleaning procedure after several sessions of range practice shooting your gun.

1. With an empty magazine in the magazine well, so that you can move the slide all the way rearward, horizontally insert into the ejection port a spent .32 shell parallel to the gun's bore axis. Position the casing to the left of the ejection port to avoid covering the extractor on the right because you have to clean under and around the extractor. See Figure 9.2.

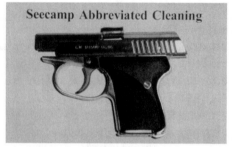

Figure 9.2

The spent casing is now holding the slide open so that you don't have to, and the gun is in the out of battery position (Figure 9.2 illustrates this.). This will free both of your hands so that you can use them to clean all interior components and the barrel without the stress of completely disassembling the pistol.

You can easily roll the casing across the open end of the ejection port to expose the opposite side of the interior that was initially covered by the case for cleaning.

2. Use a Q-Tip or the small end of a nylon toothbrush with or without a gun-cleaning patch to clean the interior of the pistol which you can now access through the ejection port which is being kept open by the spent casing.

3. Use a dry bore-cleaning brush to clean the bore of the barrel by inserting the brush into the barrel from the muzzle end and turning the brush in a clockwise direction as you push it through the barrel. Make sure that it doesn't bang into the firing pin when you bring it out through the feed ramp into the open ejection port.

Bore Brush Size. Use a bore brush designed for a .38 caliber revolver. This size brush will work in .32, .380, 9mm, .38 special and .357 magnum caliber pistols. There is a separate size bore brush for .22 and .25 calibers and a third size for .40 S & W, .45 ACP, 10mm, .45 Long Colt, .44 special and .44 magnum pistols.

4. Next, lubricate the barrel. Thread a fresh gun-cleaning patch (onto which you have first dropped 2 to 3 drops of Break Free) through the loom of your brass cleaning rod. Run the cleaning patch through the barrel several times in the same way you just used the bore brush. Then remove the patch from the loom and wipe all interior and exterior surfaces where you see dirt and debris.

5. Next, the slide rails can be lubricated from the rear of the slide while the slide is partially open. To do this, just place one drop of Break Free on each slide rail. You are going to work this Break Free lubricant and cleaner through the pistol. This will work the dirt and debris out through the front of the slide. To accomplish this, remove the casing and rack the slide back and forth about 6 times. That should do it. The idea here is similar to the procedure that we described earlier in revolver cleaning of spinning the revolver's cylinder on the barrel of the crane assembly to free dirt and debris with the Break Free lubricant and cleaner from the chambers and crane assembly.

You now have a clean Seecamp pistol! We both love our Seecamp pistols and wouldn't do anything that would damage them. This simpler, abbreviated cleaning and care procedure makes you want to clean your Seecamp after each time you shoot it. It makes it easier for you to enjoy this quality precision pistol for a lifetime.

So, take good care of your Seecamp and it will be able to take good care of you. Following S-A-F-E-S-T cardinal safety rule number 3, **F**ocus *all of your attention on what you are doing.*

Turn off the phone, forget the kids, and put down the sandwich. Pay attention to what you are doing. You can't afford to get distracted when working on any pistol, let alone the precision instrument that is the Seecamp.

You are the surgeon. Don't fail in the operation. Save money on postage by not having to return your pistol to the Seecamp Connecticut factory or worse, letting some so-called "expert" at the local gun store try to figure out how the pistol operates, keep it for 3 weeks, and then return it not functioning or damaged. This is life threatening. Take responsibility for your equipment!

Trust Must Be Earned. Therefore, trust yourself first. If a salesperson cannot clearly guide you through a pistol's disassembly and re-assembly procedure, do not purchase the pistol from that salesperson, and certainly don't trust him or her with your life.

We assure you, the procedures we've outlined are not difficult. You don't have to be a gunsmith or armorer, mechanical engineer or even a wizard to get into the habit of performing these maintenance procedures regularly.

10

Holsters

Considerable time should be spent on your holster selection. Next to your firearms training, good judgment, and choice of a quality weapon, your holster is an important part of your equipment. Your weapon transporter should be safe, secure and well-fit to provide you with quick, smooth access to your weapon. Good concealed carry holsters are designed to provide safe transportation and good concealment for your handgun.

"Custom" Vs. "Non-Custom" Holsters

Custom holsters are individually made by a master holster leather craftsman generally in a small shop with personal attention given to each detail of the holster's production. Custom leather holsters are entirely hand bench-crafted; generally of top grain cowhide or horsehide and selectively hand wet-molded to a specific handgun. Hand-carving, hand-tooling, special motifs and decorations, personalization, custom dye colors, and left or right hand models are some of the special individualized services offered by custom holster makers who make "one of a kind rigs." Some custom holster craftsmen, such as Matt Del Fatti and Lefty Lewis of Bell Charter Oak, take the time on the telephone to interview you, to learn your unique needs and preferences. Milt Sparks, Ken Null and Lou Alessi are high-end custom shops that make finely detailed, high quality holsters to meet anyone's unique individual needs. Each holster is made for a specific firearm. Also, their belt slots are usually designed to be exactly fitted to a specific size belt. It may take anywhere from 3 weeks to 3 months for a custom holster order to be fulfilled.

We recommend you log on to the web sites of the companies recommended, or call them for their catalogs, and explore what's available. You will find quality products that suit your defensive security needs.

Please note that "custom" is not for everyone. Many custom holsters do not have the more universal appeal of many of the more standard design, "mass production holsters."

The "non-custom" larger scale companies we recommend make high quality holsters. Most will have something that will satisfy anyone's needs. In most cases, their service is fast. That means you'll be likely to have your order at your doorstep within a week to two. Furthermore, some of the "larger scale" holster makers we recommend would justifiably "take issue" with the idea that they are not custom because many of them will make special rigs to order, and they have good quality control. So, we apologize to anyone we've listed if you feel we've put you in the "wrong" category.

Action-Direct *(800-667-4191 www.action-direct.com)*

Action-Direct manufactures and sells direct over 16 concealed carry products and their customer service is excellent. They are best known for their affordable, inside the pants, elastic belt-type holster rig called the "Defender." There are no clips, the rig holds the weapon very close in to your body under your shirt or blouse, and it does not print. They also make an elastic "Deep Concealment" Shoulder Holster rig. You wear it under your shirt or blouse and it distributes the gun's weight evenly for comfortable carry. As well, they manufacture and sell a number of functional synthetic and leather pocket holsters for pistols and revolvers. Give their web site a good look.

Ahern Enterprises *(706-335-5715)*

Jerry Ahern, President and CEO, is a multi-talented individual. He makes reliable, affordable and functional "custom" holsters and is also a talented non-fiction and fiction book author and "gun writer." Jerry is a generous, vast source of information and we are grateful. His designs are unique and worth checking out.

Everything is manufactured to order, specializing in: pocket holsters (the "Pocket Natural") for any handgun that can be carried in the front or hip pocket; clip-on inside the waist band rigs, belt slides and scabbards, crossdraws, inside the waistband and pocket magazine pouches, and "deep concealment" rigs. Figure 10.1 depicts the inside the pants clip-on magazine pouch, rough-side out "pocket natural" and his inside the pants, clip-on, rough-side out, leather holster.

Figure 10.1

Aker International *(800-645-AKER www.akerleather.com)*

Aker Leather is a quality holster manufacturer with excellent, prompt customer service. They make an extensive line of concealed carry and duty gear. Our favorites include: the "Express Pocket Holster" with the attached wallet shaped flap that prevents your small pocket semi-automatic from printing and the "Pocket Protector" which is essentially the same holster without the flap. Both holsters come in leather or the more exotic sharkskin. These pocket holsters keep the gun in a stable, upright position in your pocket and they work especially well with the N.A.A. Guardians and the Seecamp .32 pistol. They are a favorite of ours and Larry Seecamp for pocket carry of his Seecamp .32.

Alessi Custom Concealment Holsters *(716-691-5615)*

Lou Alessi is a master leather holster craftsman extraordinaire who has been making fine custom holsters for over 30 years. His name is synonymous with *quality*. Alessi crafts ultra-fine holsters for concealed carry use by civilians, law enforcement professionals and those who must carry duty sidearms, used by people around the country who know and desire quality. We had the opportunity to sample the following top-notch holsters:

The "Pocket Pro" for S & W J-frame revolvers is a pocket holster with an outer shell of soft garment type leather and an inner skeletal piece of regular leather to retain the holster's shape and rigidity. The interior has a cutout for the cylinder to eliminate bulk. This holster nicely stays in your pocket when you draw your revolver. It is definitely one of our favorite pocket holsters for the J-frame.

The "Close Quarter Covert-Inside the Pants" (CQC-I) for the Glock 27 is an inside the waistband holster with a double snap-on belt loop. The body of this holster is made of thinner leather with a reinforcing band around the mouth of the holster for easy reholstering. The rig also has a stitched U-shaped sight track that prevents the front sight from snagging when drawing. The added advantage of this "U-shape" at the bottom muzzle end of the holster's interior is that it keeps the muzzle of the holster from flattening out with extended use.

The CQC-S holster for a Glock 23 is an outside the pants holster that utilizes 2 snap loops that easily wrap and snap around your belt. This makes it easy to put on and take off the holster without having to undo your belt, or do a lot of twisting for those of us who have arthritis. This incredible belt scabbard rides very close to the body and is exceptionally comfortable. Unlike most easy on-easy off holsters (e.g, paddles), this rig doesn't wobble around and it cannot be ripped off in a scuffle.

The "Rough Out Pocket Holster" for the N.A.A. Guardian .32 is made of roughed out leather. It has a hook-shaped extension that hooks onto your pocket when you draw your little pistol that keeps the holster in place in your pocket. It works very well. It is also rigid enough so that you can use your thumb, index or middle finger to push off the top of the holster when you draw your weapon.

The "Talon Clip-On IWB Holster" for the Guardian .32 uses a patented injection molded nylon-fiber glass clip. The name "talon" comes from the fact that the holster has a hook on the inside bottom of the clip that catches on your pants or belt and prevents slippage of the holster when you draw your weapon.

When you want a functional work of holster art that you can depend on, you can depend on Lou Alessi, master custom holster craftsman.

Bell Charter Oak (607-783-2483 *www.bellcharteroakholster.com*)
A quality custom holster manufacturer that hand bench crafts and hand tools each and every custom leather holster. Each holster is molded to a specific firearm. Lefty Lewis, custom holster maker for BCO, is also a veteran law enforcement professional who makes sure to keep it real and who makes real practical holsters. His holsters are extremely functional and attractive and true to the tradition of the master custom holster maker's art and that of his mentor and friend, the late Chic

Gaylord. Lefty has a way with leather just as he has a way with words.

We had the opportunity to sample a number of BCO's holsters and we are very impressed with their remarkable quality and functionality. We strongly recommend the following BCO rigs:

- **The "Deep Drop Bandit Auto."** The "D.D.B.A." is a deep concealment, clip-on inside the waistband leather holster for medium and compact-sized autos. It rides so low inside the pants that you do not need a pager to conceal it. Bruce's came ready to receive a Seecamp .32. It provides a comfortable carry, an easy draw, and the little gun virtually disappears but remains securely accessible at all times.

- **The "Auto Compact Extreme."** The "A.C.E." is a small, lightweight, compact, clip-on leather holster for small semi-autos such as the Seecamp .32, the Beretta "Tomcat" .32, and the North American "Guardians" .32 and .380. It is very comfortable and convenient. The leather and talon style steel clip are high quality and the holster really stays in place. Bruce's came ready to accept his N.A.A. .380 Guardian. It's clearly the best, most secure, and unobtrusive, clip-on inside the pants holster for the Guardian we've tested. Maybe that's why N.A.A. themselves recommend them for their guns!

- **The "Deep Cover Pocket Rocket Revolver" Holster ("DCPRR").** Featuring a cut-down model for hammerless J-frame snubbie S&W revolvers and a full cover for standard hammer revolvers, this quality leather holster, as do many of Lefty's others, stem from the classic functionalist tradition of Chic Gaylord. Our Pocket Rocket holsters really stay in place in our pocket when we draw our J-frame S&W snubbies out of them. We guess the name "Pocket Rocket" is apropos because of the quickness of the draw these pocket holsters permit. They definitely provide a secure, non-printing concealed carry for the little J-frames.

- **The "Deep Cover Auto Pocket" Holster.** This is a small, convenient, and lightweight, leather pocket holster for small semi-autos. It has an ambidextrous design and a hook that keeps it in your pocket when you draw. Steve's came ready for my N.A.A. Guardian .380 and his Seecamp .32. It offers a secure, concealed pocket ride for these little guns and offers them up quickly when you need them.

- **The "Fireline."** This ambidextrous pocket holster for J-frames and for small autos has a slightly different design than the "DCPRR." It has an extended retention tab or hook to keep it in place and it works well. It has a "friction fit" to keep it in place when you draw, and is unmolded to minimize printing of the weapon's outline in your pocket. It works great with our J-frame snubbies and our Kahr MK9 semi-auto pistols.

- **The "Gaylord 8 Ball."** The late, great Chic Gaylord's 8 Ball Side Pocket Holster lives on! This holster is cut from Chic Gaylord's original die and is offered rough out or finished out in saddle brown. This is one of the smoothest deep concealment pocket holsters for a S&W J-frame we've ever tested! It is not ambidextrous. It will function equally well in your overcoat, sports jacket, raincoat, or larger-sized pocket as well as in your jeans, casual slacks or business attire.

- **The "New York Reload Double Holsters."** We've never seen rigs like these. They are amazing! Two holsters in one that allow you to securely carry two handguns muzzle tops facing each other. They are made for both small revolvers and subcompact to compact semi-autos, and for IWB clip-on or belt scabbard carry. Their "opposing butt design" gives fast access to a reserve weapon. This rig may be worn on the dominant or weak side; thus, enabling you to draw your weapon with either hand. It's a great idea that is really practical because the holsters are very lightweight, yet sturdy and functional.

BCO also offers a full line of belt slides and belt scabbards for semi-autos and revolvers that will suit anyone's preferences, needs, and pocketbook. These holsters are all excellent and worth waiting for. However, BCO's custom customer service is responsive, so the wait may be much shorter than you think for a custom holster!

Bianchi International *(800-477-8545 www,bianchi-intl.com)*
Bianchi International is recognized by shooting enthusiasts worldwide as one of the largest, leading designers and manufacturers of innovative and high-quality handgun holsters and accessories. Bianchi's many patented innovations have aggressively and consistently set the pace in holster technology. The

widely-used thumb snap feature was first innovated by Bianchi in 1960. Their broad line of innovative concealment holsters is an industry leader in comfort, function and professional styling. Bianchi's customer service and responsiveness are unparalleled. The company is capable of fulfilling large orders on tight schedules, while employing the most advanced production and quality assurance techniques in the industry.

Our favorite choices (see Figure 10.2) include the following holsters:

- **Model "3S Pistol Pocket" Inside the Waistband.** Comfortable even for wear when driving, this close and high-riding "IWB" holster easily slips behind your waistband and secures to your belt with 2 one-way snaps. The belt loop is attached to the holster with a swivel, so the holster can be adjusted to five carry modes.
- **Model "6D ATB" IWB holster.** This is a super lightweight, deep concealment soft suede holster with an adjustable thumb break with a heavy duty spring steel clip that holds the holster firmly to your belt or waistband for a secure draw.
- **Model "58L Hip Hugger" Paddle Holster.** This very comfortable paddle holster rides high and close to the body and offers easy on/off convenience.
- **Model "100 Professional."** This deep concealment IWB has a high back design that comfortably shields your side, eliminating the "biting" often associated with a gun's sharp edges. The holster's heat-treated spring steel clip slips conveniently over a belt or waistband for wear with sweats or without a belt. The clip works in unison with the non-skid suede backing to secure the holster in place when drawing.
- **Model "105 Minimalist."** As Bianchi advertises, "sometimes less is better." With minimal bulk, this holster provides stable and secure carry, quick access, and a smooth draw. A suede tab makes releasing the elasticized retention strap quick and easy.
- **Model 5 Black Widow.** This compact holster features an open muzzle design, and widely spaced belt slots to hold the gun close to the body and high on the hip for excellent concealability and easy access.
- **Model 7 and 7L Shadow II.** A classic 3-slot belt scabbard, the Shadow II is designed for comfortable all day

concealed carry, accessible and functional draw angle and excellent concealability. This holster rides close to the body to provide low profile carry.

Figure 10.2

Blade-Tech Industries

Blade-Tech Industries is one the leading manufacturers of finely crafted, super-tough, thermoplastic holsters and maga-zine/carriers for handguns. Their products are in daily use worldwide by members of law enforcement departments, special operations units, government agencies, and legally armed civil-ians. Blade-Tech holsters are very light and comfortable, yet they are durable and easily concealable, making them practical for daily carry and training.

We had the opportunity to extensively test the company's 3-Position Paddle Holsters and Inside the Waistband (IWB) holsters designed for a variety of different size pistols: the Glock line (full-size Glock 17, 22, and 31; mid-size, compact Glock 19, 23, and 32; subcompact Glock 26, 27, and 33; and the .45 caliber Glock 21, 30, and 36); the full-size .45 caliber SIG Sauer P220 and 9mm Sig Sauer 226 with and without the integrated rail; the mid-size, compact SIG Sauer P229; the mid-size, compact .45 caliber SIG P245; and the very compact 9mm and .40 caliber SIG Sauer P239.

We did not find these holsters lacking. We are happy to report to Tim Wegner, Blade-Tech's founder and President, that "these holsters are so great they're the only ones I want to wear!"

And while we have many great holsters to choose from, the statement is true. Blade-Tech makes the finest synthetic hard polymer holsters money can buy, and they are very affordable.

Their "3-position paddle holster" is a perfect choice for those looking for optimal convenience and comfort. This holster is very convenient if you do some desk work and are in and out of a vehicle all day long. Adjustable tension screws allow for precise retention. The paddle feature permits easy mounting and removal from your pants and belt. The holster may be adjusted from straight drop to muzzle forward or FBI cant.

Blade-Tech's Inside the Waistband (IWB) holster is a great choice for concealed carry. The holster holds your pistol tight to the body and there is a protective panel to prevent your shirt from interfering with the presentation of the firearm. This "body guard" also keeps perspiration off of your handgun and makes all day carry more comfortable. This IWB holster features pull-dot snap belt loops that fit 1.25, 1.50 and 1.75 inch belts.

This versatile and comfortable holster allows you to obtain a good firing grip and is easily concealed under a tee-shirt, jacket, or vest. Dual tension screws provide precise retention while the superior memory properties of Blade-Tech's thermoplastic enables easy holstering. The Glock and 1911 models allow the cant of the holster to be adjusted from "FBI" to straight drop.

To save money, Blade-Tech also makes a "One Size Fits All" IWB holster that is identical in features and specifications to the standard IWB. The only difference is that you can use the same holster for more than one Glock or more than one 1911. You can order the holster to fit all of the Glock 9mm and .40 S&W models, all of the Glock .45 caliber models, or all of the standard frame 1911s.

Blade-Tech's customer service and responsiveness are exemplary. Ordering is direct over the phone. Typical wait time until you receive your order is anywhere from a few days to several weeks. We highly recommend Blade-Tech. Also, unlike some hard polymer holsters, repeated draws will not ruin the finish on your pistol. You cannot go wrong with this company's products.

Bulman Gunleather

Bulman Gunleather offers a complete line of hand-molded and hand-detailed, concealment holsters for law enforcement professionals and armed citizens who carry concealed legally. Bulman's line of holsters provides good weapon retention. The initial resistance built into the hand-molded holster when one initiates the draw is quickly overcome as the draw is continued and the weapon presented. Josh Bulman, head of the company, has a loyal customer following who appreciate the individual attention given to each holster that assures its quality, durability, functionality, comfort and attractiveness.

Bulman makes belt holsters, IWBs, and pocket holsters for a very wide variety of handguns. Often, if you cannot find another manufacturer who makes a holster for your weapon, you are likely to find it at Bulman.

We had the opportunity to evaluate the following two holsters: "The Secret Agent" (TSA) and "The Secret Agent Practical" (TSAP). The TSA is Bulman's entry model IWB scabbard, and is similar to the Bruce Nelson "Summer Special." It can be ordered smooth side or rough side out and features dual belt loops with one way snaps, stitched in sight rails (for most autos), and a metal reinforced mouth. The TSAP is the same basic holster as the TSA, but the gun rides one inch lower in the waist. This holster also has a body guard that extends the leather on the back side of the holster to the top of the slide, for greater comfort, especially with pistols that have a thumb safety or decocking lever. We recommend that you peruse Bulman's excellent web site.

Comp-Tac

Comp-Tac is a top-of-the-line manufacturer of high quality Kydex holsters and accessories (e.g., paddle magazine carriers) for defensive firearms. Their designs are well thought out and hence, user friendly. Comp-Tac holsters provide a very stable ride on your waist, yet the holster and holstered firearm can be easily removed without the hassle of having to unthread your belt or draw your pistol out of the holster.

Comp-Tac states on their web site: "Kydex is a durable, low thermotemp plastic used in applications ranging from the aircraft industry to furniture. It has the ability to withstand solvents used on firearms and not collapse like leather... The added benefit of lowered drag on your pistol or magazine during presentation adds the need for a note of caution: This stuff is fast!"

This is true. These holsters offer a very fast draw and thus are also excellent for competition, as are the Blade-Techs. However, like the Blade-Techs, Comp-Tac's designs provide easy concealability. All of Comp-Tac's holsters are tension adjustable and an Allen wrench is included with each order.

Holster styles offered by Comp-Tac include the very stable and close-riding Comp-Tac "FBI Paddle," their "Locking Paddle," their "Gurkha IWB," their "Shirt Tucker," their "Undercover" and their "Pro Undercover."

We were very impressed with the lightweight Comp-Tac "FBI Paddle" we tested for the Glock 19/23/32. We also tested a Pro-Undercover IWB for the Glock 19/23/32 and like it very much. It has a belt clip that puts the weight of the pistol on the belt instead of the waistband of one's pants. It allows for a quick draw and one-handed re-holstering.

Finally, we tested the "Shirt Tucker" for the same guns. It can be used comfortably as a semi-concealment, inside the waistband rig. However, for deep cover, the holster can be inserted inside the waistband, the belt clip attached over the belt, and the shirt tucked in the pants between the belt clip strut and the gun. To draw the handgun, one has but to pull one's shirt tail out of the waistband. It's quick to put on and take off.

In sum, Comp-Tac makes a truly innovative, functional, and durable product that we can enthusiastically recommend.

Coronado Leather *(800-283-9509 www.coronadoleather.com)*

Coronado Leather is a leading manufacturer of leather concealment products. They make a superior line of waist packs for concealed carry of a handgun, such as their "Stealth Pac" and "Mini-Belt Pack." However, the company is best known for its attractive leather outerwear that comes with right and left inner holster pockets for safe and discreet, concealed carry of a handgun.

You can carry a small, medium and even a large handgun conveniently in these pockets, whether you purchase one of their fine Classic Bombers, a longer Driving Jacket or Car Coat, or one of their snazzier, stylish, waist length leather jackets.

In total, Coronado offers more than thirty firearm concealment products for law enforcement officers and individuals seeking safe and responsible self-protection. These quality products are all handcrafted. Attention to detail can be seen in each product.

In addition to their fine jackets and coats, Coronado's product line includes handbags, brief cases, and other types of carrying cases. All of their products are innovative, functional and designed with safety in mind. And, the company firmly stands behind everything they make. We definitely recommend that you peruse their web site. If you have a question, they'll be glad to help you, and you'll be glad you called.

Del Fatti Leather

Matt Del Fatti, owner, chief designer and craftsman of Del Fatti Gunleather, operates a truly CUSTOM shop. Del Fatti exemplifies the definition of "custom." He says it best: *"Designing and building gun leather to meet the needs of each individual customer."* He went on to tell us that *"the challenge that drives me is to make a holster that the customer will actually use and not just throw it in a box and not use."*

Each of Del Fatti's rigs are long and well thought out designs, and each design is built by Mr. Del Fatti from the ground up in individual consultation with the customer. The client confers with Mr. Del Fatti about his or her size, body type, intended use of the holster, gun type, gun details, and preferences, and is advised accordingly. Del Fatti will spend as much time as necessary with the customer in a pre-building consultation to get ALL the specifications right. The process almost reminded us of our experiences in the past of sitting down with a general building contractor to plan renovations or additions to our residences!

Every feature of the holster can be chosen by the customer: type of leather; rough vs. smooth exterior surface; very slick and smooth vs. coarser interior; color of the holster; exact angle of the cant or "rake" and whether it's adjustable by the wearer or not (e.g., 8 degrees, 10 degrees or 20 degrees?); slotted pad vs. snaps and straps vs. snaps and screws vs. sewn belt loop; type of holster mouth reinforcement for ease of reholstering; thumb retention strap vs. open top; exact height of the body/slide guard; presence or absence of a rear wing, for example, on an IWB holster or pocket holster, and the size and dimensions of the rear wing.

Fit and finish of a truly custom designed Matt Del Fatti holster is impeccable—**the** best we've seen! Stitching is elegant, sturdy and reinforced. Del Fatti holsters are designed to be worn all day without wearer fatigue. Whatever size handgun you carry in a custom-designed Del Fatti holster, you will hardly know it's there—until you need it, and then, you'll be able to acquire it with the greatest of ease.

In fact, the first sample Bruce received was a fine black leather open top IWB for his Glock 19/23 (Del Fatti's IWB-SS model) with a low-rise body/slide guard and sewn belt loops. He usually prefers snap straps or clips for ease of on/off. What a surprise! He's found himself wearing the rig all day long comfortably, and it provides confident deep concealment. He ended up ordering another one for a different pistol!

We also got to test Del Fatti's ISP-WR built for a Sig P228 9mm pistol. This rig is an open top IWB with an abbreviated rear wing and adjustable rake capability. Ours came with a slotted pad on it and with separate snap straps, with screws as an alternative.

Del Fatti builds terrific holsters for small caliber pocket pistols also. We got to test his Pocket Holster-Single Wing (PH-SW) for our Seecamps along with his Pocket Double Magazine pouch (PDM). These are designed to be worn inside the front pants pockets. The PDM is designed in such a way that it maintains a stable orientation in the pocket in the same way that its matching pocket holster is designed to behave. The key is to have your pocket pistol in your pocket on your strong side and your magazines on your support, off-hand side immediately available. In this way, both gun and spare magazines (reloads) are immediately available to your intended hand.

Del Fatti wisely points out that pocket carry should be treated in essence the same as on the belt or inside the waistband carry. You want things to be where you put them (pistol and magazines) when you need quick access to your weaponry. It is best to keep your spare magazines in your off-side pocket so they are available to your off-hand.

Another custom feature is the height of the Seecamp pocket magazine carrier. He pointed out that because of the abbreviated length of the Seecamp magazines, there can be flexibility in the height of the pocket magazine carriers. So, if you carry stuff in addition to the magazines in your off-pocket, Del Fatti can add to the amount of leather below the magazine pouch and thus, raise the magazines higher (to the same height as the grip of the gun) so they are easier to grasp. The design of Del Fatti's PDM allows the wearer to also carry keys in that off-pocket.

In sum, Del Fatti Custom Handgun Concealment Leather will meet most anyone's unique combination of needs and provide most anyone with a top of the line custom built to order holster that the user will be glad to own and use for years to come. So, buy a Del Fatti holster for each of your carry guns and leave extra space in your drawers for other stuff—like...well, those other holsters that you don't wear.

Derry Gallagher Custom Holsters *(956-686-5109)*
Derry Gallagher is a master custom leather holster maker. He was kind enough to send us two of his finely hand crafted holsters to evaluate.

The **"ADS Scabbard"** is a belt rig that has belt slots front and rear and keeps your handgun securely in position very close to the body. It is very concealable and comfortable to wear. Bruce's was made for his HK USP Compact .45. It's a natural. HK ought to sell it with this gun!

The **"Tuckable"** is a highly concealable and practical inside the waistband holster. There are belt straps in the front and rear and they are adjustable! The rig features a unique hidden hook and loop system that adjusts to fit various belt widths. Additionally, for deep concealment purposes, the straps attach to an additional leather panel which is fastened to the bottom of the holster body. This enables you to tuck your shirt between the concealment panel and the holster. The shirt covers the holster and thus conceals your weapon.

Steve received his made for his compact Glock 19. It provided him with a very comfortable, concealed carry, and a smooth draw. The holster is made for most of the popular compact to medium-frame pistols and revolvers (i.e. J-frame S&W, Para-Ordinance P10, Colt Commander, etc.). Each holster is gun specific and custom-made to your preferred angle. Highly recommended.

If you want a fine custom holster, Derry Gallagher is the right person to make one for you.

DeSantis Holsters and Leather Goods *(800-GUNHIDE)*

DeSantis is one of the best of the best among the larger, quality, holster manufacturers. The company's innovative founder and President, Gene DeSantis, puts customer and dealer satisfaction first, and quality control and good service are his passions. You can literally place a holster order today, and receive it tomorrow! We did. And you cannot go wrong with a DeSantis. The holsters all work, and they work very well. That's why DeSantis is known worldwide for making quality holsters at a very fair price that few can't afford.

The company has been one of the innovators in the holster industry and many of their patented designs have been copied or have inspired other holster makers. DeSantis holsters are like Glocks—they work great right out of the box and they last. DeSantis has an extensive and exciting catalog of products. You need to peruse their web site and their color catalog. Our favorites for concealment carry include:

- **Style 001-Thumb Break Scabbard.** In this fine leather holster, your firearm rides high. The holster's thumb break, precise molding, and tensioning device provide a secure and highly concealable carry, but the draw is smooth and fast. It comes equipped with three belt slots which allow you to adjust the cant of the weapon.

- **Style 002-Speed Scabbard.** This is essentially the same holster as the Style 001 *without* a thumb break. Because the holster holds the weapon so securely, you really do not need a thumb break for concealed carry civilian applications.
- **Style 019-Mini Scabbard.** This unique DeSantis holster has been reduced to the barest of essentials and is proof that *simple is good*. It offers a secure grip on your handgun, thanks to its exact molding and adjustable tension screw, but it also offers a very fast draw. The Mini Scabbard will accommodate medium and large frame semi-autos, but it is especially well suited for the Glock 26 and 27 pistols.
- **Style 085-Thumb Break Mini Slide.** This holster is a thumb break belt scabbard similar to DeSantis's Style 001, but it has a shorter body up and down. It was designed especially for the Glock 26 and 27 "baby Glocks" and works very well with these fine concealable weapons. It has two belt slots, a thumb break retention strap, and an adjustable tension screw.
- **Style 086-Mini Slide.** This is the same holster as the Style 085 without the thumb break retention strap.
- **Style N38-The Nemesis.** This is one great and super affordable pocket holster! Its material composition is viscous, so the holster is sort of sticky, almost like fly paper. But don't worry. It's not messy. Because of this sticky material, the holster stays in position in your pocket and when you draw your weapon. The smooth no friction draw is also aided by the slick pack cloth lining on the inside of the holster. It has an ambidextrous design. It is one of our favorites for our Seecamps, Beretta .32 Tomcats, and our N.A.A. Guardians. It is also made for comfortable pocket carry of the Glock 26/27 and the Kel-Tec P-11.
- **Style 031-The Insider.** For concealment with comfort and use with sweats or without a belt, the soft black "Insider" is the one. It is especially good with compact and sub-compact semi-autos. The heavy-duty spring steel clip stays positioned high for deep cover.
- **Style 057-Inner Piece.** This top grain leather, inside the waistband holster has few equals for performance and

comfort. A stabilizer wing insures that the holster will not rotate or shift positions. This structure is similar to the extension hooks that good leather pocket holsters have. The top of this holster is also reinforced to allow one-handed re-holstering. The holster is snapped in place around your belt with snap fasteners. This holster absolutely does not move when you draw. It's one of our favorite IWB's.

- **Style N87-The Stealth.** Made of premium padded ballistic nylon, this ambidextrous holster has a sturdy powder-coated black spring clip which keeps it securely anchored to your belt, slacks or sweats. It also has a spare magazine pouch for the semi-auto models.

- **Style R60-Original Gunny Sack.** DeSantis is the originator of the "gunny sack" for concealed carry. It is rugged, convenient, comfortable, and dependable. You can wear it anywhere without anyone knowing you are carrying a gun. It looks just like a standard hip pouch but... It has velcro access to your handgun which is kept in place inside in a holster insert which allows easy draw of your lifeline.

- **Style R72-Discreet Hip Pouch.** This rig, like the "gunny sack," lets you "hide your handgun in plain sight." It allows an easy one-handed vertical draw from a belt-looped interior pouch and can be worn on either side. It fits most small arms. It stays on your belt or sweats with a metal clip. There is also an optional hip-paddle.

- **Style N65-Pistol Pack.** This lightweight, clip-on, padded ballistic nylon, zippered pouch conveniently holds the N.A.A. Guardian models (.32 and .380) as well as most other small semi-autos, plus a spare magazine. You can wear it on your belt or beltless on your slacks or sweats.

- **Style 053-Pro Fed Paddle Holster.** This rig has an open top black "synthetic leather" ("Millennium") holster mounted on a thermal molded, self-locking, polymer paddle that's functional and durable. The holster's cant is adjustable forward to rearward. It is available with a paddle that provides for a close ride or with a "comfort paddle" that positions the holster further from the hip.

- **Style 065-Viper Paddle Holster.** This lightweight leather holster has a thumb break. It has the same thermal molded, self-locking polymer paddle as the "Pro-Fed" and is adjustable for forward to rearward cant. It also is available with either type of paddle.

Figure 10.3 pictures some of DeSantis' excellent rigs.

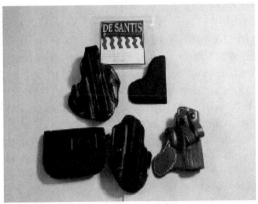

Figure 10.3

Don Hume Leathergoods *(800-331-2686 www.donhume.com)*

Don Hume is a manufacturer of a large line of quality and very affordable concealment and duty holsters. We liked all that we had the opportunity to sample and feel that you cannot go wrong with any of them. Their attentive and courteous customer service is exemplary. We liked all of the Don Hume rigs we tested a lot. The rigs we had the chance to test included:

- **The "H721 O.T." (Open Top) for Semi-Automatics.** This is a great concealment belt slide holster that features covered belt slots and a body shield between weapon and user that provides comfortable carry. The rig rides high and very close.
- **The "Front Pocket 001."** A great pocket holster. Works particularly well with the Glock 26/27.
- **"Strong Side Copy II."** This snug-fitting, double-stitched open top holster with body shield is designed for easy removal with its snap-on belt loops front and rear.
- **The "H-715M" Waistband Clip-On with or without Thumb Break.** This inside the waistband holster (IWB) is made of lightweight leather and form molded. The top of the holster is leather reinforced to aid in weapon reholstering. The design works especially well when out walking or jogging with a pair of sweats, or walking in the woods.

- **"H720 O.T." Open Top Paddle.** For revolvers as well as semi-automatics, this high riding paddle holster comes with a suede-covered metal reinforced paddle and a belt loop to hold the holster in place when drawing.
- **"J.I.T. Slide."** This "minimalist" belt slide will carry your medium to small semi-auto close to your body.
- **"PCCH IWB."** This fine inside the waistband, form-molded holster has a wide belt loop with 2 independent pull-the-dot snaps and a reinforced leather top opening for easy re-holstering. A body shield also provides comfort between user and weapon.
- **Y.S.O.** This light weight, double-stitched and form-molded "Yaqui Slide-On" rides close and has tension adjustment screws.

FIST, Inc. *(800-443-3478 www.fist-inc.com)*
FIST, Inc. of Brooklyn, New York manufactures and sells one of the best leather paddle holsters we've seen or used. Jim Murnak, the company's president and holster designer, also has invented a very unique cross-draw leather holster that can easily be used as a driving holster. The design of the belt hook allows the wearer to rotate the top open end of the rig 90 degrees clockwise down towards his or her lap for comfort while sitting at the wheel and for easy access to the gun and smooth draw. The holster also can be easily slid fore or aft to where it is most comfortable on the belt, as if the belt were a rail. Their product line also includes very durable and extremely thin and lightweight kydex, inside the waistband clip-on holsters. These include a "deep cover" model that can be hidden by the wearer's shirt. Most of their holsters are available in both kydex or leather.

Galco International *(800-USGALCO www.usgalco.com)*
Galco is an industry leader and innovator. The company manufactures and sells a wide range of attractive, functional, high quality holsters. They make one of the best horsehide pocket holsters in the industry and they are affordable. Galco's "Royal Guard" horsehide IWB is a perfect example of form following function and it's attractive too. Their "Combat Master", "FLETCH" High Ride and "Concealable" cowhide outside the waistband, belt holsters are top notch.

Gould & Goodrich Leather *(800-277-0732)*

Gould & Goodrich probably deserve the award for one of the best customer service departments in the industry. They offer a full line of holster, belt and other leather accessories that are extremely high quality, attractive, and affordable. They make some of the best, most functional and comfortable paddle holsters and inside the waistband holsters in the industry. We just love this company and their products! Give them a call and feel the Southern hospitality and charm! Their designers and skilled craftspeople have been making superior products for Police, Government and Correctional Agencies, and Sporting markets since 1980 in their 50,000 square foot factory in the heart of the Carolinas. In addition to the many innovative and attractive items featured on their web site, which you should peruse, Gould & Goodrich also design and produce custom products for law enforcement agencies.

Our factory picks include:

- **Open Top Two Slot Holster — Model 800.** This "Gold Line" product is an attractive deep definition molded, leather belt slide that fits belts up to 1-3/4 inches.
- **Three Slot Pancake Holster — Model 803.** This attractive "Gold Line," deep definition molded leather belt holster can be worn canted or straight up and fits belts up to 1¾ inches. It has a smooth "thumb break" for extra security.
- **Paddle Holster — Model 807.** This attractive, contoured, polished leather paddle holster has a suede-lined paddle with a non-slip backing and "flexible wings" that help keep the holster securely in place as you draw. The stitching and detailing are first-rate. The holster is as functional and comfortable as it is attractive. It has a smooth "thumb break" for extra security.
- **Comfort Paddle Holster — Model 817.** This is the same quality holster with thumb break as their regular paddle with the exception that this paddle provides a bit more clearance from your upper body than the regular paddle holster. Thus, it is more comfortable for many women or full-bodied men to wear.
- **Inside Pants Holster — Model 810.** This attractive open top, leather holster is designed for secure, concealed inside the pants carry. It features 2 sturdy, independent belt loops that easily snap on and off of belts up to widths of 1¾ inches. The holster really stays in place well when

you draw. It also places a body "sweat guard" between you and your weapon for more comfortable and dry concealed carry.

- **Belt Slide Holster With Thumb Break — Model B809.** This is a first-rate secure, close-riding, belt slide.

- **Inside Trouser Holster — Model 709.** This compact, open top holster with a body "sweat guard" clips to your waistband or belt and provides inside-trouser concealment. It rides very securely and stays in place when you draw. Its great for wear without a belt, as when you are in sweats. It's also easy on and easy off.

- **Grab-N-Go Holster and Magazine Case Combo — Model 707.** This is a soft leather, inside the pants, clip-on style holster with a thumb break that also has a magazine case so that you won't get caught short. It is very easy to put on and take off. Again, it's great for beltless wear as with sweats. It's a winner.

Gould & Goodrich also makes a line of attractive, firm, heavily reinforced, but lightweight, 1¼ and 1½ inch "shooter's belts" that are simply the best shooter's belts we have used—period, end of story, and they are affordable. These belts won't sag. They have brass buckles, too! So, go Gould & Goodrich and you'll be very pleased.

Figure 10.4 pictures two of Gould & Goodrich's paddle holsters; the Model 807 Paddle and the Model 817 "Comfort Paddle."

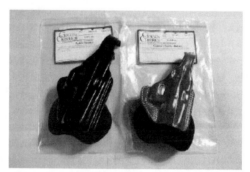

Figure 10.4

High Noon Holsters *(727-786-7528 www.highnoonholsters.com)*
If you like good leather goods and craftsmanship, you'll like High Noon's products. They provide a wide array of IWB holster

styles to choose from. We suggest you study their web site. It really is very informative and entertaining.

Their designs include "deep cover" models such as the "Hidden Impact" that has a leather extension on the main body of the holster allowing the wearer to tuck the shirt completely over the weapon and holster, and the "Down Unders" with either a clip or straps with snaps that ride extremely low in the pants for superior concealment. The clip model locks onto the belt and the snap strap model straps around the belt.

The "Down Unders" feature an open muzzle design, a stitched in sight track, a tension screw for adjusting ease of draw and tightness of gun retention, and an upward extending slide/body guard that protects the wearer's body from rubbing against the weapon's slide, hammer and rear sight. They have a slight 15 degree butt forward/muzzle raked to the rear cant.

The "Hidden Impact" tuckable IWB holster attaches to your waistband or belt with a strong, spring steel belt clip and the holster features a straight drop. The "Hideaway" with either clip or snap straps is a straight drop IWB as well and is similar to the "Hidden Impact" with the difference being that it does not tuck under a shirt. For concealment purposes, you have to wear an overgarment.

The "Tail Gunner" model with clip or snap straps has a rear stabilizer wing that keeps it from shifting position between your shirt and your pants. It also features a 15 degree forward cant and rides extremely low inside the pants for deep concealment. It's one great holster.

If you are looking for an inside the pocket holster for your small caliber, pocket semi-auto (e.g., Seecamp, Kel-Tec .32 or .380, N.A.A. Guardian, Beretta Tomcat), than you need look no further. "High Noon" makes the very unique "Pocket Grabber" line, and it isn't called "Pocket Grabber" for nothing. When you carry your little pocket piece in this rig, nobody will grab for your pockets!

Seriously, the holster features a special polymer type material stitched to the outside of the leather which (a) eliminates the outline of the weapon and (b) tends to grab the inside of your pocket so that the holster stays in its place. The design of this ambidextrous holster allows you to acquire a good grip on the gun and then draw it smoothly out of the holster and your pocket while the holster stays put. Additionally, a solid rear extension hook also keeps the holster in place by catching on the interior of your pocket when you draw your weapon. This superior design enables you to carry your pocket gun all day long without hardly knowing it's there—except if you need it. The gun stays upright and is in position should you need to acquire it.

There's nothing better than when a company takes a winning product and then makes it better. In this case, High Noon took the "Pocket Grabber" and turned it into the "Pocket Reload." This takes the famous "New York Reload" and does it one better. The New York reload is another (backup) gun. The "Pocket Reload" lets you carry your second backup gun with a spare magazine in its attached magazine pouch.

High Noon makes some great leather belt scabbards, belt slides, and paddle holsters as well for various size and model handguns. You can get the high-riding "Sky High" belt scabbard with a thumb break snap retention strap, the "Slider" belt slide with the thumb break, the sexy "Topless" belt scabbard which essentially is a "Sky High" without thumb break, and the "Slide Guard" which is a "Topless" with a high-ride slide/body guard (it's still pretty sexy!). There are just too many others to go over here. If you are interested, you are just going to have to explore their web site or request their catalog.

High Noon Holsters excels in innovative and functional holster designs.

K.L. Null Holsters *(706-625-5643 www.klnullholsters.com)*

Ken Null is a master craftsman who manufactures carefully engineered, very efficient, unique concealment holsters and accessories of exceptional quality and wearability. Every holster is flawlessly hand-crafted and wet-molded with the actual handgun using the highest quality leather. Null's motto, which he lives up to, is to not compromise on quality *"when your life depends on it."* *"Sooner or later, if you really care, you'll live with our holsters."* Here are the ones we sampled and evaluated:

The Null form-fitted "Gibralter Speed Scabbard" ("GSS") is contoured without any manual retaining devices for riding close to the body, retaining your semi-automatic pistol, and drawing smoothly. Its design provides the holster and your weapon with a stable, non-shifting ride, which is why Ken Null named it after the "Rock of Gibraltar." This holster's belt slides, as with all of Ken Null's holsters, are cut to fit specific belt sizes.

The Null Model UNS "Undercover Special" is a very easily concealed, fast drawing inside the pants holster. Like the GSS, this comfortable holster offers superior weapon retention without any mechanical devices. It molds to the curvature of your body which counters holster movement and shifting and maintains a "constant ready" position for a swift presentation of your weapon." It also has a wide bearing, close riding area that keeps wearing the rig comfortable. It offers a great concealed ride for the Kahr MK-9.

The Model SPS "Side Pocket Scabbard" is one of the best leather pocket holsters we ever tried. The Seecamp .32 feels right at home in it. It is easily drawn either by pushing off the holster with the middle finger, or by letting the hooked tab catch on the pocket. The holster does a great job of staying upright in the pocket with this little gun in it.

The "Model GBS Gibson Covert" inside the waist band holster is a favorite of undercover operatives in casual dress. It can be worn very concealed under a loose untucked shirt just forward of the hipbone. It is a comfortable, secure, and fast drawing holster. As Null aptly states: *"This deep cover unit is a lifesaver... YOURS!!!"*

Peruse Ken Null's web site and/or call or email him for a catalog. You'll be glad you did.

Kramer Handgun Leather

Having started as a "one man shop" in a garage, Greg Kramer evolved a world-class holster business through dedication, hard work and lots of talent. He states it best on his web site, which you should explore (there's a lot on there!). "Soon Ja (*Greg's wife*) and I both realize that someone's life may depend upon the products that we sell. We want our holsters to be the finest gun leather available (*they are!*). We want to provide you with a level of customer service that makes YOU feel good doing business with our company. We want you to be thoroughly and completely satisfied with your experience at KRAMER Handgun Leather."

Kramer definitely succeeds in their mission. They offer a very wide variety of innovative, functional, practical and attractive holster styles and designs. The quality of Kramer's holsters is top shelf. The name "Kramer" in fact has become legendary and synonymous with elite professionals' holsters. Kramer holsters are used by elite special forces and law enforcement groups in the U.S. and throughout the world. Each holster is hand-molded to a specific gun.

The Kramer holsters we have tested and own (Kramer's IWB #3 with snap straps for a Smith & Wesson Model 5903 TSW 9mm full-size semi-auto, and a Kramer Pocket Holster for a small S&W revolver) do all the things you expect good holsters of their type to do.

Bruce's Favorite Pocket Holster for a Small Revolver. Just as Greg Kramer claims on his web site, Bruce's Kramer black leather pocket holster for his little S&W J-frame 442 Airweight revolver really performs, and thus, gets a lot of use. It is one of his favorite pocket holsters for a small revolver. It stays in place inside his pocket. As **he** moves around, **it** doesn't. When he draws his revolver, the molded top front leather projection on the holster catches on the front inside of his pocket. This keeps the holster in his pocket and facilitates a quick, smooth draw.

Just as Kramer promises, the leather molded sight channel at the bottom front of this pocket holster prevents the black ramp front sight of his little S&W AirLite from wearing a hole in his pocket. The holster also deters his revolver's cylinder's flutes from cutting uncomfortably into his leg. Carrying his Airweight revolver in this holster ensures that his weapon won't be wrapped in a wad of pocket material if he has to grab it.

This holster also does a great job of camouflaging the shape of his revolver so that it doesn't print G-U-N right through his pocket! This is made possible by a piece of plastic laminate built into the body outside of the holster that breaks up the outline of the gun, making "the telltale bulge inside your pocket look like a wallet." The inside of the holster, which presses against your body, is smooth, comfortable, and precisely molded.

Kramer holsters are a status symbol. They are associated with good taste and judgment in concealed carry preferences. But they are more than that. They are practical, affordable, well made tools that will help you survive, and carry your handgun comfortably all day long secure in the knowledge that it is where you may need it.

Law Concealment Systems

Makes very functional, concealment leather holsters that can be used with the supplied waistband clip as a clip-on IWB, or as an inside the pocket holster. These holsters are made to fit more than one gun within a given size class (e.g., pocket pistols, subcompacts and compacts), and the same holster for the compacts also will accommodate revolvers as well as the semi-automatic pistols.

Michaels of Oregon *(800-845-2444 www.uncle-mikes.com)*

"Uncle Mike's" makes a wide range of affordable holsters and accessories that will fit every budget and most people's concealed carry needs. Their customer service is excellent and orders are fulfilled promptly.

We especially like their "Sidekick" Inside the Pocket Holster. It comes in 4 sizes for different size and model sub-compact handguns and revolvers. It is made of a moisture resistant, padded, soft suede-like material that keeps the holster in place in your pants and doesn't print the outline of the gun. We use ours (Size 3) for carrying our S&W J-frame snubbies in our pocket. For the price, nothing works better. We also use our Size 4's for pocket carry of our Walther PPK/S, SIG Sauer P-232, and Kahr Arms MK9 and MK40 pistols.

Michaels of Oregon ("Uncle Mike's") also manufactures a number of excellent, very affordable, clip-on inside the pants holsters made of soft, moisture-resistant, synthetic material that stay in place. They work well for concealed holstering of your small semi-auto or revolver when you are walking in the park or jogging with sweats or beltless slacks on.

Milt Sparks Holsters *(208-377-5577 www.miltsparks.com)*

Milt Sparks is a small, quality custom holster manufacturer dedicated to producing practical designs for everyday use. Their concealed carry fine leather holster products are handcrafted to look nice and more importantly to work well. They continuously evaluate and re-evaluate their products through their own activities in training, competition and everyday use, and through customer feedback. They really listen. So, each new or improved design is extensively wear-tested by Tony Kanaley, their President, and his staff, before it is offered for sale.

The company bears the name of its founder, the late, great and famous holster maker, Milt Sparks, who was immensely popular with the combat pistol shooters of the late 1960's and 70's. The craftsmen of Milt Sparks today are all dedicated to carrying on the tradition he began. We had the opportunity to evaluate two of their designs and are very happy with both of them. Like all of their holsters, these two are hand molded to the specific handgun.

The **"Summer Special 2 Holster"** is an IWB holster that features rough-side out construction, sight rails, a protective back-flap extension and two snap belt loops that will fit up to 1½-inch belts. It has a metal stiffener in the top band which allows for effortless one-handed re-holstering. The belt loops are secured with one-way directional snaps and the rough-side out leather grips the wearer's clothing for secure positioning while the smooth interior is easy on a gun's finish and offers a smooth fast draw. This is a winner. It works terrifically with the full size Glock 17. You almost have to remind yourself that the gun is there!

The **"PCH-RI"** is a great leather inside the pocket holster for revolvers that provides complete leather coverage of the specific revolver it is molded for. The holster positions the revolver at the centerline of the pocket. This allows a forward to rear, thin edge to thin edge profile on the holster and the unformed outer shell obscures the weapon so it doesn't print. The holster's shape, size and rough-side out construction assure that the holster will remain in your pocket when you draw your weapon.

One of the unique features of this holster is Sparks' use of a malleable wire insert which is laminated into the perimeter of the holster. This allows the user to shape and mold the outer edge as needed to achieve optimal concealment and a custom fit. The holster is designed around the hammer-less S&W 2 inch J-frame, but it's also available for 2 inch D-framed Colt Detective Specials and 2 inch Ruger SP-101's. The S&W Models 442 Airweight, 640, 337PD AirLite and 340PD AirLite all fit well in this holster. The interior front of the holster even provides enough room for the S&W 340PD's "light gathering" HIVIZ green dot front sight!

Mitch Rosen Extraordinary Gunleather (607-647-2971)

Powered by the extraordinary Mitch Rosen, this company manufactures some of the best gunleather anywhere. They manufacture and sell direct fine leather concealment holsters, gun belts, and accessories such as magazine pouches.

The customer service is excellent, and the master himself, Mitch Rosen, is usually available to consult with customers about their particular individual needs so that he can make the right holster for them. This makes his shop a "custom shop". However, Mitch Rosen also produces an "Express Line" of fine holsters that are very affordable and are much quicker to get after you place your order than his higher end line. And, the only real difference is that the higher end line sports finer detailing and there is a greater selection of items. However, all of Mitch Rosen's rigs have superb fit and finish.

For most customers who may not wish to spend $200 to $300 on a holster and belt, their needs can be very well met from within Mitch's "Express Line." Wait time for a custom Mitch Rosen holster is typically less than it is with many other custom holster makers, and with the Express Line, you can usually have your order shipped within 2 weeks.

If you like an Inside the Waistband holster you will probably love Mitch Rosen's USD-Express. This IWB holster is exceptionally comfortable, concealable and quick. It rides very close to the body comfortably. It slightly cants the weapon butt forward and muzzle raked to the rear to facilitate concealment and comfort. The standard 1.5 inch belt loop, which is interchangeable with other belt width belt loops, has a one-way snap for ease of holster removal.

This holster also has what Rosen terms his "Jig Fit" sight channel. It provides excellent fit to the weapon it is made for and excellent weapon retention and a slick friction draw. This is one excellent rig at a very affordable price.

Mitch's "5JR-Express" is a full-length, canted belt slide that offers all-day comfort and superior concealment for a belt holster. It sports an attractive smooth-fitting look but is very durable and functional. His "5JR President" is also a superior belt holster that is similar to the 5JR. Both holsters position the weapon canted muzzle raked to the rear and butt forward for optimum comfort and concealment. These holsters are available for most semi-autos.

The "Upper Limit" is a straight-drop belt holster with a high-ride feature. It is positioned to ride as high as possible, while still keeping the butt of the weapon tucked against the body and the muzzle off the hip for comfort and concealment. Worn at the side or slightly forward of the hip, the Upper Limit is also suitable for cross-draw use. It is a very versatile, comfortable and fast holster.

Mitch Rosen's "Pocket Softy" for S&W 2" J-frames and similarly sized revolvers, as well as for most small semi-automatic pistols, is a quality leather pocket holster that is made with a neoprene backing covered with suede. This effectively eliminates the visual outline of the pistol or revolver (in other words, "printing" of the weapon) and it is comfortable in the pocket. Also, the suede tends to grab the inside of the pocket, aiding in not allowing the holster to come out when drawing. The rear extension of the holster also helps keep the holster in the pocket when the handgun is drawn.

Mitch's "No. 18" pocket holster will conceal your Seecamp .32ACP or other small pocket pistol very well, and very importantly, it will keep the weapon correctly positioned in your pocket.

In sum, Mitch Rosen provides excellent, professional service to his customers and takes his business very seriously. His quality control standards are among the highest in the holster and gunleather industry. The holster manufacturing business is a very serious business—that is, manufacturing and selling rigs for carrying tools (your weapon) at the ready that you rely on to help you survive.

Pocket Concealment Systems

PCS makes some of the most functional and innovative leather pocket holsters we have ever seen. The designs they offer are well thought out and really work. A PCS holster stays in your pocket when you smoothly draw your gun. And, the holster keeps the gun upright and steady in your pocket no matter how much you move, and it does not print "'GUN' in my Pocket!"

PCS's great designs that we had a chance to evaluate and highly recommend include: the "French Curve" and "Pocket Speed Scabbard" for small revolvers; the "Redoubt" for small semi-autos that also has a magazine pouch to hold a spare magazine; the "Tomahawk, which is great for a "baby Glock" (Glock 26, 27, or 33); the "Blackbird" for small semi-automatics such as the Walther PPK/S, and the "Harpoon" for small semi-autos such as the Kahr MK9, MK40, or PM9, the Beretta .32 caliber Tomcat, the N.A.A. .32 or .380 Guardian, or the Seecamp .32 semi-auto.

The Tomahawk for the "baby Glock" (Glock 26, 27, 33) is one of the few in the pocket holsters for the baby Glock we've evaluated that actually makes it relatively comfortable to carry this little hand cannon in your pocket. It positions the gun just right for easy acquisition and a smooth draw. PCS's small revolver pocket holsters also work exceedingly well. You can choose the holster's angle of handgun cant in your pocket so that the butt of the revolver does not stick out of your pocket. And, unlike most leather revolver pocket holsters we've tried for small revolvers, the holster actually stays put in your pants during the draw!

Stellar Rigs *(561-616-5015 www.stellarrigs.com)*

Makes a really great (stellar) kydex pocket holster for the Seecamp pistol that also has a pouch for a spare magazine. Their pocket holster is extremely lightweight, thin, and functional. It prevents printing of the gun in your pocket, provides excellent retention and security, keeps your pistol upright for quick acquirement, and provides for a smooth draw. Stellar also manufactures and sells these holsters for the N.A.A. Guardians and the Keltec .32 caliber pocket pistol. We recommend that you peruse their web site.

Tauris Holsters *(315-737-9115 www.taurisholsters.com)*

Mike Taurisano is a master holster craftsman and retired law enforcement professional. His custom holsters offer quick gun access, excellent weapon retention for safety, and superior ease of re-holstering. All Tauris Holsters are made by hand, by Mike, one at a time to order, using the finest top grain cowhide. They are hand wet-molded, with a formed sight channel, covered trigger guard and exactly fitted belt tunnel or slots.

He offers an unconditional guarantee on materials and workmanship. All holsters are available in 1¼, 1½, and 1¾ inch belt widths. These holsters are highly functional, efficient, durable, long-lasting, works of art. Mike makes holsters for the law enforcement professionals in his community and he is known worldwide for his high quality custom holsters.

We got to sample and evaluate his "Double Strap 'Low Profile' In The Pants Holster" and his "Convertible ITP/Hip Holster." Peruse his web site to learn more about his great designs and rigs.

The "Double Strap Low Profile In The Pants Holster" is a precisely crafted, low profile, low riding, deep concealment, leather holster worn in the pants ("ITP"). It comes with a leather covered, metal reinforced holster mouth designed to allow quick and secure re-holstering. There is also a rigid double layer body shield between you and the weapon. Two leather straps fore and aft each with a one-way snap are used to secure the holster comfortably to your belt. This is one great concealment holster. It's made rough-side out for the full-size Glock 17 and carries it with aplomb.

An "enhanced" version of the "ITP" has an extended body fore and aft that provides more contour for greater comfort and a less observable holster outline. These "ITP's" are made with either the leather rough-side out or rough-side in.

The "Convertible ITP/Hip Holster" is the other holster Bruce sampled. It is the result of the thoughtful integration into one package of 2 holster models which combines the best of both. They are the Tauris *"Enhanced In The Pants Holster"* previously described and their *"Reinforced High Ride Belt Slide."* The latter is a low profile but high ride, hip-hugging belt slide holster.

The "Convertible ITP" allows you, the wearer, to quickly select the style you desire at any given time—it converts from one mode of holster carry to another within seconds! This is easily done by simply removing or attaching the two belt snaps by means of the one-way fasteners. This unique holster functions great in either mode. With snaps, it's an IWB holster. Without snaps, using the belt slots, it functions as a reinforced high ride belt slide holster! This is two great concealment holsters in one package. It's made for the compact Glock 23 and carries it comfortably.

Holster Companies

We list some of the great holsters companies below with their phone numbers and web site addresses.

Action-Direct	800-472-2388	www.action-direct.com
Ahern Enterprises (the "Pocket Naturals" series)	706-335-5715	
Aker Leather (e.g., the "Pocket Protector" and "Express Pocket Holster."	619-423-5182	www.akerleather.com
Alessi Holsters	716-691-5615	
Bell Charter Oak, Inc.	607-783-2483	www.bellcharteroak holsters.com
Bianchi International	909-676-562	www.bianchi-intl.com
Blade-Tech Industries	253-581-4347	www.blade-tech.com
Bulman Gunleather	814-696-8615	www.bulmangun-leather.com
Comp-Tac	713-863-9329	www.comp-tac.com
DelFatti Leather	715-267-6420	www.delfatti.com
DeSantis Holster and Leather Goods	800-GUNHIDE	www.desantisholster.com
Don Hume Leathergoods	800-331-2686	www.donhume.com
FIST, Inc.	800-443-3478	www.fist-inc.com
Galco International	800-USGALCO	www.usgalco.com
Gould and Goodrich	800-277-0732	www.gouldusa.com
High Noon Holsters	727-786-7528	www.highnoonholsters.com

Ken L. Null Holsters	706-625-5643	www.klnullholsters.com
Kramer Handgun Leather	800-510-2666	www.kramerleather.com
Law Concealment Systems	800-373-0116	www.handgun concealment.com
Michaels of Oregon	800-845-2444	www.uncle-mikes.com
Milt Sparks Holsters	208-377-5577	www.miltsparks.com
Mitch Rosen Extraordinary Gunleather, LLC	603-647-2971	www.mitchrosen.com
Pocket Concealment Systems	410-426-9004	
Stellar Rigs	561-641-6358	www.stellarrigs.com
Tauris Holsters	315-737-9115	www.tsparksolutions. com/taurisholsters/
Ted Blocker Holsters	800-650-9742	www.tedblocker.com

11

Safe Handgun Operation and Range Procedures

Our goal up to this point has been to provide you with the essential knowledge needed to develop safe and effective shooting skills. Knowing and understanding the mechanical operation of revolvers and semi-automatic pistols as well as proper maintenance procedures leads us to our next step. We want to introduce you to the equipment you will need to practice safely at the shooting range, to help you develop good firearms handling skills, and to show you how to correct common operational handgun malfunctions.

A Good Gun-Carrying Case. You need a sturdy and lockable gun case to carry your equipment to and from the range without your neighbors calling the police on you. A hard outer case that is egg crate padded on the interior gives your equipment the best protection. It doesn't have to be expensive. It can be purchased for $30 or under. The hard plastic "Gun Guard" series of cases made by Doskocil Manufacturing Company have egg crate inner foam padding to protect your weapons and come in a range of sizes. (888-70SPORT; www.gunguard.com)

Soft butterfly "rug" cases are less practical because they do not protect the sights of your firearm and compromise your weapon's value should you drop the case or if the butterfly starts to fly around in your trunk during transport. If you purchase a bigger gun case, you can also put other range accessories in it as well.

If you are willing to spend a little more (in the $50 to $150 price range) you can purchase a nice shooter's bag that is soft but has many padded compartments in which to organize your equipment, and that will carry much more equipment.

Bagmaster *(800-950-8181; www.bagmaster.com)* makes a fine line of quality shooters' and range bags. They have many different size models so that there is at least one to suit practically everyone's needs.

Eye and Ear Protection. Good eye and ear protection is essential to assure your basic physical safety when you shoot. Adequate shooting glasses should be shatter-proof and provide 180 degrees of optic coverage. Shooting glasses lenses should be made of scratch-resistant polycarbonate and not glass. Ear protection should be a minimum of 30 decibels. Ear plugs do not provide sufficient protection to the mastoid bone directly behind the outside lobe. However, ear plugs in addition to a headset will significantly reduce the chances of hearing loss.

In a self-defense shooting situation, you will be so pumped up on adrenaline that you will never hear the shots you fire in your personal defense!

Adequate Ventilation. When any firearm discharges, hot gases, spent gunpowder, and projectile particulates become airborne. These exhaust materials result from the ignition of live ammunition. They are the by-products of the hot compressed gases in the barrel that push the projectile away from the muzzle. These gases and particulates, which can include lead, are blasted away from the muzzle of the firearm in a cone-shaped pattern following cartridge ignition.

Your primary concern in choosing an indoor shooting range facility should be the air ventilation system and how it operates to vent these muzzle exhaust gases. Indoor ranges that operate with an air filtration and/or ventilation system that allegedly removes all particulates but then recirculates the internal air only tend to repeatedly expose you to those same exhaust gases. This can be threatening to your health and more hazardous to those predisposed to respiratory illnesses.

On the other hand, indoor ranges that directly exhaust the materials released during firing downrange away from the shooter and then vent the fumes and particulates up and out of the range and into the atmosphere dramatically reduce your repeated exposure to those hazardous materials. If you are feeling cool in the shooting booth from the air conditioning blowing on you, you may assume that the air within the range and the entire building is being recirculated around your respiratory system and possibly causing excessive exposure to firearm exhausts.

However, before you go into cardiac arrest or a state of paranoia about firing a weapon, you should understand that you will probably breathe in more hazardous material walking down one block of a major city street or driving behind one bus or truck.

By this time you should have memorized our cardinal safety rules. They can never be taken lightly or for granted. Next up is proper range etiquette.

Proper Range Etiquette

To lead into this, we reiterate a point from our "S-A-F-E-S-T" safe firearms handling rules. That is, that there is a good reason why the **first** cardinal rule is *Safe Direction.* As long as you always keep your muzzle pointed in a safe direction, God forbid should there be an accidental discharge, it will not cause anyone to be hurt. With that said, at the range, the first cardinal safety rule for loaded weapons is that you always point them downrange where they can do no harm, and you NEVER point them in any other direction. Firearms are a tool but never underestimate the destructive capability of a firearm. It may be your last estimate if you do.

You must always be conscious at the range of how you are holding your firearm and where you are pointing it. **That means no turning around to address others while holding a loaded weapon!**

Anytime you are not within the confines of the shooting booth, the action of your firearm should be open so that anyone approaching can tell that the weapon is unloaded and in a safe condition. If you have carry privileges in your particular locality, never produce your handgun from a holster in the range office to show the counter person what type of firearm you own. It could lead to your demise, or someone else could end up having a heart attack!

If your weapon is in a holster, leave it there until you are in the assigned shooting booth. Always follow all of the range's rules and regulations.

A follow-up would be that if upon leaving, should you decide to reload your firearm and re-holster it, only do so within the booth confines and with the firearm always facing downrange! Never reload and re-holster in the parking lot or lobby! Never, never enter a range facility in costume on Halloween saying "trick or treat." The trick may be on you, and it may be spelled "R.I.P."!

Preliminaries considered, it is now time to direct our efforts to building our shooting platform and the associated physical mechanics required.

Handgun Operational Skills

The Basics. First, we need to develop and understand the concept of "muscle memory." *Muscle memory* is defined as *involuntary, automatic, intentionally initiated* physical movements that complete an intended task without conscious thought and that involve the execution of an integrated and cohesive sequence of physical operations simultaneously. Now let's take that apart:

Involuntary and *automatic* refer to the fact that the movements have been practiced at least 2000 times so that they are cemented or imprinted into your subconscious mind. Your subconscious is the part of your mind that controls your involuntary, tactical or defensive responses in situations where slow and conscious linear thinking can get you killed because immediate and decisive action is needed NOW. *Intentional* means that your physical actions are not random but rather are all coordinated in the service of accomplishing a goal.

Orchestration is a necessity in both skill development and employment. Exhaustive mental and physical preparation assure orchestration.

Execution of an integrated and cohesive sequence of physical operations simultaneously means that you are performing a progression of actions (mental and physical) all at the same time. This requires both parallel or simultaneous as well as sequential implementation. In order to get to this point in your skill development requires lots of practice and repetition to imprint the intended action sequences into your subconscious brain and your muscles. Remember the old adage about the guy who asked someone on the NYC street corner, "How do I get to Carnegie Hall?" and who was told, "Practice, my boy, practice!" So, let's begin to develop your defensive action wall block by block.

Instant Feedback. Begin by buying an inexpensive full-length mirror. Without visual feedback, no text can adequately prepare you for the learning task. You need to have a correlating visible view of your body to give you immediate feedback about the physical actions that comprise your shooting technique.

Experience has shown that the more every day activities you can associate with shooting, the more readily you will tend to develop your talents and comfort level with the necessary operations. Being able to see yourself in the mirror often, and practice shooting techniques with the feedback that being in front of the mirror provides, will enhance your learning from our written material.

Stance and Grip

Stance. Begin with your feet and body posture. Look through the mirror and see yourself standing with your feet shoulder width apart for proper balance. Stand erect and center yourself on the mirror so you can get a direct view of yourself. Keep your shoulders straight, your head erect and balanced, maintaining clear eye contact with your mirror image. *Stance* is only an indication of foot placement. It refers to nothing else. Don't confuse the term "stance" with "sighting," "aiming," etc. It only refers to your standing position.

Strong Hand Grip. Extend your strong arm and hand directly straight out in front of you, with your elbow and wrist locked. Clench your fist and with the index finger opposing your thumb, point directly at the center of your reflection, also known as center of mass. Now imagine a handgun encompassed in your grasp and you will readily understand and feel the premise that a handgun placed within that same configuration is a natural extension of your forearm.

When you are actually holding a handgun, the top of the back strap of the handgun should be level with and lodged into the juncture between your thumb and index finger creating a natural "V" in your hand. This "V" is commonly referred to as the web of your hand. The reason that the back strap is maintained at this level position is because under recoil conditions, if the backstrap is grabbed at a lower angle, recoil will pull the handgun out of your hand, or lower the muzzle and throw your shot's point of impact low. This is illustrated in Figure 11.1.

Figure 11.1

The top of the back strap of any handgun should be flush to the meaty portion of the web of your hand as illustrated in the figure. Your index finger should be flat along the frame of any handgun and away from the trigger. Following "S-A-F-E-S-T" safety rule number 6, *keep your finger off the trigger and out of the trigger guard until you are ready to shoot.* Refer to Figure 11.2 for a clear illustration of the strong hand grip.

There are valid reasons which you must understand for keeping your wrist, elbow, and shoulder locked as you extend your strong hand straight out, down your line of sight. First, it is because a straight line is the shortest and truest distance to the target. Second, and of equal importance, is the fact that your arm must be locked in order to maintain your point of aim despite the gun's recoil. This is because your arm will act as human shock absorber as it moves upward and then back downward to its original point of aim, if it is locked correctly. If it isn't locked correctly, you should have bought a shotgun because with handgun shooting technique, you will lose your point of aim.

Figure 11.2

Strong hand grip should be maintained with approximately 20 pounds of pressure; not a death grip, but firm, so that your handgun cannot be readily pulled from your hand. Also refer to Figure 11.2 for a clear illustration of the one-handed shooting grip.

These measures are critical for accurate one-handed shooting. A break in your wrist, elbow or shoulder weakens your shooting foundation and leads to an inaccurate response to a criminal threat.

Two-Handed Grip. The two-handed grip is the most accurate form of handgun shooting. (See Figure 11.3.). Your dominant strong hand needs the support of your nondominant supporting hand to maintain point of aim and recoil reduction. The length of your support arm needs to be pushed to its furthest extension so as to equal the length of your strong arm which it meets in what we call the "mono-grip." An easy visual for this is the isosceles triangle, which is equal on two sides, that project upward from the triangle's base to the triangle's apex, which is where the firearm is held firmly in the mono-grip position.

The two-handed grip must be projected simultaneously once the weapon has been drawn from the holster. This is accomplished by bringing the support hand up to meet the strong hand holding the weapon at the level of your belly button. Some experts have called this position at your belly button the "close ready" or "ready gun" position. It actually is a safe position to maintain if you are in a situation where you've drawn your gun but are not ready to employ it combatively immediately. It allows you, as its name suggests, to be ready to simultaneously push the weapon out and up to eye level with both hands and then pull (actually press or squeeze) the trigger if necessary.

Figure 11.3

In other words, we are talking about every movement flowing from one movement to the next in one continuous fluid motion. This can only be realized effectively and functionally through practice and more practice.

We bet you thought up to this point that your belly button was a useless physical commodity. It actually serves two essential functions in handgun defensive training of which you've been told one. The other is reloading a revolver which we will cover later.

The "Mono-Grip." We use the term the *"mono-grip"* to refer to the idea of one ideal grip for *all* handgun types. To accomplish this, here's what you do. First, establish a strong-hand grip as we described earlier. Then take the center knuckles of your support hand and align them directly under the trigger guard overlapping the center knuckles of the middle, ring and pinky fingers of your strong hand. The heels of your hands should meet at the backstrap, and the thumb of your support hand should be pressed firmly and directly on top of the thumb of your strong hand. This, in effect, establishes a human mechanical vise that prevents downward muzzle movement under firing conditions by preventing downward movement of the frame.

This is the *"mono-grip."* Again, refer to Figure 11.3 for a clear illustration of the mono-grip. Your support hand should apply double the pressure of your strong hand or about 40 pounds per square inch (psi). As we said earlier, the mono-grip is formed in one continuous motion by bringing the support hand up to meet the strong hand holding the weapon at the level of your belly button in the "close ready position." Then you can project the gun outward towards the target in a straight line (actually one straight linear motion) if you are ready to fire.

Ineffective Grip Positions. Outdated and ineffective is the "cup and saucer" method of gripping your handgun. That means you're cupping your shooting hand with your support hand. It was once a standard FBI grip that had been used for years. Upon firing the weapon, it provided absolutely no lateral support for controlling handgun recoil and maintaining defensive second and third shot recovery. What happens is that your shooting hand is propelled up and away from your cupped support hand creating what is in effect a flying cup! So, unless you have an **S** on your chest, leave the cup and saucer at the restaurant where it is more practical and eliminate it from your repertoire of shooting techniques.

Second on our list of gripping "no-nos" is the support hand grabbing either forearm or wrist. This does not prevent the wrist from moving left to right and breaking the plane of sight alignment. The wrist is the weakest joint in the body and if not supported properly from the apex of either the isosceles or Weaver positions, it will break down into helter-skelter inaccuracy.

The "Isosceles Stance." The entire stance and grip from head to feet is now in place and is referred to as the *isosceles shooting stance*. One advantage of the isosceles stance is that from this position, you can engage multiple targets rapidly within 180 degrees of movement by turreting your torso from one side to the other in a 180 degree arc. A second advantage is that this stance requires you to push the gun outward. This helps to counter recoil and is also a natural response in a high stress situation because it is simple and effective. Figure 11.4 clearly illustrates the isosceles stance.

Remember to keep your arms, elbows and wrists locked. Should you relax your elbows to a flapping "chicken wing configuration," shots will have a tendency to go darned near anywhere because you have no support for the firearm. Without maintaining true lockup, you can expect totally inaccurate shooting.

Figure 11.4 (Front)   **Figure 11.4 (Side)**

"Resilience Under Fire." Isosceles shooting is infinitely less fatiguing on the body and one can therefore easily fire hundreds of rounds in a shooting day without suffering from the muscular effects of recoil fatigue. No matter what type of firearm you choose to purchase, it requires no change or modification from this grip position. Any handgun regardless of caliber can be accurately fired and controlled when the mono-grip has been correctly implemented.

The "Weaver Stance." Imagine yourself walking down the street one leg in front of the other with your holster on your strong hip. You are confronted by a criminal adversary! You step back about 12 inches with your holstered strong side leg. Your unholstered support side leg is 12 inches in front of your holstered strong side leg.

You draw your weapon from your holster and as you bring it up, your support hand meets your strong hand in the "mono-grip" just above and beyond the "close ready" position. However, as you continue to push your weapon out in front of you to acquire your target, your support arm is now bent at a 90 degree downward angle pulling back against your strong hand. Your strong arm is also slightly bent at approximately a 130 to 150 degree angle horizontally, and is pushing forward against your support hand. Rather than cocking your head to acquire your sights, you bring your mono-grip up toward your head so that your head is as straight as possible.

This is a truly isometric shooting position, using the body's power of push and pull to maintain accuracy and reduce recoil. Figure 11.5 illustrates the Weaver stance.

Figure 11.5 (Front)   **Figure 11.5 (Side)**

Your weapon is pointed directly at your assailant. Okay. Are there any problems with this technique? Yes, there are. The main problem with the Weaver technique is tremor and fatigue. Holding an isometric position (muscles in counter-tension opposing each other) for any length of time will cause muscle fatigue, tremor and weakness.

It is most natural to instinctively push your weapon forward and out towards your adversary in the more balanced "isosceles stance." The "Weaver" requires too much fine motor coordination of the upper and lower extremities for high stress situations.

Weaver is uncomfortable and not conducive to prolonged or accurate shooting. From hundreds of students, Steve has never encountered a Weaver shooter he couldn't make better by using Isosceles. Most people have a natural tendency with the Weaver to cock their head down toward the gun to acquire a sight picture and aim. This has to be resisted. In a combat scenario, this would reduce your peripheral visual awareness and it could get you killed!

Another disadvantage of the Weaver is that any firing of rounds in excess of 50 is usually extremely fatiguing and hard to continue and maintain comfortably. Experience has shown us

that most Weaver shooters who fire in competition large numbers of rounds significantly in excess of the average person,
experience chronic elbow fatigue (a.k.a., "tennis elbow").

Despite the limitations of the Weaver technique, it still makes
sense for you to know how to use it. It will make you a more
complete shooter to experience it for yourself since both of the
above stances are equally important in your total handgun
tactical repertoire. Fatigue does need to be a premium concern
when we are talking about personal defense. The idea of the
weak foot being positioned in front of the strong side foot in the
Weaver emanates from martial arts or boxing techniques and
lore. It is supposed to give you greater balance. However, since
the majority of people who shoot are not martial artists or boxing
experts, it seems unnatural to expect to be able to use this
stance in a stress situation. This goes back to our original idea
that those things that are common to you and natural in your
everyday life lend themselves better to being efficient and your
being proficient under high stress.

Additionally, when speaking about engaging multiple targets,
the Weaver actually reduces your 180 degree arc to 90 degrees.
Try it and you will see what we mean. Also try retreating from
the Weaver position. You'll find yourself hopping like Bugs
Bunny or falling over your own feet. It is for these aforementioned reasons that we prefer the Isosceles and results have
shown it to be superior for most shooters. However, as we advise
you in relation to all of the techniques described throughout our
text, do not accept anyone's word, including ours, with blind
faith or obedience.

Experience, test, and evaluate these techniques for yourself
and make your own judgments based on your own experience
which is the truest teacher. Recognize that inevitably the choices
you make and how you practice will determine how you respond
in a survival oriented critical incident.

An Important Qualification. In close quarters combat encounters, or if you are accosted in a motor vehicle, you will not
be able to position yourself for optimum tactical marksmanship
response. Therefore, in such circumstances, for which you
should be prepared and proficient, you do the best you can with
what you have—and you have practiced. Remember (we know
there's a lot of remembers) that you have to practice to build a
muscle memory. There is no quick substitute for practice to
build a muscle memory. So you can practice shooting defensively in any type of situation, and you can thus prepare yourself in
the event you are caught in one.

How often should you practice? The answer is as often as your time and your budget allows. You should practice different scenarios so that you are prepared and proficient well before they ever occur, and hopefully they will never occur.

If you cannot afford regular trips to the range, then dry-firing and practical simulations within your own home or apartment are whole-heartedly recommended **as long as your handgun is empty!**

True Sight Alignment

With your dominant hand, push your empty weapon (that you've repeatedly checked and re-checked) straight out in front of you to eye level, using either your *one-handed* or *two-handed mono-grip* hold. Now, employing your mirror image as a target, observe that you have to focus on three items collectively and simultaneously to achieve an accurate point of aim on your reflection's center of mass. This is *true sight alignment* incorporating the following 3 elements:

1. The rear sight which is shaped in a "U" pattern.
2. The front sight which is a single blade.
3. And the target beyond on which you should be focusing at its center of mass.

However, since your eyes can only focus clearly on one object at a time, the most prominent and important of the three is the front sight, because that is inevitably where the bullet's path of travel begins and ends—where the front sight is pointing. However, you cannot afford to forget the alignment of the front sight with the *rear sight* to maintain a level firearm.

What follows is a quick illustration of what constitutes proper sight alignment. Do the following exercise:

Draw a 3-inch circle in the center of an 8½ by 11-inch sheet of blank paper. As illustrated in Figure 11.6, draw the letter "E" lying on its back with its legs of equal length extending upward into the circle's center. The length of the back of the E should equal the circle's diameter and span the entire lower half of the circle. This simple diagram illustrates proper sight alignment on a target for point of aim/point of impact *center hold.*

Proper Sight Alignment. It is helpful to use the letter "E" as a visual to interpret proper sight alignment. The top of the front sight, or center leg of the "E," must be level with the tops of the rear sight blades. It must also be centered between them. This will produce equal amounts of light between each of the rear blades and the front sight. This is also illustrated in Figure 11.6.

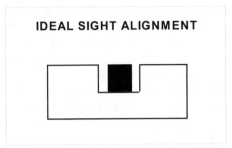

IDEAL SIGHT ALIGNMENT

In ideal sight alignment, the front post is centered in the rear notch and the tops of the front and rear sights are level. However, in *defensive* sight alignment, you may fire whenever the post is visible <u>somewhere</u> in the rear sight blade notch.

Figure 11.6

Closing your support eye is the only way to clearly observe proper sight alignment with your "shooting eye." Please note that your "shooting eye" should always be on the same side as your strong or shooting hand. Using the opposing eye will usually foster shooting across the target inaccurately rather than into the target's center accurately.

Now, with both eyes open, you are much more likely to see two sights—double vision. In this case, two is definitely NOT better than one and doesn't double your pleasure. For shooters who do shoot with both eyes open, the correct technique is to squint with both eyes equally as if you were looking into the sun. That will eliminate the unwanted double vision effect.

Shooting with both eyes open does help you to maintain peripheral vision, still using the sights of the firearm. Using sights is especially important in defensive shooting because it avoids "moon shots" over the adversary's head. Should you shoot over the adversary's head, he is still a threat, so proper procedures to avoid this must be utilized.

Determining Your "Dominant Eye." This term refers to your "stronger eye" which is your preferred eye because it's the one you rely on instinctively to do most of the sightwork. A shooter should always use his or her dominant eye for aiming, making the front sight crystal clear.

To determine which is your dominant eye, do the following. Look on the wall for a stationary object that's about 3 to 4 inches high. Don't get out your ruler. Just use your closed fist as a guide. Then move yourself so that you are about 15 feet away from it (about 4 to 5 paces) and face the object. Now, fully extend both your arms directly in front of you, and place one hand over the other so that the middle knuckles of your index fingers are lined up one on top of the other. Let your thumbs overlap each other. You should have now created a triangular gap between your hands. With both your eyes open, hold the triangular gap of your hands so that you can see the object in it. Now keep your hands, arms, and body very still. Then close your left eye. Can you see the object? Reopen your left eye, then close your right. Can you see the object? Whichever eye permits you to see the object without moving your hands, is your dominant eye. Whenever you're establishing sight alignment, *always* bring your weapon to your dominant eye, not vice versa. This means that you must move your sight picture on your weapon to your dominant eye, not the reverse. Your head must remain well balanced and erect, not cocked to the side.

The perfect situation is when your dominant eye corresponds to your dominant shooting hand (i.e., right-eyed dominant-right-handed and vice versa). However, it is not a perfect world. We must all live with our limitations. So, if your dominant eye and dominant hand do not correspond, you can go to the "cross dominant shooting technique." Years ago, instructors taught shooters with this challenge to switch their strong shooting hands. Today we emphasize the following technique:

"Cross Dominant Shooting Technique." This is a term that applies when your dominant eye is the eye opposite your dominant shooting hand. Because you must use your dominant eye to aim, "cross dominant shooting" means that you are crossing over from your dominant hand to your opposite side dominant eye.

"Cross dominant shooting" is an effective technique for acquiring center of mass target acquisition when you have no other choice. By keeping your head erect, well balanced and supported by your neck, your sight focus should be clear and accurate. If you were to turn your head toward your sight, shots will be thrown off-center of mass either left or right depending on whether you are a right-handed or left-handed shooter. Keep your head straight towards your target. *Always bring the sights to your dominant eye, do not turn your head.* You must maintain a steady balance and you will establish accurate shot placement and consistent center of mass accuracy with "cross dominant shooting."

The single most vexing problem with this technique arises if you are shooting from behind a barricade. This is because it forces you to expose more of your head to the adversary. The solution is to don a bullet-proof helmet. No, seriously—practice what's best for you because we all have physical limitations that prevent us from shooting textbook perfect. The best tactical advantage is to find the best compromise that least compromises your security and maximizes your response effectiveness. Keep it real, remain unpredictable, and stay safe!

Proper Sight Picture. Once your sights have been aligned properly, that in conjunction with your point of aim on your target is defined as "sight picture." "Sight picture" involves three components. They are (1) front sight, (2) rear sight, and (3) the target. A proper sight picture is when you see a *crystal clear* front sight centered between a slightly blurred rear sight and centered on a slightly blurred target.

"Play Statues." To effectively train yourself in utilizing proper sight alignment in conjunction with sight picture or target acquisition, *you must trust your sights*. This may be termed "shooting on faith." However, you cannot ignore your target. It must remain in your visual field. Nevertheless, it will be blurry and you should be relying primarily on your sights.

Do not lose sight of your sights out of anxiety by looking for the shot. This means that you are taking a quick peek at your target before you take your shot to make sure that the target is still there. It normally results in a low shot. Just trust your sights and maintain a total body hold. "Play statues." See Figure 11.6 again for illustrations of proper and defensive sight alignment.

Keep It Real. Keep Moving and Seek Cover and Concealment. Now, so as not to confuse several issues, we must clarify a few things. In a defensive combative situation, whenever possible, you always want to seek cover and concealment. From behind cover, you can "play statues" for brief moments as you take aim at your attacker. However, you also need to keep moving in a combative situation so that the bad guy cannot "get the make on you." You need to retain the element of unpredictability and surprise.

You NEVER want to just stand there exposed in the line of fire! So, you need to train in shooting on the move. Of course, this is an advanced technique that you need to work up to, as you practice and perfect the basic techniques first.

One more important point. If you could take only one shot, you obviously don't want to throw that shot away. You must make it count. Therefore, ask yourself the following question. Does it make more sense to take the extra nanosecond to obtain a good sight picture on your adversary's center of mass, or does it make more sense to "point shoot" that one shot? Point shoot means you are looking at your target, not using sights, just pointing the firearm at the target. This usually results in a "moon shot." You need to maintain peripheral vision of your firearm to keep it level with the ground, and the adversary in the direct line of fire.

There probably is no absolutely right or wrong answer here. We can only tell you that data collected from police shootings reveal that veteran police marksmen have missed their attackers in the extreme stress of a life and death combat situation when they *didn't rely on their sights*! In fact, there are documented instances where expert police marksmen missed their first shot, that they had point shot, took a bullet, and then managed to use their sights to stop the criminal attacker. So, think this through and come to your own conclusion.

The Sights Are the Only True Indicator of Where the Shot is Directed. When practicing looking over the sights to see what a fine job you are doing on the target, you are not helping yourself to learn proper sighting procedures. Looking over the sights only tends to foster dropped shots, otherwise known as lower than desired impacts. On the other hand, by shooting on faith (in your sights) you let the tool do the job it was designed to do. By maintaining crystal clarity on the front sight, accurate shot placement is an inevitable conclusion. Your shots will go through the same hole each time if every component of your shooting technique is applied properly.

Controlled Breathing. When you have all the time in the world to aim and place a shot on the range, you have the luxury of practicing breath control. Proper breath control is inhaling a full breath, releasing half, and hold your breath just before the trigger is squeezed. This is usually over-emphasized by most instructors. Tighter groups are achieved with proper sight alignment and proper trigger control, nothing else. In a tactical or defensive scenario, your adrenaline will be pumping and dumping, consequently, your heart rate and blood pressure will be raised and your breathing will be short and rapid.

For these reasons, controlled breathing is the least significant element of defensive shooting. So, be aware of this in your practice at the range. If you should ever be so unlucky to have to use your firearm in a life or death situation, you will be prepared and understand your body's natural automatic defensive reactions. You will not be surprised. You will be thoroughly prepared and thus, you will adapt, overcome and survive.

Sight System Configurations. Firearms have two distinctive sight system configurations.

1. The first one is the *fixed sight* which is defined as the rear sight being permanently cut into the back of the top strap just above the hammer or the rear of the slide, and the front sight being permanently affixed to either the top front of the barrel or slide directly above the muzzle.

2. The second type of sight system is the *adjustable sight system*. This means that with the application of a quality screwdriver to the rear sight, either elevation, up and down movement, or windage, left and right movement, can be changed and controlled by turning the adjustment screws one way or the other.

Hold Positions. One is the "6 o'clock hold." This is illustrated in Figure 11.7. This indicates that when the front and rear sights are aligned at the 6 o'clock position of the most inner circle of a target, the projectile will correspondingly hit the center of the target. In other words, 6 o'clock point of aim results in center point of impact.

The other position is the "center hold" or "point of aim / point of impact" position illustrated in Figure 11.8. This means that when the front and rear sights are aligned at the center of the target's inner core, the projectile (bullet) will correspondingly hit that point in the center of the target if all other variables are correct in the sequence (grip, stance, sight alignment, trigger control, and follow-through).

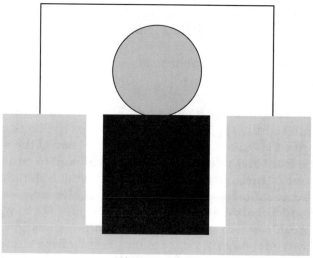

Figure 11.7

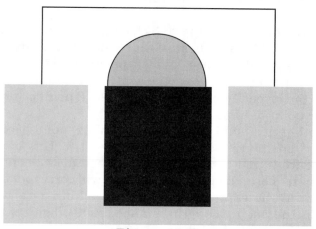

Figure 11.8

By adjusting the rear sight for either elevation or windage, impact can be directed as desired, most usually to a center hold position corresponding to the center of the target or center of mass. When adjusting adjustable sights, you must turn the adjustment screw to **move the rear sight in the direction of desired point of impact**.

You won't know which of these adjustments you have on your firearm straight out of the box until your first testing session at the range.

"Quick Sight Acquisition" and "Point Shoulder Shooting"

A VERY important survival element that you must remember about sights is that when you see a white dot or red ramp on the front sight or the like (e.g., it could be yellow or green!), that it is designed for *quick target acquisition*. That means that in a stressful encounter, moving the dot or ramp in one continuous motion from your holster or close ready position to your eye level aimed at the center of your adversary's chest or mass is a quick way to align your shot placement and get off an accurate effective shot, thus neutralizing the threat.

Most mistakes occur during point shoulder shooting because of an additional essential element; that is, the shooter does not maintain peripheral awareness of the relationship between the firearm and the ground to maintain a parallel alignment of gun and ground to target. Bending your wrist slightly either up or down will tend to throw your shots either up or down defeating your tactical response.

Some of the most practical self-defense, concealed carry handguns because of their small, pocket size (e.g., the Seecamp .32, Beretta .32 and N.A.A. Guardian .32, as well as the S&W J-frame .38 specials) have either no sights on them (the Seecamp) or sights that are so small that they are practically irrelevant in a defensive situation. To effectively be able to use these superior tactical weapons, you **must** master point shoulder shooting. With practice, you can accomplish this.

When you practice, you must train yourself (so that it becomes a "muscle memory") to maintain peripheral awareness of the relationship between your handgun (small .32 pistol or snub nose revolver) and the ground to maintain a parallel alignment of your gun and ground to target. Practice makes perfect. Practice and you will be pleasantly surprised at how easy it is to point shoot with one of these defensive pistols or revolvers for close tactical encounters.

Point shoulder shooting is most effectively used for close-up and personal defensive encounters and as suppression fire while moving to cover and concealment. Always keep in mind, that in a combat situation, you have to keep moving to stay safe and survive. Get off quality shots and keep your butt moving!

Anatomical and Positional Defects During Sight Alignment. A physical feature that often manifests itself and that often interferes with accurate sight alignment and proper focus is the tilting of the head. If your chin is tilted into your chest, you are slightly cutting off the blood supply to your brain which blurs your vision. Extending your chin skyward slightly reduces your oxygen supply which can also cause blurred vision. **Don't tilt your head. Keep it straight**. Maintaining a straight, level and balanced head in more ways than one, equals crystal clear sight performance.

If you tilt your head to locate a sight picture, the shots will be thrown away from your point of aim at the center of mass because it creates an optical illusion.

Usually the shots are thrown either high or low. If you tilt your head down, the shot will be thrown high. If you tilt your head upwards, the shot will be thrown low.

Practice, Stay Safe and Survive. All of these suggestions and techniques can readily be practiced in front of your full-length mirror. Practice assures professionalism and criminals do not like and are scared of professionals. Professional conduct negates criminal attack. *So practice, stay safe, and survive.*

Fundamentals of Marksmanship

Good accuracy with any handgun is defined by placing your shots where you intend to place them. Accuracy is affected by several interrelated factors that collectively form the fundamentals of marksmanship: proper stance and grip, proper sight alignment, sight picture with the front sight on the target, trigger control, and good follow-through. We have already covered stance, grip and sight alignment. Now we move on to trigger control and follow-through.

Trigger Control and Follow-Through

The fleshy pad of your index finger on your strong hand (where they get your fingerprints) up to the first joint of the finger should be the only portion of your trigger finger to touch the trigger. By centering that finger pad or first finger segment at the trigger's center, it fosters a 90-degree straight back rearward pressure on the trigger. The trigger has to be pressed straight back (notice we said *pressed* and not *pulled*) to get consistently accurate shot placement.

Once you have committed to rearward movement of the trigger, do not release the trigger until a split second has passed after the ammunition discharges and the gun fires. This is termed "follow-through." It takes that split second for the projectile (bullet) to emerge from the crown of the barrel through the muzzle, and we do not want to disturb the shot by slapping, jerking or excessively yanking the trigger's rearward movement.

We actually want to apply continual pressure on the trigger as it is taken up in its rearward travel to that point where the trigger disengages the sear and releases the striker or hammer onto the firing pin. At that furthest trigger take-up point in the trigger's rearward travel, you want to hold the trigger back for a split second before letting the trigger reset. Then you want to "ride" the trigger back as it resets. Again, no slapping, jerking or yanking please—just straight back rearward pressure, hold ever so briefly, and then ride the trigger forward on trigger reset.

When firing a revolver, let the trigger push your finger forward. Your goal is to never let your finger come off the trigger while you are firing multiple shots. Doing otherwise will disturb your shots and widen your groups.

When thinking about trigger control, it helps to imagine touching an infant's cheek. You would be gentle and light. Yet, you want to really *feel* the trigger. That is part of getting to really know your handgun. Different amounts of trigger pressure will be necessary on different handguns depending on the degree of trigger tension.

Isolating the Trigger Finger. When using proper trigger control, your body must "play statues" while you let the gun do the work. Your only job is to watch the front sight while pressing the trigger gently to the rear, fostering a clean, continuous movement as you take up the creep in the trigger. Do not squeeze with your entire hand. Your trigger finger should be the only digit moving on your shooting hand. For a right-handed shooter, too much trigger finger on the trigger results in shots pulled to the right. Conversely, too little trigger finger on the trigger results in shots pushed to the left. This is reversed for left-handed shooters.

If you have wide center groups, your support hand is not being applied tightly enough to your shooting hand in forming your two-handed mono-grip. If you drop your left elbow, shots will pull to the left. If you drop your right elbow, shots will pull to the right.

Drawing From Your Holster

Your platform for producing your firearm in a tactical situation is established at the holster with your initial grip of the firearm, high on the backstrap and your finger off the trigger (See Figure 11.9). Locked in that position, you can feel assured that once the weapon is pulled, it will be held in a straight line as you stretch your arm out to its fullest extension—also known as pointing towards the target's center of mass.

Draw your weapon from your holster with your strong shooting hand. Your draw should be implemented in one quick, smooth continuous motion from the holstered position to where it is trained on the target. These are the steps which meld into one fast continuous flow. (See Figure 11.10.)

It must be noted that you should wear your holster on your strong hand side wherever it is easiest and quickest for you to reach and react. So, your holster may be positioned anywhere from just behind your hip bone, at your hip bone, to slightly in front of your hip bone—whatever works best for you.

Figure 11.9

Recognize that you have to be comfortable with your equipment and practice with it regularly to develop techniques that you feel most comfortable with as long as they are safe.

Even with the safest product line of items we've described or recommended, if you don't use and apply proper techniques correctly, accidents can happen, **AND YOU CANNOT AFFORD TO HAVE A FIREARMS-RELATED ACCIDENT! NEVER EVER EVER!!!**

Safe Training. You should always do your utmost to prevent accidents by only *training in your drawing techniques with unloaded firearms*. That way

Figure 11.10

you'll notice any failures of your technique, areas where you need improvement and development, and no one will get hurt or killed. Uneducated persons and media already have predetermined that you are already reckless by wanting to own a firearm to protect yourself.

Please don't contribute to the negative statistics they quote by being an imbecile and causing yourself or anyone else to be maimed or killed innocently and stupidly. You have a grave responsibility to society and yourself by assuming the rights we all share as law-abiding citizens to defend ourselves. Give your responsibility the attention and respect that it deserves.

Safe Holster Drawing Technique

The safe holster drawing technique steps are:

1. Sweep your shooting hand back and up towards the grip of your holstered gun.

2. Wrap your pinky, ring and middle finger around the grip of your gun with your thumb opposing these fingers and pointing towards the muzzle against the inside of the frame. Your index finger should be pointed towards the muzzle, parallel to the outside of the frame. With your index finger outside of the trigger guard, you control the weapon versus the weapon controlling you. It also avoids accidental discharges with light trigger action firearms.

3. Your grip should be firm enough (about 20 pounds of pressure) so that you have a good handle on your weapon and it can't be pulled easily from your hand. You must stay conscious of your weapon retention at all times in a tactical situation.

4. If your holster has a thumb retention strap or "thumb break" around the hammer of your revolver or the back of the slide of your semi-auto, do the following: Snap the thumb break open with the back of your thumb by striking downwards on the flap as you simultaneously grip and remove your firearm.

5. Lift your weapon straight up and out of your holster, drawing it out of the holster at the same angle in which the holster is canted. As part of your training, you must evaluate how your holster needs to ride on your side for you to accomplish the most natural, comfortable, effi-cient, and smooth draw. Should your holster be canted so that the gun's muzzle is raked to the rear and the butt is forward? If so, how much rear rake do you need? Or, are you better suited for a straight upright or high ride? Again, you must determine this for yourself by *safely* experimenting with an *unloaded* weapon to learn which position best allows you to draw straight out of the holster in one smooth continuous motion.

6. For two-handed shooting, bring your firearm up and out as if you were assuming the "ready gun position" which is where your support hand meets your shooting hand. Then from that position, push the gun straight out towards your target/adversary. This, as we previously stated, happens in one smooth transitional flow.

7.   If you are shooting close range one-handed, you are going from holster directly to arm's length and straight out to the target.

Cautionary Note. To be safe, any of the techniques we describe or mention have to be learned and practiced under the tutelage of a concerned, qualified firearms instructor with whom you have rapport so you feel comfortable and confident as you are learning. It is the instructor's job to teach you the correct way to perform the techniques, and also to spot problem areas in your performance.

You cannot fully learn safe and effective shooting techniques by yourself from this or any other book. You can practice by yourself, but without a concerned qualified instructor, you are not going to be able to identify what you are doing wrong. You need that third eye because you cannot see the common errors that you will make (and most of us make), if you are concentrating on everything else at the same time. You need appropriate interactive feedback from an instructor. The best place to make mistakes is while learning and practicing in a range setting—not in actual combat!

You'll find that even in a range setting, you still will have adrenaline pumping. You can quickly identify this by the sweating of your palms. Don't be concerned. This is normal and it goes away with practice.

Some texts will illustrate an example of purposively developing an adrenaline rush—bringing it on on purpose. We believe that this idea is invalid. Even though you may be able to manufacture adrenaline to the same degree during training exercises, no one has ever been able to tell us how you can associate or input the fear level of an actual attack in conjunction with a training exercise. They are two totally different experiences. The experience of being under a real attack cannot be simulated in most practical training situations outside of hard core police combat training. However, even then, the trainees know that they are not facing live ammunition or enemies with deadly weapons. They also understand that they get to go home at the end of the day's training.

Stop Jerking! This brings us to another important point that we might as well raise here. Practice at the range with snap caps (Lyman Products Corporation) inserted into some of your revolver's cylinder chambers, or intermixed with the live rounds in your semi-auto's magazine. This will allow you to notice if you are jerking the gun while squeezing the trigger, thus throwing your sight alignment and aim off. This is the best way to eliminate jerking—*establish better trigger control and follow through.* A corrective measure in improving trigger control is to slow down as you're squeezing the trigger from front to rear—slow, steady, uninterrupted pressure. The "mantra" is: eye on the front sight, mid-tip touch the trigger, squeeze slowly and steadily, and hold the trigger at its most rearward position momentarily, allowing the bullet to clear the barrel.

Loading A Revolver

Loading a revolver can be most easily accomplished as follows (right-handed):

1. Place the revolver in the palm of your support hand so that your center 2 fingers (middle and ring fingers) are directly beneath the cylinder, your index finger below and supporting the barrel, and your pinky supporting the frame just below the hammer.

2. Depress the cylinder release latch (differs with each manufacturer) with your strong thumb and simultaneously push the cylinder with your middle two fingers into your support thumb. Another way to visualize this is to make your support hand like a shadow puppet on the wall—2 ears and the center 2 fingers touching your thumb. See the illustrations in Figures 11.12 through 11.15.

Figure 11.12

3. With the open cylinder facing your belly button and close to your stomach at a downward 45-degree angle, loading is accomplished quickly with the help of gravity whether it be

in light or darkness by feel. Your focus should never leave your adversary while reloading. Staring at an open cylinder on your revolver will only diminish your survival by getting you shot in the head or chest. Loading is best done behind cover and concealment. A bowed head is only good in your nearest religious prayer place.

4. Using the "shadow puppet" configuration or technique as pictured, rotate the cylinder counterclockwise (away from the frame to avoid crushing your supporting middle fingers should you have chosen to do it clockwise) with your support thumb as you load each chamber with a round.

Figure 11.13

Figure 11.14   **Figure 11.15**

5. Now close the loaded cylinder gently, and your weapon is loaded.

Unloading A Revolver

1. After you've fired all of your rounds, fully open and support the cylinder as you did in loading using the

"shadow finger puppet technique" described and previously illustrated. Now rotate your revolver to a 90-degree upright angle with the muzzle facing the sky. At this point, make sure that with your two middle fingers you are pushing the cylinder to its outermost position so that it fully clears the frame. With your support thumb, press down firmly on the ejection rod. Make sure that the ejection rod star does not catch on the frame. If you are pushing the cylinder to its outermost position with your support hand middle fingers, you'll achieve the necessary clearance of the cylinder from the frame.

2. Now, if you have adequate cylinder clearance from the frame, one firm downward push on the ejection rod will eject all spent casings simultaneously.

3. Should a casing get caught on the star, pull it off manually *before* releasing the downward tension on the ejection rod and allowing the spring tension to return the ejection rod to its forward original resting position. Now you are unloaded!

CAUTION #1. Do not pump the ejection rod like you are making butter! Because that will only tend to catch a spent casing beneath the star which reduces you to having a very expensive hammer instead of a firearm! It's extremely difficult to pry spent casings from under the star especially under stress! You avoid this by pressing the ejection rod firmly down ONCE to its fullest rearward extension allowing gravity to work by pushing the spent casings down and out of the cylinder's chambers onto the ground.

CAUTION #2. Never ever catch brass in your hand while training. Let the brass fall to the ground so that you establish and imprint a "muscle memory" for this technique. How you train will establish what you do on the street in a lethal confrontation. When police officers in their range practice are trained to catch brass to facilitate a nice clean range area, they tend to do this same thing when unloading and reloading on the street! Data from police street shootings have shown that when officers who have trained to catch brass have been shot during reloading in a street confrontation, post-incident investigators have found their dead hands clenched around spent brass casings! In other words, poor muscle memory had been developed and imprinted and implemented where and when it should not have been.

CAUTION #3. Never bang down or slap with the palm of your hand the tip of the ejection rod to eject spent casings! If you do so, you may end up impaling your hand, or at the least drawing blood. So, it's a bad idea especially because fired casings expand within the chambers!

* * * CAUTION #4 * * * This one is especially critical. Should you inadvertently, against all common sense and judgment, use the single action mode of your revolver in a defensive situation, how do you return the hammer to its resting position once you have not had to fire? The safest and most practical way to accomplish this critical maneuver is as follows:

1. Take your support thumb and position it between the frame and the cocked single action hammer with your support thumb nail facing the hammer.

2. Momentarily depress the trigger with your strong index trigger finger, and allow the hammer's weight to fall onto your support thumb.

3. Remove your trigger finger from the trigger guard so that you don't inadvertently or accidentally disconnect the internal safeties on the revolver, and with your strong thumb lower the hammer to its resting position inside the frame.

This safe technique has saved lives in incalculable home defense incidents where novices have cocked to single action mode in error and didn't know how to release the hammer without firing their weapon. We don't know how many accidental unintended shootings have resulted from the lack of knowledge and training in this procedure. The point is that we do not want YOU to have such an accident.

If you have a shrouded hammer, it makes it a little more difficult, but you still can do it:

1. Hold the cocked hammer securely with your shooting thumb.

2. Pull the trigger while at the same time removing your finger from the trigger guard and lowering the hammer manually.

Of course, these methods described should be tried and practiced **ONLY WITH AN UNLOADED FIREARM WELL BEFORE AN INCIDENT EVER OCCURS!** If you blow this procedure one or two times, don't worry about it because you are practicing with an **UNLOADED WEAPON!!!** Right?

Semi-Automatic Loading Procedure

1. Sit down and make yourself comfortable. With your support hand, grasp your magazine tube securely and hold it so that its floorplate rests solidly on the table in front of you with the front or rounded edge of the magazine tube facing your strong hand.

2. Looking down at the top of the magazine tube, you will see 2 parallel edges taking up approximately half of the length of the magazine opening at the top of the magazine. These parallel edges are known as the lips of the magazine. With a round of ammunition between your strong thumb and your index finger and with the projectile facing your strong palm, press down on the follower (the plastic or metal support for the ammunition within the magazine tube which once the last shot has been fired on a quality semi-automatic, locks the slide to the rear) just forward of the lips and push downward and rearward.

3. The second and subsequent rounds will be a little more difficult to load because now you are pressing one rounded ammunition casing on top of another and you are also increasing spring tension within the magazine with every additionally compressed inserted round. To assist yourself, you can use the *thumb-to-thumb method.*

> Use the thumb of your support hand to press down the rear of the previously loaded casing. While pressing downward, use your strong thumb to press the rear of the casing you are loading down on to the front top of the previously loaded round and rearward into the magazine tube. This compresses the new round on top of the lower round.

Visualize a magazine as one large "Pez" dispenser. It operates in a similar fashion.

4.   Tap the rounds to the rear of the magazine. This is known as "stacking." It is accomplished by tapping the flat edge or rear of the magazine tube against your support palm or another flat surface. Commonly in combat footage, you will see infantrymen tapping the magazine against their helmet which accomplishes the same task. However, we do not want you banging or slapping on your head for any reason whatsoever.

5.   With our magazine stacked and loaded, it's time to complete the firing train within our semi-automatic pistol. Insert the loaded magazine into the butt or hollow end of the grip until you feel a locking click or cannot tug the magazine from the magazine well without pushing or compressing the magazine release button.

6.   At this point it must be understood that the semi-automatic pistol has 2 sitting phases of loading as you see it laying flat in front of you on the table. (1) If the slide is completely forward on the frame, the firearm is called *in battery*. (2) If the slide is locked rearward by the slide stop lever on the frame, it is called *out of battery*. To load from a magazine in either of these 2 positions, that is, to "charge the weapon," you must grasp the slide by the serrations at the rear of the slide which function as friction grooves.

7.   By pulling the slide to its most rearward position, compressing the guide rod spring assembly, and letting the slide go forward with its own momentum "into battery," the center rail of the slide will strip a round off the top of the magazine propelling the round between the barrel's feed ramp and hood into the barrel's breech, also known as the chamber. This is called racking the slide and chambering a round, or colloquially as *charging the weapon*.

The Semi-Auto's Sequence of Operation. The above loading procedure allows consistent feeding of ammunition rounds one after the other as the magazine's spring is gradually decompressed following the pistol's loading, firing, extraction and ejection operations. Once you charge the pistol and fire it, the pistol has fired, extracted, ejected, and reloaded a round instantly, easing spring pressure as the rounds are being exhausted with each press of the trigger.

Slide Stop Lever Operation. For those friends of yours who have a habit of releasing the slide with the slide stop lever when the pistol is out of battery, we want to direct your attention to one common sense consideration. Should you continually release the slide's forward momentum from the out of battery position using this slide stop lever, you will eventually cause material fatigue of either the slide stop cutout (the right angle in the slide that collectively with the slide stop, locks the pistol out of battery) or the slide stop lever itself. We call it a slide "stop" lever, not a "release."

Chambering a Round. To correctly load or *chamber* a round and "charge" any semi-automatic pistol from the "out of battery" position, you must manually pull the slide back from its static position on the slide stop lever, past the out of battery position. *You will notice that the slide moves rearward at least another eighth of an inch and* **drops the slide stop lever out of the way** *before forward momentum of the slide begins driving it forward into battery.* Once the slide stop lever has dropped, then let go of the slide. The gun will go into battery and will be ready to shoot.

Remember that heavy spring tension is demanded to reliably chamber a round of ammunition. Alternatively, if you baby the slide forward with your support hand, you retard its forward spring tension release, and 90 percent of the time, this will result in an "out of battery" malfunction.

For those enthusiasts who are now going into cardiac arrest because of our statement, let us acquaint you to one simple fact. When a weapon is fired under live ammunition pressures, we as human beings cannot see the operation happening visually. By pulling the slide to its most rearward extension and releasing it, we cannot possibly cause any damage to the pistol whatsoever. This is because we can come nowhere near to producing or simulating the pressures produced under live fire.

Slide Stop Release With An *Empty* Magazine. On a quality semi-automatic pistol, the follower of an empty magazine engages the slide stop lever locking the slide rearward out of battery. Therefore, to put the slide back into battery, it is necessary to compress the follower to disengage the slide stop lever lock and thus allow the slide's forward movement into battery. To accomplish this, you have to press down on the slide stop lever with your strong thumb while holding the slide rearward with your support hand on its friction grooves. This allows the follower to be compressed downward, and when you release the slide stop lever and the slide simultaneously, the slide is allowed to move forward into the in battery position.

Slide Stop Release *Without* **A Magazine**. With no magazine in the magazine well, and the weapon locked out of battery, all you have to do to place the weapon back into battery is to pull the slide back about an eighth of an inch past the slide stop lock and let go. The forward momentum of the slide will release the slide stop. This is called racking the slide.

Slide Stop Release *With* **A Fully-Loaded or Partially-Loaded Magazine**. With a magazine in the magazine well that is loaded with one or more rounds, and the weapon locked out of battery, all you have to do to place the weapon back into loaded battery is to follow the above procedure exactly. The rounds in the magazine are compressed within the magazine once the top round has been stripped and loaded into the breech by the slide's center rail. This releases the forward momentum of the slide racking the slide back into the loaded in battery position.

Locking the Slide Out of Battery Without A Magazine. To accomplish this task, with the grip in your strong hand and your support hand pulling rearward on the friction grooves to the slide's most rearward position, your strong thumb can now push the slide stop lever up into the slide lock securing the pistol out of battery.

By following our recommended procedures, you can avoid incurring mechanical damage to your pistol and thus protect your investment and your life. Check it out and come to your own experienced, informed and educated conclusion.

12

Safe Handgun
Shooting and Survival Procedures

At this point, we are ready to apply all the building blocks of information we've covered to help you develop practical defensive shooting techniques and procedures. These techniques can become your lifelines to self-preservation. They can be imprinted in your brain and made indelible by reading and re-reading this chapter and practicing regularly at the range.

▶ **What are the main differences between revolvers and semi-automatic pistols?**

1. Revolvers have a simpler action mechanism and make it easy to learn loading and unloading procedures.

1a. Semi-autos are more complex mechanically, require more training time for unloading, safe handling, disassembly and malfunction clearance.

2. Revolvers are more difficult to learn to shoot and reload efficiently.

2a. Semi-automatics require less training time to shoot accurately and reload rapidly.

3. Revolvers are less maintenance sensitive and less critical of ammunition types and ammunition quality.

3a. Semi-autos are more militaristic and as such, can survive in mud, sand, and other extreme climactic conditions without operational failure. Proper ammunition is critical and magazines must be maintained flawlessly.

4.   Revolvers are less durable in long-term use especially with heavy loads (e.g., +P, +P+ and magnums).

4a. Semi-autos are much more durable as they are usually designed to be carried as a sidearm along with a submachine gun of the same caliber—ergo, the same ammunition.

5.   Revolvers have a much smaller ammunition capacity and are slower to reload.

5a. Semi-autos have a greater ammunition capacity and are faster to reload. Regardless of lighting conditions or movement, they maintain a better continuity of fire.

6.   Revolvers can be cleaned without disassembly. Anything other than basic maintenance requires a trained armorer.

6a. Semi-autos can be field-stripped by their user, cleaned, re-assembled and be back in combat in a matter of minutes.

7.   Revolvers are unlikely to malfunction in limited use conditions if they are properly maintained. However, if a malfunction does occur with a revolver, it is usually much harder to solve and can seldom be done in the field.

7a. Malfunctions with semi-autos are easily cleared in the field and under any other conditions.

8.   Revolvers are much more forgiving of careless handling. They are relatively foolproof when dealing with large numbers of people of varying ability, intelligence, and carefulness.

8a. Semi-autos are a more efficient type of weapon requiring more thorough and frequent training.

▶ **What are the basic techniques of defensive shooting?**

The purpose of this section is to explain "defensive shooting." Defensive shooting means properly using *cover* and *concealment*. **Cover** enables you to be protected from incoming fire. **Concealment** only enables you to be hidden from an adversary's visual senses.

Ideally, cover and concealment should be sought together each and every time it is practical and possible. Inevitably, you can rely on the fact that some situations may arise when one may be obtained but not the other.

In defensive combat shooting, a major emphasis must be placed on safety because as you change positions, moving to cover and concealment, your finger must be outside the trigger guard until you are ready to shoot.

Cover and concealment positions enable you to defend yourself or others with minimum danger by presenting the smallest possible

Figure 12.1

target to an adversary. They also increase your ability to shoot accurately. This is because you are more able to get off well-aimed and unrushed shots when you are tactically secure ("playing statues").

When using cover in a defensive situation, it is imperative that you protect your body as much as possible and still be able to return accurate fire to the oncoming threat. To accomplish this, you must use your strong eye in concert with your strong shooting hand which reduces your exposure. Full head exposure with both of your eyes open increases your exposure which you want to minimize and avoid.

When shooting from a barricade position, it is imperative that you do not rest the weapon's action against the barricade. When using a revolver, you must keep the barricade from interfering with the rotation of the cylinder. When using a semi-auto, you must prevent the barricade from impeding the motion of the slide.

We have indicated throughout this text that you should stay flexible. That means that in terms of barricade shooting, 3 positions should be applied *irregularly* and *unpredictably* to confuse and confound the aggressor.

1. Kneeling offers a good, adequate shooting platform which also reduces the shooter's exposure and profile as a target. See Figure 12.2.

Figure 12.2

2. Standing behind the barricade hides the majority of your silhouette and reduces your exposure to your shooting eye and hand, which are readily movable.

3. Prone is the third position which reduces your body silhouette to an even greater degree. See Figure 12.3.

4. **Always be conscious of where the muzzle is being pointed and that your trigger finger is outside the trigger guard until you are ready to shoot and return fire.**

Figure 12.3

We recommend, based on our experience, that no more than 2 to 3 shots should be fired from any one position as it gives the adversary a point of aim should the fight be prolonged to any longer than 2 to 3 shot bursts. This is especially crucial in dim light conditions where muzzle flash is a primary concern.

Please note that most jams on semi-automatic pistols are shooter-induced from ineffective practice of arm and wrist lock-up and firing techniques.

"Stoppages" and "Malfunctions." A *stoppage* does not mean a weapon malfunction. It means that, for one reason or another, a round was *stopped* from feeding into the chamber, thus preventing the weapon from being charged for the next shot. A stoppage *stops up* the action.

A stoppage can result from a number of factors which can include a dirty, poorly maintained weapon, limp wrists while shooting, or clothing interfering with the pistol's operation. All of these things are under the shooter's direct control.

On the other hand, a *malfunction* is a mechanical failure of either the pistol or the ammunition. *Stoppages* are the result of **shooter** error, while *malfunctions* are the result of **mechanical** failure.

When drawing your handgun one-handed to defend yourself in a close combat position, you must have a good 3 finger grip on the gun and you must keep your trigger finger outside the trigger guard until you are ready to fire after acquiring your target.

Crouch Shooting for Quick Defensive Response. "Crouch shooting" means you are bending your knees slightly to lower your body profile and prepare yourself to shoot and then immediately move laterally to cover and concealment. It is also known as quick instinctive shooting. We are here talking about two-handed versus one-handed point shooting. Note that two-handed shooting is much more controlled and thus, more accurate and dependable. It works more effectively at greater distances within the defensive space than does one-handed point shooting which works acceptably really close up.

While you are engaged, you must be looking left and right with your peripheral vision to locate cover and concealment and any further threat while keeping your eyes focused on your adversary or attacker. At the same time, you must be preparing for your next immediate move to cover. Remember this isn't the "OK Corral" where you stand and fight holster to holster straight on and fall down. The "Big S" stands for SURVIVAL and not Superman.

"Crouch shooting" is advisably practiced at 21 feet or less when you are in the open and **moving**. If you are in a barricaded position on the other hand, you have more time to adjust for a proper sight picture and control your trigger squeeze to get off a more accurate shot.

However, when responding to an instantaneous threat right in front of you, a certain amount of accuracy must be sacrificed in exchange for a quick response to protect your life.

As a defensive shooter, your life and those of others under your protective blanket depend on the speed with which you can draw and fire a well placed shot at close range. Once an adversary has crossed your point of danger line (approximately 21 feet) and invaded your boundaries, it's up to you to produce your defensive firearm and defend yourself in a matter of nanoseconds.

Going into the crouched position means you are establishing your double-handed mono-grip at waist level and then in one continuous motion, pushing your weapon directly out to chin level with your arms locked ready to fire double action only. Both eyes are open. Remember, you have but a split second to react, make a defensive decision, and then fire, once your adversary has crossed your life line of limitations regarding your personal survival.

Initially in a confrontation, you don't have time to get a perfect sight picture by bringing the weapon up to eye level using your strong eye only. Both of your eyes must be open and focused on your adversary's center of mass. Peripheral vision must also be simultaneously maintained to ensure the firearm is level and to prevent shooting over the adversary's head or at the ground resulting from a slight bend or tilt in your wrists. The immediate goal here is to fire the few rounds necessary to allow your relocation to a place of cover and concealment.

Scanning. Whichever position you have chosen for your personal defense, it is immediately important that once you have fired a string of rounds to protect your life, you transition to the scanning position. The *scanning position* is when you drop your firearm from chin to chest level, stiff-armed in the mono-grip shooting stance, traversing your exposed area 180 degrees from left to right using your waist as the pivot. Once a secondary threat has been identified, you raise your weapon back up to chin level and address the threat until your adversaries have been defeated, neutralized or have surrendered. You cannot continue to fight and fire once they have given up or their threat is gone.

Night Fire. When seeking a training facility, you must find one that will teach you how to operate in night fire shooting conditions. Statistically, it has been proven that more trained police officers have been killed during the hours of darkness due to ineffective training, and limited to poor technique for operating under night conditions, than for any other reason.

You, our reader, must be taught to identify the threat and effectively stop and counter it. The use of low light conditions can actually be a blessing as opposed to being a detriment. By following and practicing what we are about to describe, you can transform the adversity of low light conditions into your tactical advantage or strategy.

There are essentially 2 low light illumination levels:

1. Ambient light which allows you through a haze of low light to identify your threat and still have visible control over your sights. Use this condition to your best tactical advantage.

2. Dark conditions which mean that there is no ambient light. Here, the rule of survival is that *if it is dark, keep it dark.* Your night vision will be acquired within a matter of 30 seconds, and that, in addition to your other senses, can easily enable you to pick up movement. Only then should you think about using any of the flashlights we've described earlier. Then too, your flashlight should be positioned in front and away from your body, unless you are using an exotic integrated system such as Insight Technology's M6 Tactical Laser Illuminator M6-TLI.

Despite our recommendation against doing so, searching your home may be a necessity due to circumstances like your remoteness or limited police capacity, so in searching for someone inside your residence or wherever you are caught short, inevitably you will be moving from light to dark conditions. Make your judgments about your next move well ahead of your movements. Apply the darkness to achieve and maintain your best possible concealment.

In a lit area, on the other hand, light the area up more. You cannot react to a threat unless you can see it. It is tactically significant and most important in dim or dark conditions that you employ cover and concealment to your best possible advantage when dealing with an armed adversary.

You must use your flashlight beam briefly, and only when tactically sound, to either blind your adversary and make your tactical retreat, or beat him over the head if he comes up on you. Maglites are great for this given their weight and size.

Keep your flashlight off and only use it when these 4 reasons dictate:

1. To see where you are going.
2. To locate and identify the attacker or suspect.
3. To blind the attacker and interrupt his night vision, making him more vulnerable.
4. And, to shoot if necessary.

Once you are satisfied that your defensive area has been cleared of intruders, do a double-check to make sure you did not miss anything or anyone. The concept of searching and clearing an area in the darkness is a DANGEROUS one! NEVER take it lightly. Only use it when you can't maintain a barricaded position and only until the arrival of the police or backup (if you are the police).

You should buy a good quality flashlight, preferably one that is charging on your wall so that you know it will be there when you need it. The lights manufactured by Streamlight and Mag Instrument Company described earlier are very capable and reliable tools to serve these functions.

Remember to only move to change your cover and concealment when your flashlight beam is off so that you are not an illuminated target. Blinding your adversary is accomplished by placing your flashlight at a fixed position at eye level away from yourself inside your barricaded position should the invader enter. If you are attacked within distances of 12 feet or closer, use your unlit flashlight as a defensive baton to swing and sweep in front of you as you prepare to fire and neutralize the imposing threat. You are working to push the threat back and get your gun out on him. The flashlight serves a number of defensive purposes; as a baton and as a flashlight. Everything you can use to increase your longevity is a valuable tool.

It should be noted that you never enter to search and clear a building or dark area without a flashlight no matter what time of day it is. Being able to locate and identify the threat or threats as early as possible is critical to your survival. You must have the capability to penetrate through the darkness around you to locate the threats. Minimally, the brightness level of your chosen light should fall in the range of at least 20,000 to 40,000 candle power. Your light should also have a 3-button position switch which would be: off, on, and manual blink. This last position gives you intermittent discretionary lighting as you are moving from one position to another. Here, again, we endorse the attributes of the M6-TLI with its multiple features which enhance defensive flexibility.

Before starting a prolonged check of any area, remember to have backup batteries and an extra flashlight in case your primary flashlight fails. You must be prepared for the fact that a flashlight can fail at any time. So, you must have backup light that you check periodically for functionality. We do not recommend matches, candles or a key ring light in a high stress situation.

▶ **What types of ammunition failures can occur?**

In a world where everything worked correctly, you would load your ammunition into your firearm and it would function when you press the trigger. However, as a result of manufacturing and storage defects, certain problems can arise which you should be aware of and know how to handle. These include misfires, hangfires, and squib loads.

▶ **What is a "misfire"?**

"Misfires" happen when you pull the trigger and you have neither report (that is, no sound) from the ammunition or recoil from the firearm. This indicates that you either have a defective, corroded or otherwise non-functioning primer or a moisture-saturated or chemically-altered smokeless gun powder. For example, spraying your handgun with WD-40 will corrode the primer pockets of the ammunition you use in that gun, causing malfunctions that are avoidable.

To insure that a misfire is not a hangfire, hold your weapon safely downrange for a period of one minute. In a combat defensive situation, your thoughts should not be on *why the gun didn't fire*. You should be solely focused on ridding yourself of the defective round and moving on to the next live round.

▶ **What is a "hangfire"?**

"Hangfires" occur due to contamination of either the primer or the gunpowder. As a result, ignition is slow to take place and usually occurs within a period of 1 minute. The easiest example to illustrate this is that of a moist firecracker fuse. When lit, it sparks and burns intermittently and then finally causes the fire-cracker to ignite and explode.

So, in the case of your handgun, if ignition does not occur within a 1 minute period, most likely the gun will not fire and you have a "misfire." If it occurs, but is delayed, then it is a "hangfire." Once again, in a defensive combat situation, don't wait around to find out which it is. Just eject and get rid of the defective round and move on to the next live round.

▶ **What is a "squib load"?**

A "squib load" occurs when, during the manufacturing process, the gunpowder has inadvertently been left out of the shell. You would never be able to recognize this or spot the problem from the exterior. It is common that once you have one squib load in the box of ammunition, you are likely to have several others. So, the best thing to do is to either discard that box or return it to the manufacturer should you be given the opportunity.

With any defective ammunition problem, you should notify the manufacturer because it could jeopardize other people's lives. On the flap of any box of ammunition is the date/shift code which tells the manufacturer on which shift and date the ammunition was produced. This enables the manufacturer to segregate problem loads.

It must be noted that the ignition primer will provide sufficient enough force to lodge the projectile in the barrel. However, it will get stuck there and cause a blockage. Squib loads are easily identifiable by their actions. You squeeze the trigger and you get the pop of a child's cap gun, yet there is no perceivable recoil.

Should a squib load happen to you while you're in a defensive combat situation, you can do nothing to clear it. You've reduced yourself to having an expensive club. Let those feet fly to fight another day, unless you've tactically planned in advance and have a secondary backup handgun.

Ammunition failures do not occur all that often. At the very least, you should inspect every round before you load your revolver or the magazine of your semi-auto, checking for primers that have been installed incorrectly, cracks in the cartridge casing, collapsed hollow points, or other damage to the projectile. By checking your rounds externally as well as possible, you are doing your utmost to make sure you do not suffer the results of an ammunition-related problem.

▶ **What is "muzzle flash" and "firing shock"?**

"Muzzle flash" from an adversary's weapon can cause destabilizing effects on your psyche which is termed "firing shock." You must understand and be prepared for this. If you are not prepared, the sudden flash and shock can be intense enough to make you freeze momentarily or worse, permanently. Remember that muzzle flash and your psychological reaction (i.e., "firing shock") cannot injure you, but the bullets you will receive if you freeze definitely will!

Muzzle flash from both your and your adversary's gun create two main problems:

1. It illuminates you and thus can give away your position. So you must move after rounds have been exchanged.

2. It can interfere with your night vision. This is mainly caused by ammunition that has excessive flash on detonation (i.e., super high velocity ammunition combined with low bullet weight such as +P+).

Our recommendation is to use a slower moving, heavier projectile, which will produce a lower level of muzzle flash from your gun. It will not aid the adversary by illuminating you. In other words, your body's fingerprint silhouette will not be as readily exposed.

Therefore, when your buddy, Bubba, who gets off on the 3-foot muzzle flash coming out of his firearm offers you ammo, turn it down with a, "No thank you, Bubba. If I wanted to see the bright lights, I'd go into show business!"

Your adversary's muzzle flash can on the other hand help you by revealing your adversary's location and verifying your own sight alignment. You should always keep both eyes open while scanning and searching. When scanning in the dark, and not pulling the trigger, keep your eyes moving and use off-centered peripheral vision—look left, right, above and below the area scanned. That negates the effects of your adversary's muzzle flash.

▶ **What types of common function failures can occur with a revolver?**

Revolver malfunctions are fairly rare. Usually it's a mechanical part inside of the revolver that suffers breakage as a result of either material fatigue or improper care, such as dropping the revolver on a concrete surface or using it as if it were a hammer. The old song, "If I had a hammer, I'd hammer in the morning ..." refers to a real hammer, not to a revolver.

Most common causes of a malfunction in a revolver are improperly manufactured ammunition such as where the primer is not seated deep enough inside the cartridge casing which causes the casing to scrape and rub against the recoil plate retarding or stopping the cylinder's rotation.

Ammunition failures are easily corrected by replacing the defective ammunition. On the other hand, if a revolver has a true mechanical failure, it can usually only be solved by taking the revolver to a qualified, certified armorer or gunsmith for repairs.

One other simple problem that occasionally occurs with revolvers is loosening of the ejection rod through continuous use. Hot rounds can do this, as well as loosen other parts of a gun through extreme vibration. A loose ejection rod will manifest itself in that the cylinder cannot be freely released with the cylinder release latch. Here again, correction must be made by an armorer to avoid damage to the gun.

Should you notice binding problems of any kind with a new revolver, do not hesitate to ship it back to the factory for correction. Turn around time is usually very quick with a quality manufacturer such as Smith and Wesson. So, don't settle for carrying a weapon that has spotty problems when you first begin to use it—get it fixed!

Due to the numbers produced, not every firearm comes out perfect. Quality manufacturers are more than happy to take care of you and accommodate your legitimate defensive needs. The cylinder of your revolver should rotate smoothly with and without rounds in the chamber, action open or closed, and with action closed, whether double or single action is applied.

▶ **What types of common function failures can occur with a semi-automatic pistol?**

Dirt. Improper maintenance procedures and neglect are the number one cause of malfunctions with a semi-automatic pistol. Cleaning agents that bind the mechanisms of your pistol can lead to your demise. From personal experience, we don't believe that relying on ultrasonic tanks alone are the solution to the problem. As we have indicated repeatedly throughout the text, a very short time has to be devoted regularly to assuring that your pistol is clean and operational.

Failure to Feed. Always go for the least complicated and most inexpensive solution first to try to solve the problem. Failures to feed usually result from damaged magazine lips which usually occur as a result of slapping the magazine upwards into the magazine well on reloading, just as seen in the movies, or dropping the magazine onto a hard surface crushing the magazine's lips.

Additionally, there are many after-market magazine manufacturers. Some are completely inferior and do not function reliably enough to rely on in defensive situations. Finally, improper ammunition length, as much as several thousandths of an inch, is enough to cause failures to feed. That either means the rounds were manufactured improperly, or you chose the wrong specific caliber of ammunition (e.g., amongst 9mm ammunition, there's no comparison between 9mm Luger and 9mm Largo).

Failure to Go Into Battery. Because your body provides the platform for a semi-automatic to function correctly, failure to lock up your arms and wrists in the proper shooting position can unnecessarily cause a failure for your pistol to go into battery. Additionally, dirt either in the chamber, slide rails or feed ramp can retard the necessary spring action for ammunition to be propelled from the magazine into the barrel's breech and for the slide to move back into battery. Last, but not least, is the weak recoil spring. Should that fail, immediately replace it because you can make no adjustments, and it will not regain its tensile strength by wishing.

Failure to Fire.

> **Three of the six common problems that can cause failures to fire are firing pin related.**
>
> 1. Dirt in the firing pin channel retarding the forward movement of the firing pin. Therefore, we never advocate lubrication of the firing pin channel because it acts as a "dirt magnet."
>
> 2. A weak or defective firing pin spring or striker spring. This spring surrounds the firing pin or striker and provides the pressure needed to propel the firing pin or striker into the primer for ignition.
>
> 3. A broken, worn or bent firing pin or striker tip. If you have a weak or defective spring or tip, the defective part *must be* replaced.
>
> 4. The weapon is slightly out of battery as a result of firing limp-wristed. This prevents the firing pin or striker from contacting the primer because the slide has not gone completely forward into battery.
>
> 5. A hard or deeply recessed primer. Hard primers result from a manufacturing defect where the primer is made of material that the firing pin or striker cannot dent and ignite. A deeply recessed primer is a compression of the primer so that it is pushed below the cartridge's base level position. In a recessed primer, the firing pin cannot reach the primer with enough force. As a result of either of these defects, the firing pin does not develop enough energy to incur ignition and detonation.
>
> 6. A bad primer as we indicated under ammunition-related failures. This causes a misfire and that round can never be used effectively again in a combative situation. Because it is not readily identifiable from the exterior, this defect is unknowable until you try to fire the round.

Failure to Eject. Most commonly, dirt and poor maintenance are associated with failures to eject. However, there are 3 additional reasons why failures to eject can occur. One is a broken or worn ejector which must be replaced as soon as it is discovered. Underpowered ammunition which usually occurs with your buddy Bubba's reloads means you get very light recoil for target shooting but you get unreliability in defensive situations. Lastly, limp-wristing, poor shooting technique, and/or not have the correct pistol lock-up can cause ejection failures.

Failure to Extract. The extractor removes the empty, fired casing from the barrel breech. Then the casing is ejected by the ejector. The extractor is most often defeated by poor maintenance and neglect which allows dirt to accumulate under the extractor. This negates its proper grip on the cartridge casing. A weak extractor can further be identified by a broken or weak extractor spring. Replacement is a necessity. Chipped or worn extractors also must be replaced after inspection by a certified armorer or gunsmith.

Under or overpowered ammunition can also cause failures to extract. Underpowered ammunition does not provide sufficient physical force or speed for the extractor to pick up and pull the spent cartridge casing from the breech. Overpowered ammunition provides so much pressure and speed that it forces the extractor to override the spent cartridge casing within the breech.

Failure to Lock Out of Battery. Most but not all quality semi-automatic pistols are designed to lock in the out of battery position once the last round is fired. For those that have the lock-out feature, some common problems associated with failure to lock out of battery are: (1) a broken slide stop lever; (2) a weak magazine spring; and (3) a broken or defective magazine follower. These three conditions can only be corrected by replacement parts.

Three additional associated problems with failure to lock out of battery are: (1) poor maintenance and lubrication procedures resulting in a dirty, binding slide; (2) underpowered ammunition; and (3) incomplete shoulder lock up and dropping your elbows which defeats the slide's rearward inertia for proper lock-out of battery.

Excessively Heavy Trigger Squeeze. The most common reason that trigger squeeze increases over time is because of poor maintenance and lubrication procedures. These corrected, there are two additional mechanical problems that can additionally increase trigger squeeze. One is a kinked or broken trigger

spring or trigger return spring, and two is galling or binding of
the trigger bar at the connector. These two problems have to be
repaired by an armorer or gunsmith and are usually indicative
of excessive wear or material fatigue.

Incorrect Point of Impact. If you haven't been taught correct
sight alignment and trigger squeeze in conjunction with all of the
other methods we have previously described, you are most
probably not going to attain proper point of impact with your
first shooting experience. You need to know how to use your
gun's sights, how they can be adjusted, and by whom they
should be adjusted, if you cannot adjust them yourself. Also,
you must understand how elevation and windage changes affect
point of impact.

Usually, on adjustable sight firearms, sight elevation (height)
and windage (left-right centering) can be changed by making a
simple adjustment with a screwdriver. On fixed sight firearms,
it usually requires a special tool that only a gunsmith or armorer
has.

So, if you have a question about your firearm's point of
impact, talk it over with and get it appraised by your trusted
firearms instructor so that you understand what the problem is
and why it is happening.

Other factors that can affect point of impact are weather
conditions (meaning wind speed) and shadowing of the target
surface as the sun changes direction throughout the day. This
can be distracting and create optical illusions.

Inaccurate Shooting. Assuming you have developed proper
technique; the proper stance, trigger squeeze, sight alignment,
grip and follow-through, there are only three common reasons
for inaccuracy to occur.

1. A broken, loose, or missing sight should be your first
   option to check for obvious reasons.
2. Faulty ammunition, which means that some manufacturers do not precisely size the bullet head. This
   translates into the bullet wobbling down the bore of the
   barrel instead of spinning with the lands and grooves out
   towards the target. This causes the bullet to have an
   inaccurate and unreliable trajectory and flight, and point
   of impact.
3. People who use lead ammunition on a regular basis to
   save a few pennies, and who do not follow proper
   maintenance procedures will experience the effects of the
   lead residues binding onto the lands and grooves of the

barrel bore. This unintentionally alters the bullet's flight trajectory. A good substantial cleaning will resolve this unnecessary problem.

▶ **What types of jams occur most often with semi-automatic pistols?**

Operator-Created Errors. This is where the shooter either fails to seat and lock the magazine properly in the magazine well, has not chambered a round at all, or has not chambered a round completely, which is termed "out of battery." In any of these cases, once the trigger is squeezed, nothing happens. A simple check to prevent this from happening is to press the magazine floorplate upward into the magazine well insuring that it is locked, and then tug on the floorplate to make sure that it indeed stays locked.

In the case where the round is not fully lodged, or the slide is out of battery, simply tapping the rear of the slide forward should seat the round and force the gun into battery. If not, follow the "tap, rack, bang" procedure described below.

As we have indicated, always chamber a round correctly by using the heavy spring tension supplied by the slide of the pistol to chamber the round. Should the round fail to fire when you squeeze the trigger, extract and eject the round because in most cases, you have a misfire. Who cares why it doesn't work! Replace it with a fresh round. If this happens, however, do be suspicious about the remaining rounds in the box from which that round came.

For emphasis, we reiterate three of the most common operator created errors:

1. Pressing the trigger too hard.

2. Squeezing with the whole hand rather than with just the trigger finger.

3. Watching the target rather than maintaining a crystal clear sight picture.

"Tap, Rack, Bang." The common industry vernacular for the procedure of correcting stoppages is "tap, rack, bang."

1.   ***Tap*** refers to what you do to make sure that the magazine is seated in the magazine well fully—you **tap** the baseplate of the magazine up into the magazine well so it is fully seated.
2.   ***Rack*** means pulling the slide to its furthest rearward position and then letting it go into battery, seating the round in the chamber by heavy spring momentum.
3.   ***Bang*** means only fire again if the situation indicates or dictates that the threat to your survival is still immediately present. If it isn't, then you must desist from firing and remain in the "challenge position" until you are sure that the incident has been defused or terminated.

With any of the malfunctioning clearing procedures, they are best performed for obvious reasons behind good cover and concealment.

A "Stovepipe." A "stovepipe" is when an empty or spent cartridge casing is partially extracted from the chamber's breech and is pulled to a 90-degree vertical angle perpendicular to the ejection port of a semi-automatic pistol. It's called "stovepipe" because it resembles an old potbellied stovepipe or chimney. "Stovepipes" are caused by underpowered ammunition, a weak or dirty extractor, or poor lubrication of the pistol. The "stovepipe" is illustrated in Figure 12.4.

It is essential to know how to quickly and efficiently clear this type of stoppage. Your life could depend on it. Learn the procedure and practice it regularly with orange training rounds or snap caps and an empty cartridge casing.

To effectively clear a stovepipe, do the following (see Figures 12.4 through 12.6):

1.   Hold the pistol in your strong hand. Form your support hand into a karate chop configuration.
2.   Starting just behind the front sight with your support hand palm touching the top of the slide, sweep your support hand rearward dislodging the spent cartridge casing out of the ejection port.

Ninety percent of the time a new round will be chambered from the top of the magazine into the barrel's breech. Should that not occur, go back to "tap, rack, bang."

Figure 12.4

Figure 12.5

Figure 12.6

The Reasoning Behind This Procedure. You don't have to sweep rearward with a lot of force. You just need to form a rigid karate position with your support hand and start from behind the front sight. If you don't form a karate type stiffness with your support hand, one of 2 things can happen as you are sweeping rearward. You can either become cut by the spent cartridge casing, or the meat of your fingers can get entangled in the ejection port.

Do the procedure correctly and you'll leave without injuries and learn a valuable survival tool. Do it incorrectly and you'll go away with several boo-boos and you'll never practice it again. Besides the physical damage to your hand if you do it incorrectly, you might also fail to survive by failing to clear the stoppage and chamber a fresh round.

A "Double-Feed." "Double-feeds" as illustrated in Figure 12.7 occur when the spent cartridge casing within the barrel's breech fails to be extracted; however, the slide is propelled far enough rearward to pick up a fresh round that is now pressing against the spent casing inside the breech. To correct it: "rip, work, tap, rack, and bang."

Figure 12.7

"Rip." Take the thumb of your strong hand and depress the magazine release button, while simultaneously with the support hand grabbing, yanking, or *ripping* the magazine floorplate out and away from the pistol.

Do not expect the magazine to drop free! You have to understand that your slide pressure is forcing the round on top of the magazine up against the spent casing inside the barrel's breech. The only thing you can rely upon is that the round inside the breech has indeed been fired, otherwise the slide would have never come back to pick up the second round. **So, you have to rip the magazine out.**

"Work." Place the magazine against the grip and under the thumb of the strong hand. With the support hand *rack* the slide, commonly called *working* it, until the spent casing either falls out of the ejection port or magazine well.

"Tap." Re-insert the magazine with the support hand and *tap* the floor plate upward into the magazine well.

"Rack." *Rack* the slide to chamber a fresh round from the magazine.

"Bang" or "Challenge Position." If necessary, should the situation still require a live fire response, then squeeze the trigger, and make the pistol go *bang!*

"Double feeds" are caused by either weak or underpowered ammunition, dirt under the extractor, a broken or chipped extractor, a defective recoil spring, or limp-wristing the pistol. Unless there is a mechanical malfunction of the pistol, "rip, work, tap, rack, and bang" should clear 100 percent of non-mechanically related stoppages.

In any situation, one of the two methods described above must be applied to clear the pistol, and you should always start with the least complicated first. So, progress in numerical order: (1) *tap, rack, bang,* or (2) *rip, work, tap, rack, bang.* If you try any other sequence of operations for clearing the pistol, you may just end up compounding or complicating the existing problem. Also, remember that you should always clear a stoppage from behind cover and concealment.

Remember that "Rip, Work, Tap, Rack, Bang" or "RWTRB" is our RSVP with a vengeance!

One further term that should be explained is "tapping the magazine up into the pistol." Unlike in the movies, you shouldn't smack the magazine into the pistol because you can damage the magazine's lips creating an irreversible mechanical problem. Tap means just that—light pressure on the floorplate of the magazine to lock it into the magazine well. Be sure not to create mechanical problems you didn't originally have.

Remember: Practice promotes survival. So, practice, practice, practice! It's very important that you take the time to practice these drills so that they are in your muscle memory if you should ever need to use the techniques. Positive responses are generated through positive practice.

Now that we have gone over the "RWTRB" and "TRB" drills for clearing pistol stoppages, please recognize that pistol mechanical malfunctions can never be predicted, and that when they do occur, they usually cannot be remedied on the spot. That is why we extol the virtues of buying quality handguns that have proven track records of reliability. That means that you can basically count on a handgun with an excellent reliability record (just as with cars that are rated tops in "Consumer Reports") unless you use Uncle Ferd's WWII ammunition, or the cheapest Soviet product now clogging our marketplace, or if you clean your gun with Uncle Andy's Goiter Compound.

Another pointer is that if you carry a backup gun, you are essentially giving yourself insurance for those rare times when a mechanical malfunction does occur. We realize that many people will never even carry a primary gun let alone a secondary one. But, should *you* choose to carry defensively and legally, you deserve to know and understand your alternatives.

By practicing the above drills with training rounds, you can readily discover if your chosen pistol has any specific inadequacies well before you need to handle them in a combative situation. You can always revise your choice of defensive weapon or make an additional purchase should your primary choice of a defensive firearm be lacking.

Supplemental Sighting Systems

Night Sights. Night sights add between $50 and $100 additional cost to your handgun. They permit you to obtain sighting with a 3-dot glow in limited lighting conditions. They will usually last for 7 to 10 years without malfunction. Their advantage is that they allow you to use your front sight at night or in the dark to acquire your target quickly. However, they do not provide target identification; just quick target acquisition. Therefore, they are no substitute for being sure of your target which is still going to be in the dark. Good flashlight equipment supplemental to night sights are therefore an additional tactical advantage.

Tactical Flashlights. We cannot affirm emphatically enough how effective tactical flashlight products by both Streamlight and Mag Instrument Corporation ("Maglites") are in strengthening your defensive capabilities in a tactical situation. It is our personal and professional opinion however, that the tactical use of the flashlight at night, most specifically in a home defense situation, is best accomplished by NOT having the flashlight attached to your gun. Having a continual, static light beam emanating from your gun makes you a target *unless* the manufacturer has built in a switch which permits you to toggle the high intensity light beam on and off intermittently. Then you can toggle the light on briefly to acquire your target and turn it off again so as not to become the target. Each time you toggle the light on and off, you have to move and use cover and concealment. However, the location and design of the toggle switch on the rail-mounted tactical flashlight *must* enable you to operate it with your support hand without changing your grip on your weapon. This is critical. Remember that under the stress of a life or death situation, fine motor coordination is one of the first things to go.

If you are going to use a rail-mounted, high intensity tactical illuminator, you had better practice with it. Remember: repeated practice imprints a procedure into muscle memory and your subconscious. You are going to have to practice operating the toggle switch so that it becomes automatic and you are going to have to practice defensive moving so as to not give away your position to the bad guy(s).

If a gun-mounted high-intensity illuminator with a toggle switch also incorporated a laser sighting device that you could use or not use (toggle on and off with or without the light illuminator) depending on the circumstances, it would make an even more valuable defensive fighting tool.

Actually, there is such a product on the market, and it is called the "M6 Tactical Laser Illuminator." It is a reliable, high quality product manufactured by a company called Insight Technology, a premier designer of quality white light illumination systems **(Insight Technology.** *3 Technology Drive, Londonderry, NH 03053. Tel: 603-626-4800. Fax: 603-647-7234; www.insight lights.com).*

Use of the M6 can indeed provide a real tactical advantage to a home defender as well as to law enforcement personnel. The product is backed by the company's comprehensive limited warranty. Given that Insight has been around since the 1980's and its products are used by elite law enforcement and military personnel around the world, their commitment to customer satisfaction means something.

The M6 Tactical Laser Illuminator offers a unique, compact, mobile, integrated laser/high-intensity torch light system. It is easily attached to the bottom of your pistol frame's dust cover if your pistol has a rail. If not, Insight makes adapters to fit specific pistols. The M6 has a 4-position Mode Selector switch which allows you to choose one of four laser/light combinations: off position; white flashlight alone; laser alone; or light and laser.

Once you select the mode, you can set the unit's bilateral "rocker on/off switch" to one of two modes: either "steady on" or "momentary." The latter is the toggle option. For "steady on," or continuous operation, you can either push the right side of the rocker switch (on the right side of the trigger guard) *down* with your trigger finger, or you can push the left side of the rocker switch (on the left side of the trigger guard) *up* with your support hand thumb. The switch will stay in the continuous on position and the light will stay on continuously until you return the switch to its neutral position.

For "momentary" or toggle operation, use your trigger finger to push and hold the right side of the rocker switch *up*, or your off hand, support thumb to push and hold the left side of the rocker switch *down*. The light will stay on until you release the upward pressure of your trigger finger on the switch, or if you are using your off thumb, until you release the downward pressure of your off thumb on the switch.

The 3.4 inch long by 1.6 inch wide by 1.9 inch high unit is powered by two 3 volt lithium 123 batteries and has a tungsten halogen, xenon filled lamp. Peak light output is a blindingly bright 90+ lumens and the light has a range of 25 meters. The unit only weighs 3.7 ounces with the batteries.

The light beam can be focused by turning the bezel surrounding the lens until the desired focus is reached. The laser aiming module does need to be zeroed in, or calibrated, for the particular weapon on which the M6 is mounted. The process is simple, and clear instructions are given in the accompanying manual. However, should you have any questions whatsoever, friendly and helpful technical support is readily available during business hours at the company.

Insight also manufactures the M3 Tactical Illuminator which is the light without the laser. Naturally, it is much less costly. Both the M6 and M3 are readily compatible with Glock handguns that have accessory rails, as well as with other popular pistols such as the Beretta Model 92/96 and SIG P226 and P220.

Compact and lightweight, the powerful M3 and M6 both offer fast and clear identification of the target, and the M6 in addition, offers the advantages of a laser—its deterrence effect and the ability in a high stress situation to quickly acquire your target and laser-point shoot. It has been our experience that these devices are useful tactical tools that with adequate practice and preparation, will not hamper shooter performance.

One other thing, the M6 TLI and the M3 attach and detach from your handgun exceptionally fast. This makes them suitable for reacting to split-second-decision-making situations. They are valuable defensive fighting tools to add to your survival strategy that can stack the survival deck in your favor.

With all of that said, a flashlight on your gun makes you a target. You may be able to see the criminal but he can also see you. Many seasoned gun writers and firearms instructors teach tactical flashlight techniques where the flashlight is held in your hand with your handgun or is attached via rails to your gun. All of them emphasize the importance of not remaining static (i.e. keep moving) and of not keeping the light on continuously so as to avoid being a static lit target. Having to turn the light on and off as you move under cover and/or concealment adds another thing to think about and coordinate in a high stress situation,

unless, like Insight Technology's rail-mounted tactical illumina-
tors, the light has an easy-to-access toggle.

We believe that simpler is better, meaning more effective.
That's why we teach and practice the technique of using the
flashlight as a way of bathing the entrance to the room or area
with light keeping the flashlight in front of and pointed away
from you and towards where the aggressor will be coming from.
When you are behind the light, you can see whatever comes up
in front of it. This aids you in target identification and
acquisition and avoids making you a target. Don't enable your
adversary; disable him!

Now, with good tritium night sights as made by Trijicon or
Mepro Light, you can get a better sight picture and alignment
with your target lit up by your flashlight which is positioned
away from you and on him. It also frees your hands from
multiple operations and allows you to maintain proper grip and
control of your firearm. Remember that under the stress of
combat, fine motor coordination is the first to go.

Laser Sighting Systems

We recently tested the LaserMax LMS 1000 Series laser
sighting system. The installation directions are manageable and
easy to follow for a competent firearms person and testing went
without one single problem or glitch.

Experience with this system has taught both of us that it is
a worthy addition to your quality pistol. In fact, when used
properly, it can turn out to be a life saver. Permit us to explain.

For one, the LaserMax makes target acquisition from the
point shoulder position easier and more accurate. Every shot
aimed at the laser dotted target in our range tests, hit within a
2 inch group from our point of aim at 50 feet. That is remarkable
data! As a firearms instructor who has been teaching and
emphasizing front sighting without laser systems for over 30
years, Steve experienced the LaserMax's performance firsthand,
and was very impressed with it.

With the LaserMax installed in our Glock 27 and 23 pistols,
we found our quickness and accuracy increased remarkably in
a very short period of time using point shoulder shooting. We
rolled, ran, jumped, went prone and sat with our laser equipped
Glocks, and the LaserMax performed flawlessly.

It is our evaluation that the LaserMax is a very welcome
addition to any professional who has to be conscious of the
surrounding critical area and crowds. It helps you avoid tunnel
vision on your front sight so that you can be more aware,

responsive, and effective. However, do not make the mistake of thinking that a laser sight can be a substitute for good fundamental shooting skills and technique. It cannot. It is a useful supplement.

It must be pointed out that the LaserMax we tested was an out of the box tool that was not specially strengthened or modified for our tests. We unwrapped it, installed it and shot with it, so we know this to be true.

The LaserMax system configuration is integral to the pistol's operational components. In our tests, the heart of the laser unit replaced the pistol's spring guide rod assembly and takedown lever. It eliminated exterior add-ons that can bulk up the pistol and become easily jarred or snag on holsters or clothing (See Figure 12.8).

Having a laser sight system does not eliminate the necessity of maintaining proper grip, stance, trigger control and follow-through. The LaserMax system which is true to point of aim, given that the laser beam emanates from right below the barrel, does make it unnecessary to aim using front sight alignment. However, you still can shoot using your front

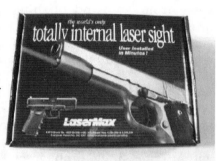

Figure 12.8

sighting if you so choose and your laser beam pinpoint will be right on target confirming the accuracy of your point of aim and your sight alignment. We still recommend sighting and using the laser to confirm accurate sighting if you are aiming for a smaller area such as the criminal's head.

Alternatively, you can just point and shoot. You do this by pointing the beam on an area within the target's center of mass (e.g., the chest). However, to hit accurately, you must be sure to have good grip, steady hand with controlled movement arc (you can see your arc of movement by watching the laser beam's pinpoint), and good trigger control and follow-through.

The advantage to point shooting with the integrated Laser Max as a pointer is that you can more easily and effectively keep your eyes on your adversary. This eliminates tunnel vision.

The Laser Also Serves As A Strong Deterrent! No adversary wants to hang around under the moving pulsating beam of the LaserMax. Hopefully, this deterrent value will make it unnecessary for you to have to be involved in a post-shooting incident. In fact, data from police departments around the country indicate that the use of laser systems does reduce the frequency of police shootings. Criminals are cowards, but many of them are also not stupid!

In addition, the LaserMax system, given its accuracy, provides you with a way of getting instantaneous feedback when you are dry-firing your unloaded snap cap equipped gun for practice. It allows you to develop muscle memory for point shooting and sighting positions. It also helps you see if you are shaking and how much you are jerking the trigger when you are pressing the trigger in firing.

13

People and Guns: Safety and Survival

You will survive when you keep your secrets alive,
And your personal business to yourself.
— The Authors

▶ **Why you should NOT broadcast that you own firearms or that you carry concealed**

It is best NOT to tell people that you own firearms, have training, or if you carry concealed, that you do so. Let's examine why.

First of all, if you broadcast that you own or collect firearms, believe it or not, this could make you a target for burglars intent on stealing your prized possessions. Firearms on the black market are valuable commodities for criminals who can sell them at a premium price to other criminals who cannot purchase a firearm legally.

Therefore, it is prudent to let as few people as possible know that you have a firearm in the house with the exception of your homeowner's insurance agent (your weapons should be insured) and your firearms/self-defense instructor. With these people, you should have a professional, fiduciary relationship which ethically (and in some cases legally) should bind them to keep your personal business confidential. It's privileged information!

What to Broadcast. It is wise to broadcast via stickers on your windows and/or mailbox that you have a home or business security alarm system. This serves as a deterrent. No one will try to steal your burglar alarm system nor could they. Burglars and criminals are opportunists. They would much rather go to a house or business that offers them less of a challenge and chance of getting caught than a house or business that is protected by a security alarm system that is directly connected to the local police department. The system can be configured so that when your burglar alarm goes off, unless you call the security alarm company that monitors your system (or the police) and give a secret code, the police are at your door within minutes to catch the crook.

If you have a dog that functions as a watch dog or guard dog, it is prudent to broadcast this, too, via a sticker on your door and/or windows that says something such as *Beware of Dog*. Having a dog or dogs can be a great alarm and security system!

The Element of Surprise. When it comes to defensive weapons such as firearms and knives, pepper spray, etc., it is best to capitalize on the element of surprise. Always keep potential assailants guessing. Let them deal with the uncertainty of not knowing how or the degree to which you are prepared to respond to a criminal attack. Just broadcast that you are prepared by carrying yourself confidently and remain aware of your immediate environment and your surroundings at all times. And there is no reason why you should not *feel* confident. If you have digested and practiced the material in this book, and you own and know how to operate and maintain handguns, you practice at the range on a regular basis, and especially if you do carry concealed, you will be a formidable defender and opponent to any criminal.

Bear in mind that the element of *surprise* has won many of history's major battles and more importantly wars (e.g., "D-Day" and the invasion of Normandy during World War II and the United States using the atomic bomb on Hiroshima and Nagasaki). A shocked and surprised opponent is a weaker and ultimately a defeated opponent. Make sure that you are prepared for any contingency and make sure that anyone who dares to attack you is surprised and defeated.

We never let anyone know how or with what we are armed, how or where we are carrying, and to what extent we are armed. The elements of unpredictability and surprise are always on our side. Therefore, it behooves you to learn different carry modes, different self-defensive techniques, and the use of different defensive weapons. Don't just rely on one thing. It behooves you to vary what you carry and do, just as you should vary your routines and routes, to keep people guessing. If potential evil doers think you are predictable and you are not, that is okay too. The surprise will be where it should be—on them!

The Defensive Attitude

All the worst elements of human behavior are implemented by an offender during a criminal attack. It would be great to believe that all of us would respond in kind for our personal survival, but in many cases, that just isn't so. Survival must be a self-taught methodology, a practiced determined motivation and attitude that begins today.

Having to face a criminal and violent aggressor is a frequent street occurrence for many non-combative and peace-loving individuals who live in different environments. Having to face a violent criminal intent on making you his prey while you maintain a normal human value system is impractical and unrealistic. Many of us have grown up in a world without this everyday street dilemma. Our emphasis is not to turn you into a common street fighter, but rather an individual, who being exposed to the worst of humanity, muddles through by appropriately realistic thought, action and feelings.

The message is SURVIVAL. The means is by any you can employ to accomplish SURVIVAL without relinquishing your life. So, dig in. Use your training and equipment to the best of your abilities, and continue to develop your defensive abilities. When confronted by an aggressive criminal, respond with greater vengeance and neutralize the aggressor's power and tactics. Remember that surviving a criminal assault is all about POWER. You keep it. Practice and follow your personal defense training methods and survive.

Adapt a defensive attitude and lifestyle. That means being prepared for anything that might arise. It doesn't mean being paranoid, but it does mean being wary and suspicious. Let people earn your trust through their actions. Don't divulge unnecessary information to anyone. Give people information on a *need to know basis*. As Marlon Brando, playing Don Corleone, said to his sons in the movie version of Mario Puzo's "The Godfather," *Don't let other people know what you are thinking.*

When you let people know what you are thinking, you give them an extra edge to use against you, if they have reason to, because they have a better idea about how you are going to respond if they do *X*. Now, of course, we are not referring to intimate trusting relationships, although even there one can get hurt and be surprised how, years later, information you once freely gave can be used against you.

However, the good news is that people can change. So, if you have made the mistake of sharing information about yourself that you later regret, you can keep in mind what you divulged and always change your responses in the future should the need arise. In that way, you still have the element of surprise in your favor. People are much less predictable than are animals or plants. So, if you feel that you have projected yourself in a less than desirable way up until now, you can start acting and feeling differently from this moment on! This can even work in your favor. If criminal or sociopathic elements think you are an easy mark, boy, can you have a surprise ready for them!

Concealed Carry

The reason why there are *concealed carry* laws is that when you have a permit or license to carry a deadly weapon such as a firearm you do not want to broadcast to the world that you are armed and dangerous. First of all, this can make you a target as we stated earlier. There are foolish people who just might want to take the weapon from you. So, *concealed* means concealed— hidden, out of sight, masked and obscured. Your weapon/s must not be blatantly displayed. At the least, they should not even be obvious to a trained eye; that is, they shouldn't "print" through your clothing.

Secondly, other people do not know that you are licensed to carry and that you are a law-abiding citizen who is carrying for self-protection. Did you know that when you carry a gun, as a law-abiding citizen, you have a legal and ethical obligation, to know what you are doing? That means you must know how to effectively and safely operate your weapon and you must always be safety conscious.

Whether you are a legally armed citizen carrying a weapon or even a plainclothes cop who is not in a police uniform, no one else will know that you have a concealed carry permit or that you are a cop. You will scare people if they see your gun. They may think that you are a criminal or a nut. This could lead them to mistakenly do something stupid or deadly. It could even get you killed! At the least, it could lead to a lot of embarrassment when you are told to put your hands up and drop to the floor by several shotgun-wielding police officers called to the scene.

Furthermore, while it could be argued that it is desirable to let people know that you carry, so that they will think twice about messing with you, the truth is quite the opposite. People are likely to think that you are paranoid or worse, a nut. They are likely to avoid you, and at the first sign of trouble, suspect that you are to blame.

In conclusion...

Do not let people know that you own guns or that you carry!

▶ **What should you do if you've been involved in a defensive shooting?**

You are justified in using lethal force in self-defense of your life or someone else's *only if* **you feared for your life or the life of the other person**. The law does not require you to submit and die if someone launches a violent attack against you, or threatens to do so imminently. The imminent or immediate threat of grave bodily harm is recognized as adequate and defensible justification for employing lethal force to save yourself from an attacker.

If you've been forced to use lethal force in defense of your life, do not expect the aftermath to be easy. The legal system can operate in cruel and twisted ways. You must be prepared to continue your self-defense even after your physical attacker has been stopped.

Here are some guidelines for defending yourself if you have been involved in a shooting incident:

1. **Make sure your attacker is no longer a threat.** Once you are completely sure that your attacker no longer is a threat to you, you should check yourself for injuries. Then, visually secure your attacker's weapon, but *do not tamper with any evidence at the scene*. **If at all possible, without compromising your safety, assuming the possibility of accomplices or neighbors sympathetic to the downed perpetrator and who are not concerned with the truth or your survival, you must maintain all the elements of the crime scene intact until the arrival of the police**.

   If you feel that your life is still in danger in light of possible further threats, then you must do whatever you have to do to assure your survival. Retreat if possible. However, you must also take whatever action you in the moment deem necessary to prevent the perpetrator's weapon from being subsequently used against you.

2. **Call "911" or the local police.** Call "911" or the local police ASAP. Report what has taken place and where you are located. Ask for emergency medical assistance. Do NOT give

too many details over the phone that can be misinterpreted and misused!

3. **Secure your weapon.** Put away your own weapon and keep it out of sight. You do not want the police when they arrive to mistake you for a perpetrator! Do as the police tell you to do. Don't argue with them or question them! Expect to be treated as a suspect. The police will be doing their job and that means they have to secure the scene, sort things out, and make a report.

4. **Call an attorney to represent you.** You should make no statements to the police or anyone else until your attorney is present. This is just good common sense. It is your constitutional right to remain silent and not say anything that can be misconstrued, taken out of context, distorted, and held against you!

5. **Get appropriate medical treatment.** When the paramedics or EMTs arrive, get medical treatment for yourself and anyone else that was involved in the incident. If you are lucky enough not to have been physically injured, you still will be experiencing an "acute stress reaction" or "psychogenic shock." Recognize that this is a *normal* reaction to an abnormal and extraordinary event in which you faced the possibility of death.

6. **Stay away from the news media!** Whatever else you do or don't do, stay away from the news media. They are looking for a story pure and simple. They have no authority and you do not have to talk to them. Let your attorney make any statements for you.

7. **Do NOT apologize for what happened!** Do not apologize or express regrets for what happened. Such statements will wrongly be interpreted as an admission of guilt, and if you acted purely in self-defense, you are guilty of nothing. In a court of law, where you can expect to end up eventually, such statements will be used against you.

8. **Seek appropriate psychological support.** Related to #5, seek appropriate post-critical incident psychological support, and if necessary, treatment to help you deal with the *acute traumatic stress*. Expect to experience acute traumatic stress

symptoms which can include: **cognitive symptoms** such as confusion, disorientation, and memory loss; a peculiar (but normal) sense of detachment (technically termed "dissociation"); **emotional symptoms** such as feelings of guilt, sadness, anxiety, and panic; and **physical symptoms** such as shaking, palpitations, hyper-irritability and jumpiness, restlessness, sleeplessness, nausea, diarrhea, headaches, pain of one kind or another, and an exacerbation or aggravation of any ongoing chronic medical symptoms you may already have.

Having such a reaction and experiencing such symptoms are normal. If you do not seek appropriate help, they will only get worse. So, make sure to seek appropriate help from a qualified, licensed mental health professional with experience in treating post-traumatic stress, such as a licensed psychologist, clinical social worker, psychiatrist or pastoral or mental health counselor.

14

Top Quality Manufacturers

For your convenience, in this chapter, we provide manufacturers whose products are discussed in this text. Many of these companies supported our project from its inception. Top individuals in these companies took valuable time out to be available to explain their products and assist us in our research. They also were willing to provide us with the opportunity to evaluate some of their selected products.

Every manufacturer listed in this text produces quality, durable, reliable and affordable products that can make the difference between surviving or not. They all take this commitment very seriously.

Most provide excellent customer service. They are responsive, easy to get a live person on the telephone, and in most cases have clear web sites and product literature.

Tactical Flashlight Manufacturers

Mag Instrument, Inc.
1950 South Sterling Avenue, Ontario, CA 91761
Tel: 909-947-1006 - Fax: 909-947-3116
www.maglite.com
Affordable, quality high illumination, tactical flashlights ranging from miniature carryables to giants that you can also use as a club and a re-chargeable system.

Streamlight
30 Eagleville Road, Eagleville, PA 19403
Tel: 800-523-7488 - Fax: 800-220-7007
www.streamlight.com
Cutting edge company with a large line of high illumination, tactical flashlights of various sizes and configurations.

Pepper Spray Manufacturers

Spitfire
8868 Research Blvd., Suite 203
Austin, TX 78758
Tel: 800-SPITFIRE - Fax: 512-453-7504
www.1800spitfire.com
    Manufactures a powerful and effective pepper spray product deterrent that is ergonomically dispensed.

Firearms Manufacturers

Beretta U.S.A. Corporation
17601 Beretta Drive, Accokeek, MD 20607
Tel: 301-283-2191 / 800-636-3420 - Fax: 301-375-7677
www.berettausa.com
    Beretta is the oldest existing firearms manufacturer in the world. They have a full product line that is extensive and reliable. Their line of .22 (21A Bobcat) and .32 caliber (3032 Tomcat) sub-compact pocket pistols are affordable and very carryable. They also offer a full line of full-size, medium and compact, large caliber pistols.

Glock Inc. USA
6000 Highlands Parkway, Smyrna, GA 30082
Tel: 770-432-1202 - Fax: 770-433-8719
www.glock.com
    Durability, accuracy, simplicity and reliability are synonymous with the name, Glock. Glock was the first designer of polymer firearms in the early 1980's and this has since become the standard throughout the firearms industry. A wide variety of calibers and pistol sizes (subcompact, compact, full-size, and full-size target/competition) exist throughout the Glock line to suit anyone's defensive, law enforcement, competitive needs.

Heckler & Koch
21480 Pacific Blvd., Sterling, VA 20166
Tel: 703-450-1900 - Fax: 703-450-8160
www.hecklerkoch-usa.com
    Manufacturer of pistols having all the bells and whistles and also highly functional and effective, defensive and combat-ready weapons. Accuracy, fit and finish are impeccable. In addition, the company supports and enhances their products with professional firearms training programs.

Kahr Arms
P.O. Box 220, Blauvelt, NY 10913
Tel: 845-353-7770 - Fax: 845-353-7833
www.kahr.com
　　Kahr Arms has designed a line of small subcompact, defensive pistols (the MK9 in 9mm and MK40 in 40 S&W series) with excellent machining and care to detail.

　　With the acquisition of Auto Ordnance, Kahr's product line has expanded to single action 1911 .45 ACP caliber pistols as well as the famous Thompson semi-automatic .45 caliber carbines.

Kel-Tec CNC Industries, Inc.
1485 Cox Road, Cocoa, FL 32926
Tel: 321-631-0068 - Fax: 321-631-1169
www.kel-tec.com
　　Affordable, quality pistols. Manufactures the .32 caliber P-32 pocket pistol and the P-11 9mm pocket pistol—a semi-automatic, locked breech pistol that is one of the smallest and lightest made. All products are warranted for life.

Kimber Manufacturing Company
2590 Highway 35, Kalispell, MT 59901
Tel: 800-880-2418 - Fax: 406-758-2223
www.kimberamerica.com
　　Manufactures 1911s in the classic full-size and in various subcompact and compact sizes. The Kimber 1911 pistols have all the bells and whistles while remaining highly functional and effective. Their accuracy, fit and finish are superb.

North American Arms
2150 South 950 East, Provo, UT 84606
Tel: 800-821-5783 - Fax: 801-374-9998
www.naaminis.com
　　Produces effective, highly concealable, criminally resistant, quality firearms. N.A.A. offer numerous customization options in terms of sight systems, grips and holster choices. Guardian .32 and .380 caliber sub-compact pocket pistols—sleek, sturdy, reliable, accurate and affordable. Also offer their famous line of mini-revolvers in .22 LR and .22 magnum, as well as a black powder version.

L.W. Seecamp Company
301 Brewster Road, Milford, CT 06460
Tel: 203-877-7926 - Fax: 203-877-3429
　　Makes superior small pocket pistols. The L.W. Seecamp Company has been manufacturing the basic design of the

Seecamp LWS .32 ACP handgun since the company's establish-ment in 1973. It remains unchanged with the exception of a caliber upgrade from .25 ACP since around 1981. Among the pistol's many unique features is the following safety aspect: when the magazine is removed, the trigger is blocked and the slide cannot be pulled rearward far enough to hand-chamber a round.

Larry Seecamp is totally committed to producing a quality defensive weapon. Each gun produced receives personal and careful attention before it leaves the factory. As such, it is highly unlikely for a gun with defects to leave the Seecamp factory after their extensive reliability and performance checks.

SIGARMS

18 Industrial Drive, Exeter, NH 03833
Tel: 603-772-2302 - Fax: 603-772-4795
www.sigarms.com

SIGARMS manufactures high quality .380 ACP, 9mm, 40 S&W .357 SIG and .45 ACP semiautomatic pistols, and is the producer of the famous SIG Sauer series. Their firearms have a well deserved reputation for superior quality and engineering. Reliability and accuracy of SIG pistols are outstanding.

SIGARMS also runs a highly reputable firearms training academy at their site in Exeter, New Hampshire.

Smith and Wesson

2100 Roosevelt Avenue, Springfield, MA 01104
Tel: 800-331-0852 - Fax: 413-747-3317
www.smith-wesson.com

Extensive product line of revolvers and semi-automatic pistols. Smith's prices are fair and products are impeccable. Each S&W revolver we tested had superior actions and accuracy. Fit and finish were excellent and light years ahead of any competition. Their professional training academy and armorer school in Springfield, Massachusetts, is deservedly world-renowned.

Their collaborations with Walther of Germany has also contributed fine pocket pistol designs.

Sturm, Ruger & Company

200 Ruger Road, Prescott, AZ 86301
Tel: 928-541-8820 / 888-220-1173
www.ruger-firearms.com

Ruger's product line is extensive. They make quality, durable and high strength revolvers and semi-automatic pistols in the medium price range.

Ruger is also known for the emphasis the company has always placed on firearms safety education and awareness campaigns.

Ammunition Manufacturers

Federal Cartridge Company
900 Ehlen Drive, Anoka, MN 55303-7503
Tel: 800-322-2342 - Fax: 763-323-2506
www.federalcartridge.com

High quality manufacturer of an extensive line of quality ammunition in a whole range of calibers. Designed to make your defensive weapon work to its fullest potential.

Federal "Hydra-Shok" rounds are unique because of their function oriented construction. They have a notched post situated in the center of the hollow point cavity which is surrounded by a notched metal jacket.

Customer service and accountability is excellent.

Fiocchi USA
6930 N. Fremont Road, Ozark, Missouri
Tel: 417-725-4118 - Fax: 417-725-1039
www.fiocchiusa.com

Fiocchi USA manufactures and sells affordable, quality ammunition in all of the major calibers. Fiocchi imports ammunition from its parent company, Fiocchi of Italy, for sale in the United States. Products sold through authorized distributors and dealers.

Product line includes: full metal jacket training ammunition; jacketed hollow point duty and defensive ammunition; shotgun birdshot, buckshot, and slugs; frangible and non-toxic pistol ammunition, and rifle ammunition. Many of the calibers feature full metal jackets and hollow point bullets of the same weight which "allows shooters to practice with economical FMJ's and switch to defense or duty use with little or no change in point of aim/point of impact."

Remington Arms Company, Inc.
870 Remington Drive, P.O. Box 700
Madison, NC 27025-0700
Tel: 1-800-243-9700   Fax: 1-336-548-7801
www.remington.com

Remington's Golden Saber Brass Jacketed Hollow Point (BJHP) handgun ammunition may be one of the most technologically advanced self-defense cartridge designs manufactured today. The cartridge is constructed to ensure that, after the bullet is launched, its jacket and core remain locked together for maximum weight retention and core/jacket integrity. The brass jacket encasing the Golden Saber's hollow point bullet also has a unique design -- the cuts on the bullet jacket's nose go completely through the jacket for better initiation of mushrooming on penetration of flesh and tissue.

Reduced bullet nose diameter directly ahead of the bullet's "driving band", as with a bottle-necked cartridge, promotes precise bore alignment, for reduced barrel friction and enhanced ballistic accuracy. The cartridge's nickel plated case also promotes enhanced reliability in different types of handguns, and the powders used are treated to suppress muzzle flash. Finally, the primers are triple inspected during the manufacturing process for improved reliability.

Golden Saber in .38 Special is empowered by a 125 grain +p bullet. In 9mm, it is offered with 124 grain, 124 grain +p, and 147 grain bullets. In .40 S&W, Golden Saber comes in 165 and 180 grain, and in .45 ACP, it comes in 185 grain, 185 grain +p, and 230 grain.

Speer Gold Dot Federal Cartridge Company
900 Ehlen Drive, Anoka, MN 55303-7503
Tel: 800-322-2342 - Fax: 763-323-2506
Technical information: Tel: 800-627-3640
www.speer-bullets.com

Speer "Gold Dots" are a precisely engineered quality jacketed hollow point self-defense round that delivers superior per-formance in accuracy, expansion and penetration across the range of calibers. Speer's "Uni-Cor" manufacturing process bonds the jacket to the core, thus minimizing core/jacket separations which are a common cause of handgun bullet failures. Speer Ammunition is owned by the same quality company that owns Federal.

Winchester Ammunition
East Alton, IL 62024
Tel: 877-838-3700
www.winchester.com

Founded in 1866, the company manufactures a very extensive line of ammunition for all calibers and types of firearms. Two of their best known defensive rounds are their Winchester "Super-X Silvertips" and "Supreme SXT" handgun ammunition. Can be counted on to provide reliable functioning, good accuracy, controlled recoil, optimum penetration and uniform bullet expansion.

"Custom" Holster Makers

Ahern Enterprises
P.O. Box 186, Commerce, GA 30529
Tel: 706-335-5715 - Fax: 706-335-6259

Jerry Ahern is a multi-talented individual. He makes reliable, affordable and functional "custom" holsters. His designs are unique and worth checking out. Manufactures everything to order. Specializes in: pocket holsters (the "Pocket Natural") for any handgun that can be carried in the front or hip pocket; clip-on inside the waistband rigs, belt slides and scabbards, cross-draws, inside the waistband and pocket magazine pouches, and "deep concealment" rigs.

Aker International
2248 Main Street, Ste 6, Chula Vista, CA 91911
Tel: 800-645-AKER - Fax: 619-423-1363
www.akerleather.com

Quality holster manufacturer with excellent and prompt customer service. They make an extensive line of concealed carry and duty gear. Makes and sells great pocket holsters for the pocket pistols. Especially useful is their pocket holster with the wallet flap that prevents printing through your pocket.

Alessi Leather
2467 Niagara Falls Blvd., Amherst, NY 14228
Tel: 716-691-5615 - Fax: 716-691-5639

Lou Alessi is a master leather holster craftsman extraordinaire who has been making quality custom holsters for over 30 years. Makes ultra-fine holsters for concealed carry use by people around the country who know and desire quality.

The "Pocket Pro", "Close Quarter Covert-Inside the Pants" (CQC-I), CQC-S, "Rough Out Pocket Holster", "Talon Clip-On IWB Holster" are some of the holsters made here.

Bell Charter Oak, Inc.
P.O Box 198, Gilbertsville, NY 13776
Tel: 607-783-2483
www.bellcharteroakholsters.com

Quality custom holster manufacturer that hand bench crafts and hand tools each holster. Each holster is functional, attractive and molded to a specific firearm. Also offers a full line of belt slides and belt scabbards for semi-autos and revolvers.

Derry Gallagher Custom Holsters
P.O. Box 720536, McAllen, Texas 78504
Phone/Fax: 956-686-5109
www.dgallagherholsters.com
    A highly recommended master holster maker. Each holster is gun specific and custom-made to your preferred angle.
    The **"ADS Scabbard"** and the **"Tuckable"** are concealable holsters made by Derry Gallagher.

K.L. Null Holsters
161 School Street NW,
Hill City Station, Resaca, GA 30735
Tel: 706-625-5643 - Fax: 706-625-9392
www.klnullholsters.com
    Manufactures carefully engineered, efficient, unique concealment holsters and accessories of exceptional quality and wearability, flawlessly hand-crafted and wet-molded with the actual handgun using the highest quality leather.

Milt Sparks Holsters
605 E. 44th Street, #2, Boise, ID 83714
Tel: 208-377-5577 - Fax: 208-376-7386
www.miltsparks.com
    Quality custom holster manufacturer producing practical designs. Continuously evaluates their products through their own activities in training, competition and everyday use, and through customer feedback.

Mitch Rosen Extraordinary Gunleather, LLC
300 Bedford St, Manchester, NH 03101-1102
Tel: 603-647-2971 - Fax 603-647-2973
www.mitchrosen.com
    Manufacture and sell direct custom leather concealment holsters, gun belts, and accessories. Also produces an "Express Line" of fine holsters that are very affordable and are much quicker to get. All of Mitch Rosen's rigs have superb fit and finish.

Tauris Holsters
Michael P. Taurisano, 3695 Mohawk Street,
New Hartford, N.Y. 13413
Tel: 315-737-9115
www.taurisholsters.com
    All holsters are handmade by Mike. His holsters offer quick gun access, excellent weapon retention for safety, and superior ease of re-holstering. They are hand wet-molded, with a formed sight channel, covered trigger guard and exactly fitted belt

tunnel or slots. He offers an unconditional guarantee on materials and workmanship. Makes the "Double Strap 'Low Profile' In The Pants Holster" and his "Convertible ITP/Hip Holster."

High Quality Larger Scale Holster Manufacturers

Action-Direct
14285 SW 142nd Street, Miami, FL 33186
Tel: 800-667-4191
www.action-direct.com
    Action-Direct manufactures and sells over 16 concealed carry products as well as functional synthetic or leather pocket holsters. Excellent customer service. Best known for their rig called the "Defender."

Bianchi International
100 Calle Cortez, Temecula, CA 92590
Tel: 800-477-8545 - Fax: 909-676-6777
www.bianchi-intl.com
    Bianchi International makes a wide variety of holsters for concealment and law enforcement. One of our favorite inside the waistband (IWB) holsters is their Model 38 Pistol Pocket. Comfortable even for wear while driving, the "Pistol Pocket" slips into your waistband and secures to your belt with two one-way snaps. The belt loop is attached to the holster with a swivel so the holster can be adjusted to five carry angles or cants. Their products are impeccable and their customer service outstanding.

Coronado Leather
1059 Tierra Del Rey, Suite C. Chula Vista, CA 91910
Tel: 800-283-9509 - Fax: 619-216-9338
www.coronadoleather.com
    Leading manufacturer of over thirty quality, handcrafted concealment products with a superior line of waist packs, such as their "Stealth Pac" and "Mini-Belt Pack." Best known for attractive leather outer wear that comes with inner holster pockets. All of their products are innovative, functional and designed with safety in mind.

DeSantis Holster and Leather Goods
P.O. Box 2039, New Hyde Park, NY 11040
Tel: 800-GUNHIDE - Fax: 516-354-7501
www.desantisholster.com

Quality Holsters, great affordability, excellent gun retention and security with a very quick draw . Makes the "Nemesis" line of ambidextrous pocket holsters. They are made of a viscous, sticky material so the holster positively does not come out of your pocket when you draw your pocket pistol!

Don Hume Leathergoods
P.O. Box 351, Miami, OK 74355
Tel: 800-331-2686
www.donhume.com

Don Hume makes positively one of the best clip-on inside the waistband (IWB) leather holsters in the world, the Model H715-M and H715-MT.B (with thumb break safety strap). Model PCCH IWB with snap belt loops is also extraordinary. It is functional, attractive, durable, reliable and affordable. They make it for most of the popular models of pistols (subcompacts, compacts and full-sized) and small revolvers. Check out their web site and peruse their full line of quality, affordable concealed carry and duty sidearm holsters. Their customer service is exemplary.

FIST, Inc.
35 York St, Brooklyn, NY 11201
800-443-3478
www.fist-inc.com

Manufacture and sell one of the best leather paddle holsters we've seen or used. Also has a very unique cross-draw leather holster that can easily be used as a driving holster. Their product line includes very durable and extremely thin and light-weight kydex, inside the waistband clip-on holsters. These include a "deep cover" model that can be hidden by the wearer's shirt. Most of their holsters are available in both kydex or leather.

Galco International
2019 West Quail Ave, Phoenix, AZ 85027
Tel: 800-874-2526 - Fax: 800-737-1725
www.usgalco.com

Manufactures and sells a wide range of very attractive, functional, high quality holsters.

Gould & Goodrich Leather
709 East McNeil Street, Lillington, NC 27546
Tel: 800-277-0732 - Fax: 910-893-4742
www.gouldusa.com
Offers Southern hospitality and charm along with their excellent customer service and full line of holster, belt and other leather accessories that are extremely high quality, functional, innovative, attractive and exceptionally comfortable.

High Noon Holsters
P.O. Box 2138, Palm Harbor, FL 34682
Tel: 727-786-7528
www.highnoonholsters.com
Excels in innovative, functional holster rig designs to choose from. Their designs include the "Hidden Impact", the "Down Unders" and the "Tail Gunner". Also makes the very unique "Pocket Grabber" line with the "Pocket Reload." In addition they offer some great leather belt scabbards, belt slides, and paddle holsters for various size and model handguns.

Michaels of Oregon (a.k.a. "Uncle Mike's")
P.O. Box 1690, Oregon City, OR 97045
Tel: 800-845-2444 - Fax: 503-655-7546
www.uncle-mikes.com
Makes excellent, affordable, and highly recommended holster products for the concealed carry civilian and the law enforcement sectors. Their customer service is exceptional.

Stellar Rigs
PO Box 22132, West Palm Beach, FL 33416
Tel. 561-616-5015
(www.stellarrigs.com)
Makes pocket holsters that are extremely lightweight, thin, and functional. Prevents printing of the gun in your pocket, provides excellent retention and security, keeps your pistol upright for quick acquirement, and provides for a smooth draw.

Handgun Accessories

Barami Corporation "Barami Hip-Grip"
P.O. Box 252224, West Bloomfield, MI 48325
Tel: 248-738-0462 - Fax: 248-738-2542
www.hipgrip.com
Barami makes the "Hip-Grip" which has been around for a long time for good reason. It makes it possible for you to comfortably and conveniently carry your snub-nose revolver inside your waistband without a holster and with **great con-**

cealment. The pair of hip-grips in a set replace the original grips on your revolver. The right grip panel has an extension that flares away from the frame slightly creating a surface that when inserted inside the waistband, securely hooks over it. This is an excellent product that can be used with J and K frame Smiths (round and square butt), and small Colt, Taurus, Charter 2000 and Rossi revolvers. The Barami is very concealable, which is a very important consideration. We strongly recommend this product, and especially like it for a concealed carry of Smith snubbies.

Crimson Trace Corporation
8089 SW Cirrus Dr., Beaverton, OR 97008
Tel: 800-442-2406 - Fax: (503) 627-0166
www.crimsontrace.com
   Crimson Trace manufactures one of the best laser products on the market in the form of replacement grips for your defensive handgun. The grips contain the laser. When you establish your firing grip with these on your handgun, the laser is activated, the laser comes on, and this facilitates instant target acquisition and pinpoint accuracy. Extremely easy to use and instinctive, it's essentially point and shoot. Therefore, this tool is also effective in low light situations when you cannot see your front sight. The laser has also proven to be a powerful deterrent allowing de-escalation in potential lethal-force encounters. Further, installing this product on your handgun permits use as a visual training tool for improving trigger control and accuracy. Crimson Trace's clear, bright, long-lasting laser beam puts you on target at the speed of light so you can shott faster and more precise in a defensive situation.

Pearce Grips
P.O. Box 40367, Fort Worth, TX 76140
Tel: 800-390-9420 - Fax: 817-568-9707
www.pearcegrip.com
   This is the company that makes quality grip extensions for the Glock and other semi-automatic pistols.

Pachmayr Grips
Lyman Products Corporation
475 Smith Street, Middletown, CT 06457
Tel: 800-423-9704 - Fax: 860-632-1699
www.lymanproducts.com
   This is the company that produces high quality rubber pistol and revolver grips that will absorb the recoil instead of your hand absorbing it. These grip replacements for those that come out of the box with your new handgun will especially be useful

if you have a high caliber pistol or revolver with a lot of recoil—they will dampen it. Also, if your handgun has small or uncomfortable grips, you should be able to find a Pachmayr replacement that will make the grip more comfortable and your gun more pleasant to shoot. This is a reliable company that stands behind all of its products and provides excellent and prompt customer service.

LaserMax

3495 Winton Place, Bldg. B, Rochester, NY 14623
Tel: 585-272-5420 - Fax: 585-272-5427
www.lasermax-inc.com

LaserMax is a reliable, customer oriented company that produces a quality laser sighting system for Glocks, SIGs, and other quality semi-automatic pistols. The company's motto is that your gun equipped with their laser *"stops suspects dead in their tracks without firing a shot."* We agree that the sight of the pulsating pinpoint laser beam pointed on any criminal intent on doing no good will quickly give him the motivation to think again. This deterrent effect obviously is a good thing.

The LaserMax is not for beginners to shooting. It will not substitute for well learned and practiced skills. However, in the hands of the experienced shooter, it will facilitate aiming accuracy and rapid target acquisition, both indoors and outdoors, and from dusk to dawn. In our test systems for our Glock 27 and 23 models, the system replaced our pistols' factory guide rod spring assembly inside the barrel. It could not be knocked out of alignment just as the company's advertising states. We found it easy to install and then easy to turn on and off (the "on-off switch" is incorporated in the Glock's takedown lever).

We feel that the LaserMax is also useful for honing one's "instinctive" shoulder point shooting skills and for dry-firing practice. We highly recommend LaserMax.

Tyler Manufacturing & Distribution Company

P.O. Box 94845, Oklahoma City, OK 73143
Tel: 800-654-8415
www.t-grips.com; www.kaeskorner.com

Tyler is the manufacturer and distributor of the famous "Tyler T-Grip Adapter" that extends and adapts your revolver's grip to your hand to eliminate recoil and improve your shooting comfort. It extends your revolver's "grip-ability" and hence, its shootability. It works especially well with the Barami "Hip-Grip."

Safes

American Security Products Company
AMSEC: 11925 Pacific Avenue, Fontana, CA 92337
Tel: 800-421-6142
www.amsecusa.com

AMSEC manufactures an extensive line of heavy-duty, quality gun safes and handgun strong boxes such as the portable "Pistol Packer." Their products range from safes of moderate size and weight (starting at 375 pounds) to heavy weight behemoths that require a tractor trailer to move in or out. Owning an AMSEC permits you to safely secure all of your firearms in Fort Knox in your own home.

DAC Technologies
1601 West Park Drive, Suite 4-C
Little Rock, AR 72204
Tel: 800-920-0098 - Fax: 501-661-9108
www.dactec.com

DAC manufactures portable, affordable, battery-powered, quick-opening digital gun safes that can comfortably hold up to 4 medium-sized handguns and spare magazines or ammo. These safes are easy to conceal and are built to last. They will allow you to safely secure your handguns away from those who shouldn't get near them, but they won't break the piggy bank!

Organizations

Gun Owners of America
8001 Forbes Place, Springfield, VA 22151
Tel: 703-321-8585
http://gunowners.org

Gun Owners of America is the foremost national membership organization in the ongoing battle to protect our Second Amendment freedom, to keep and bear arms. GOA lobbies for the pro-gun rights position in Washington and is also involved in firearm issues in the states. GOA's work includes providing legal assistance to those involved in lawsuits with the BATF.

GOA's Executive Director and Founder, Larry Pratt, is an author, editor, columnist, scholar, syndicated radio talk show host, and former state representative. Through his energetic leadership, GOA operates on multiple levels to preserve American citizens' gun rights. The **GOA Political Victory Fund** raises funds to support the election of pro-gun candidates at all levels of government. **Gun Owners of California** operates solely in California where it was founded by Senator Bill Richardson to address the pivotal gun rights issues in that state. **Gun Owners**

Foundation is the research arm of GOA. Its activities include sponsoring seminars to inform the public, legislators, the media and government officials about key issues affecting the Second Amendment. GOF also publishes books, articles, and a newsletter concerning gun issues as they impact people throughout the world in their pursuit of liberty and freedom.

International Defensive Pistol Association
IDPA: 2232 CR 719, Berryville, AR 72616
Tel: 870-545-3886 - Fax: 870-545-3894
www.idpa.com
IDPA is dedicated to the promotion and perpetuation of defensive pistol shooting as a viable sport.

"Defensive pistol shooting is quite simply the use of practical equipment including full charge service ammunition to solve simulated 'real world' self-defense scenarios. Shooters competing in Defensive Pistol events are required to use practical handguns and holsters that are truly suitable for self-defense use. No 'competition only' equipment is permitted in Defensive Pistol matches since the main goal is to test the skill and ability of an individual, not his or her equipment or gamesmanship." (from the IDPA Web site, 2002)

IDPA provides practical shooters with a forum for competing with their practical equipment (their service sidearms or concealable carry weapons and concealed carry holsters) employing practical defensive shooting techniques and courses of fire.

"If you are interested in using truly practical pistols, drawn from practical holsters to solve challenging and exciting defensive shooting problems, then Defensive Pistol is the sport for you."

IDPA promotes and tests the skills and abilities of individuals, not their equipment or gamesmanship. IDPA promotes the safe and proficient use of guns and equipment suitable for self-defense use. It offers a competition forum for standard factory produced service pistols and revolvers which have been customized for carry. IDPA competitive shooting events provide shooters "with practical and realistic courses of fire that simulates potentially life threatening encounters or tests skills that would be required to survive life threatening encounters."

In sum, IDPA promotes a practical shooting sport that allows competitors to concentrate on the development of their defensive shooting skills and that promotes education, safety, and fellowship. IDPA holds friendly, competitive events that offer simulations of actual or possible "real world" confrontations and test both accuracy and speed.

"Physical condition has very little to do with your performance in a Defensive Pistol match."

International Practical Shooting Confederation
IPSC: P.O. Box 972
Oakville, Ontario, Canada L6J 9Z9
Tel: 905-849-6960 - Fax: 905-842-4323
www.ipsc.org

Founded in Missouri in 1976, this international organization is dedicated to the promotion and perpetuation of the competitive sport of safe, accurate, powerful, and fast pistol marksmanship. IPSC sponsors competitive shooting events around the globe.

National Rifle Association of America NRA
11250 Waples Mill Road
Fairfax, VA 22030
Tel: 800-336-7402
www.nra.org

Every gun owner should join the original national organization that is dedicated to firearms education and safety, protecting our gun rights and Second Amendment freedoms, preserving true democracy, and perpetuating the shooting sports. Peruse their web site and consider subscribing to their free e-mail legislative and other alerts.

The NRA publishes a series of instructional guides on firearms and firearms safety that should be in every shooter's personal library for personal reference. These include the following informative publications: *NRA Guide to the Basics of Personal Protection in the Home; Basics of Personal Protection; The Basics of Pistol Shooting; The Basics of Rifle Shooting; The Basics of Shotgun Shooting;* and *Home Firearm Safety.*

15

Recommended References and Reading

Ahern, Jerry (1996). *CCW: Carrying Concealed Weapons: How to Carry Concealed Weapons and Know When Others Are...* Chino Valley, AZ: Blacksmith Corporation Publishers.

Applegate, Col. Rex & Janich, Michael D. (1998). *Bullseyes Don't Shoot Back: The Complete Textbook of Point Shooting for Close Quarters Combat.* Boulder, CO: Paladin Press.

Artwohl, Alexis & Christensen, Loren W. (1997). *Deadly Force Encounters: What Cops Need to Know to Mentally and Physically Prepare for and Survive a Gunfight.* Boulder, CO: Paladin Press.

Ayoob, Massad F. (1980). *In the Gravest Extreme: The Role of the Firearm in Personal Protection.* Concord, NH: Police Bookshelf.

Ayoob, Massad F. (1987). *The Semiautomatic Pistol in Police Service and Self-Defense.* Concord, NH: Police Bookshelf.

Ayoob, Massad F. (1984). *Stressfire.* Concord, NH: Police Bookshelf.

Ayoob, Massad F. (1992). *Stressfire II: Advanced Combat Shotgun.* Concord, NH: Police Bookshelf.

Ayoob, Massad F. (1994). *The Truth About Self Protection.* New York: Bantam Books.

Ayoob, Massad F. (2002). *The Gun Digest Book of Combat Handgunnery (5th Edition).* Iola, WI: Krause Publications.

Barnes, Frank C. (2000). *Cartridges of the World-9th Edition.* Iola, WI: Krause Publications. *The Basics of Pistol Shooting.* (1991). Fairfax, VA: National Rifle Association of America. *The Basics of Rifle Shooting.* (1987). Fairfax, VA: National Rifle Association of America. *The Basics of Shotgun Shooting.* (1985). Fairfax, VA: National Rifle Association of America.

Bass, Joseph L. (1999). *A Little Handbook on the Second Amendment: What the American Aristocracy Doesn't Want You To Know*. Suffolk, VA: The Downhome Enterprise.

Bird, Chris (2000). *The Concealed Handgun Manual: How to Choose, Carry, and Shoot a Gun in Self Defense*. San Antonio, TX: Privateer Publications.

Bloodworth, Trey & Raley, Mike (1998). *Hidden In Plain Sight: A Practical Guide to Concealed Handgun Carry*. Boulder, CO: Paladin Press.

Boatman, Robert H. (2002). *Living With Glocks: The Complete Guide to the New Standard In Combat Handguns*. Boulder, CO: Paladin Press.

Boston T. Party (2002). *Boston's Gun Bible*. Ignacio, CO: Javelin Press.

Branca, Andrew F. (1998). *The Law of Self-Defense: A Guide for the Armed Citizen*. Acton, MA: Operon Security, Ltd.

Cassidy, William (1975). *The Complete Book Of Knife Fighting*. Boulder, CO: Paladin Press.

Cirillo, Jim (1996). *Guns, Bullets, and Gunfights: Lessons and Tales from a Modern-Day Gunfighter*. Boulder, CO: Paladin Press.

Clapp, Wiley (2002). *Concealed Carry: The Shooter's Guide to Selecting Handguns*. Boulder, CO: Paladin Press.

Conlon, Francis M. (2002). *The "How" of Criminal Law*. New York: Looseleaf Law Publications.

Cooper, Jeff (1989). *Principles of Personal Defense*. Boulder, CO: Paladin Press.

Cooper, Jeff (1998). *To Ride, Shoot Straight, and Speak the Truth*. Boulder, CO: Paladin Press.

Crews, Jim (2002). *Some of the Answer, Handgun: An Advanced Handgun Technique Manual*. Stevensville, MN: Jim Crews.

de Becker, Gavin (1997). *The Gift of Fear*. New York: Dell Publishing.

Duran, Phil L. (1999). *Developing the Survival Attitude: A Guide for the New Officer*. New York: Looseleaf Law Publications.

Eimer, Bruce N. & Torem, Moshe T. (2002). *Coping With Uncertainty: 10 Simple Solutions.* Oakland, CA: New Harbinger Publications.

Enos, Brian (1990). *Practical Shooting: Beyond Fundamentals.* Clifton, CO: Zediker Publishing.

Farnam, John S. (1998). *The Farnam Method of Defensive Rifle and Shotgun Shooting.* Boulder, CO: DTI Publications.

Farnam, John S. (2000). *The Farnam Method of Defensive Handgunning.* Boulder, CO: DTI Publications.

Farnam, Vicki and Nicholl, Diane (2003). *Teaching Women to Shoot: A Law Enforcement Instruction Guide.* Boulder, CO: DTI Publications.

Fjestad, S.P. (2002). *Twenty-Third Edition Blue Book of Gun Values.* Minneapolis, MN: Blue Book Publications.

Forker, Bob (2000). *Ammo & Ballistics for Hunters, Shooters, and Collectors.* Long Beach, CA: Safari Press.

Givens, Tom (2000). *Fighting Smarter: A Practical Guide for Surviving Violent Confrontation.* Memphis, TN: Rangemaster.

Grover, Jim (2000). *Street Smarts, Firearms, & Personal Security: Jim Grover's Guide to Staying Alive and Avoiding Crime in the Real World.* Boulder, CO: Paladin Press.

Hayes, Gila (2000). *Effective Defense: The Woman, The Plan, The Gun (2nd Ed.).* Onalaska, WA: The Firearms Academy of Seattle.

Home Firearm Safety. (1990). Fairfax, VA: National Rifle Association of America.

Janich, Michael D. (1993). *Knife Fighting: A Practical Course.* Boulder, CO: Paladin Press.

Kappas, J. Scott (2002). *Traveler's Guide to the Firearm Laws of the Fifty States.* Covington, KY: Traveler's Guide.

Klein, Chuck (1998). *Klein's C.C.W. Handbook: The Requisite For Those Who Carry Concealed Weapons.* St. Louis, MO: Accurate Press.

Klein, Chuck (2004). *Instinct Combat Shooting - 3rd Edition.* New York, Looseleaf Law Publications, Inc.

LaPierre, Wayne & Baker James Jay (2002). *Shooting Straight: Telling the Truth About Guns In America.* Washington D.C.: Regnery Publishing.

Lauck, Dave (1998). *The Tactical 1911: The Street Cop's and SWAT Operator's Guide to Employment and Maintenance.* Boulder, CO: Paladin Press.

Lonsdale, Mark V. (1998). *Advanced Weapons Training for Hostage Rescue Teams.* Los Angeles, CA: S.T.T.U.

Lott, John R. (2000). *More Guns, Less Crime: Understanding Crime and Gun Control Laws.* Chicago, IL: University of Chicago Press.

Lott, John R. (2003). *The Bias Against Guns: Why Almost Everything You've Heard About Gun Control Is Wrong.* Washington D.C.: Regnery Publishing.

Lovette, Ed (2002). *The Snubby Revolver: The ECQ, Backup, and Concealed Carry Standard.* Boulder, CO: Paladin Press.

Lovette, Ed & Spaulding, Dave (2005). *Defensive Living - 2nd Edition: Preserving Your Personal Safety Through Awareness, Attitude & Armed Action* New York: Looseleaf Law Publications.

Marshall, Evan P. & Sanow, Edwin J. (1992). *Handgun Stopping Power: The Definitive Study.* Boulder, CO: Paladin Press.

Mattera, John (1998). *Up to Speed: A Practical Guide to Handguns and How to Use Them.* Oxford, Mississippi: Zediker Publishing.

Moses, Steve (2002). *Carbine and Shotgun Speed Shooting.* Boulder, CO: Paladin Press.

Mroz, Ralph (2000). *Defensive Shooting for Real-Life Encounters: A Critical Look at Current Training Methods.* Boulder, CO: Paladin Press.

NRA Firearms Fact Book—3rd Ed. (1993). Fairfax, VA: National Rifle Association of America.

Poe, Richard (2001). *The Seven Myths of Gun Control: Reclaiming the Truth About Guns, Crime, and the Second Amendment.* Roseville, CA: Prima Publishing.

Ramage, Ken (2003). *Handguns 2003 — 15th Annual Edition.* Iola, WI: Krause Publications.

Rauch, Walt (2002). *Practically Speaking: An Illustrated Guide. The Game, Guns and Gear of the International Defensive Pistol Association with Real-World Applications.* Lafayette Hill, PA: Rauch & Company.

The Right to Keep and Bear Arms: Report of the Subcommittee on the Constitution: U.S. Senate 97th Congress-2nd Session. Washington, D.C.: U.S. Government Printing Office.

Shapiro, Irving (2002). *The New Dictionary of Legal Terms.* New York: Looseleaf Law Publications.

Smith, Guy (2002). *Gun Facts: Version 3.1.* Alameda, CA: Second Amendment Sisters and Guy Smith; home.attbi.com/~guys/guns.html

Spaulding, Dave (2002). *Handgun Combatives.* New York: Looseleaf Law Publications.

Spear, Robert K. (1996). *Military Knife Fighting.* El Dorado, AZ: Desert Publications.

Suarez, Gabriel. (1996). *The Tactical Pistol: Advanced Gunfighting Concepts and Techniques.* Boulder, CO: Paladin Press.

Suarez, Gabriel. (1996). *The Tactical Shotgun: The Best Techniques and Tactics for Employing the Shotgun in Personal Combat.* Boulder, CO: Paladin Press.

Suarez, Gabriel. (1998). *The Tactical Advantage: A Definitive Study of Small-Arms Tactics.* Boulder, CO: Paladin Press.

Suarez, Gabriel. (1999). *The Tactical Rifle: The Precision Tool for Urban Police Operations.* Boulder, CO: Paladin Press.

Suarez, Gabriel. (2001). *Tactical Pistol Marksmanship: How To Improve Your Combat Shooting Skills.* Boulder, CO: Paladin Press.

Suarez, Gabriel. (2003). *The Combative Perspective: The Thinking Man's Guide to Self-Defense.* Boulder, CO: Paladin Press.

Supica, Jim & Nahas, Richard (2001). *Standard Catalog of Smith & Wesson.* Iola, WI: Krause Publications.

Taylor, Chuck (1994). *The Gun Digest Book of Combat Hand-gunnery (4th Ed.).* Iola, WI: Krause Publications.

Winokur, Jon (1985). *Master Tips.* Potshot Press. A Division of Epsilon Press.

Wood, J.B. (1999). *The Gun Digest Book of Firearms Assembly/ Disassembly-Part I: Automatic Pistols (2nd Ed.).* Iola, WI: Krause Publications.

RECOMMENDED SUBSCRIPTION MAGAZINES

American Handgunner. www.americanhandgunner.com. Tel: 858-605-0253.

Combat Handguns. www.combathandguns.com. Tel: 800-2COMBAT.

Concealed Carry Magazine. www.concealedcarrymag.com. Tel: 262-677-8877 or 877-677-1919.

Gun Tests. The Consumer Resource For The Serious Shooter. www.gun-tests.com. Tel: 800-829-9084.

Guns & Ammo Handguns. www.gunsandammomag.com. Tel: 800-800-4486.

Guns & Weapons For Law Enforcement. www.guns-weapons.com. Tel: 888-444-GWLE.

Soldier Of Fortune. www.sofmag.com. Tel: 800-877-5207.

S.W.A.T. Magazine: Weapons, Tactics & Training For The Real World. www.swatmag.com. Tel: 800-673-4595.

Tactical Knives. The Cutting Edge Of Survival. www.tacticalknives.com. www.harrisoutdoorgroup.com. Tel: 212-807-7100.

16

Quality Products

We provide you with the following chart of the current products on the market.

Any quality manufacturers or products that have been inadvertently left out are invited to contact us via our publisher, or email, so that we may be able to include them in the next edition.

Holsters Criteria	Manufacturers and Products
IWB clip ons	Don Hume Waistband Clip-Ons "H-715-M" and "H715-MTB" (with thumb break); FIST "#1 Clip"Holster, and "#6 Rounded Front Clip Holster"; Lou Alessi "Talon Plus"; High Noon "Hideaway"; Bell Charter Oak "Auto Compact Extreme" (A.C.E.), Mitch Rosen "Clipper"; Aker "Spring Special Executive"; C.A.C. and "Scorpion"
IWBs with snap strap loops	Matt Del Fatti ISP-SS; ISP-WR, ISP-3; Mitch Rosen "USD Express"; Mitch Rosen "ARG-Express"; Kramer IWB #1-$^1/_2$, #2, and #3; Milt Sparks "Summer Special" and "Summer Special 2"; Milt Sparks "Ex-Executives Companion"; Don Hume "PCCH"; Bianchi "3S Pistol Pocket"; FISH "#20 Adjustable IWB"; Blade-Tech "I.W.B."; DeSantis "Inner Piece," Lou Alessi "CQCI"; High Noon "Down Under," "Hideaway" and "Tail Gunner"; Galco "Summer Comfort" and "Royal Guard"; Bulman Gunleather TSAP; Gould & Goodrich Inside Pants; Bell Charter Oak "Defender IWB"
IWBs with tunnel belt loop	Matt Del Fatti ISP-SS; ISP-WR, and ISP-3; Mitch Rosen "ARG"; Kramer "IWB #1-½, #2 and #3."

Holsters Criteria	Manufacturers and Products
Belt slide scabbards	Matt Del Fatti "ComTac" and "ComTac Light Weight," "LP," "LP-HTL," "SLP" and "SLP-2," and "SSK" and "SSR-N"; DeSantis "Speed Scabbard," "Thumb Break Scabbard," "Mini-scabbard," and "Mini-slide"; Mitch Rosen "SJR-Express"; "SJR-Pres"; UPL-Express; Don Hume "Open Top Double Nine," "H721-O.T. Open Top Double Nine," "H722" series, "H721 Double Nine," and "007K Concealment Holster"; FIST Basic High Noon "Sky High," "Topless," "Need For Speed" and "Slide Guard"; Gould & Goodrich Gold Line "Open Top Two Slot" and "Three Slot Pancake"; Bulman Full Belt Slide; Kramer "Vertical Scabbard" and Kramer "Belt Scabbard," "Vertical Scabbard"; Galco "Combat Master," "Fletch High Ride," and "Avenger"; Bell Charter Oak "Dragon Wing Scabbard"
Snap on belt scabbards	Lou Alessi "CQC/S"; Bulman "Quick Release Holster"; FIST "Easy On"; Del Fatti "LP-QS"; Milt Sparks "Nelsons Patriot."
Paddle holsters	FIST Paddle; Blade-Tech Paddles; Gould & Goodrich "Paddle and "Comfort Paddle"; Uncle Mike's Kydex; Comp-Tac "FBI Paddle" and "Locking Paddle"; Don Hume "H720" series, Desantis "Viper"; High Noon "Spanky" and "Speedy Spanky"; Kramer "MSP Paddle"
Pocket holsters	Pocket Concealment Systems; Kramer Handgun Leather "Pocket Holster"; High Noon "Pocket Grabber" and "Pocket Reload"; Ken Null; DeSantis "Nemesis"; Michaels of Oregon "Inside the Pocket" Don Hume "Front Pocket 001"; Bell Charter Oak "Deep Covers"; Aker "Express" and "Pocket Protector" Mitch Rosen "Pocket Softy"; "No.18"; "COZY"; Alessi; Bulman "Front Pocket Pal"; FIST #5 Pocket Holster
Thermo-plastic & Kydex Holsters	Blade-Tech; Comp-Tac; FIST; Michaels of Oregon; Desantis
Best gun belts	Gould & Goodrich
Fit and finish	Mitch Rosen; Don Hume; DeSantis; Bianchi; Del Fatti; Kramer; Alessi, Gould & Goodrich; Galco; Bulman; FIST; Comp-Tac; Blade-Tech; High Noon; Milt Sparks; Pocket Concealment Systems; Bell Charter Oak

Holsters Criteria

Manufacturers and Products

Criteria	Manufacturers and Products
Best customer service	Mitch Rosen; Don Hume; DeSantis; Bianchi; Matt Del Fatti; Kramer; Michaels of Oregon; Gould & Goodrich; FIST; Milt Sparks; Bell Charter Oak
Fastest to fulfill order	DeSantis; Don Hume; Galco; Bianchi; Michaels of Oregon; Gould & Goodrich; FIST; Mitch Rosen
Most affordable	Michaels of Oregon; Don Hume; DeSantis; Blade-Tech; Bianchi; High Noon; Gould & Goodrich; Mitch Rosen Express Line

Revolvers Criteria

Manufacturers and Products

Criteria	Manufacturers and Products
Quality and reliability	Smith and Wesson
Largest selection	Smith and Wesson
Best customer service	Smith and Wesson
Fit and finish	Smith and Wesson
Accuracy	Smith and Wesson

Pocket Pistols Criteria

Manufacturers and Products

Criteria	Manufacturers and Products
Quality and reliability	L.W. Seecamp; Beretta .32 Tomcat; Kahr Arms MK9
Most powerful caliber	Kahr Arms MK9, PM9, and MK40; North American Arms .32 N.A.A. Guardian and .380 Guardian
Heaviest trigger pull	North American Arms Guardians
Lightest trigger pull	Beretta .32 Tomcat
Smoothest double action trigger	Kahr MK9 and MK40
Longest DA trigger pull	Kel-Tec P-32

Pocket Pistols Criteria	Manufacturers and Products
Most concealable	L.W. Seecamp; Kel-Tec P-32
Simplest to operate (Fewest mechanical controls)	L.W. Seecamp; Kel-Tec P-32; Kahr MK9/MK40/PM9
Best customer service	Kel-Tec; L.W. Seecamp; Beretta; Kahr Arms
Easiest to shoot	Beretta .32 Tomcat; Kahr MK9
Easiest to clean	Beretta .32 Tomcat; N.A.A. Guardians; MK9/MK40
Best performers	L.W. Seecamp; Beretta .32 Tomcat; Kahr MK9/MK40
Most collectable	L.W. Seecamp
Most affordable	Kel-Tec .32 P-32
Fit and finish	L.W. Seecamp; Beretta .32 Tomcat; Kahr MK9/MK40
Accuracy	L.W. Seecamp; Beretta .32 Tomcat; Kahr MK9/MK40

Subcompact Pistols Criteria	Manufacturers and Products
Quality and reliability	"Baby Glocks" (26/27/33); SIG Sauer P232; Kahr MK9/MK40
Most powerful caliber	Glock 27 (.40 S&W); Glock 33 (.357 SIG); Kahr MK40
Most concealable	Kahr MK series; Kahr PM9; Kel-Tec P-11 (9mm)
Best customer service	SIGARMS; Glock; Kahr Arms
Simplest to operate (Fewest mechanical controls)	Glocks; Kahr MK9/MK40/PM9; Kel-Tec P-11
Easiest to shoot	SIG P232; Glock 26 (9mm)

Subcompact Pistols Criteria | Manufacturers and Products

Subcompact Pistols Criteria	Manufacturers and Products
Easiest to clean	SIGARMS; Glocks; Kahr MK9 and 40
Best performers	Glocks; SIG P232; Kahr MK9 and 40
Most collectable	Glocks; SIG P232
Most affordable	Kel-Tec P-11; Glocks; SIG P232
Fit and finish	Glocks; SIG P232; Kahr MK9/MK40
Accuracy	"Baby Glocks" 26 and 27; SIG P232; Kahr MK9

Compact Pistols Criteria	Manufacturers and Products
Highest quality and reliability	HK USP Compacts; SIG Sauer P239, P228, P229, P245; Glock 19/23/30/32/36; Smith & Wesson 3913, S&W 457; Kahr K9
Most powerful caliber	HK USP Compact .45; SIG P245; Glock 30/36 (.45 ACP); Smith & Wesson 457 (.45 ACP); Kimber Ultra CDP II; Para-Ordnance Para Carry 6.45 and 7.45 LDA series
Most concealable	Glock 36; SIG P239; Kimber Ultra CDP II; Kahr K9; S&W 3913LS; Para-Ordnance Para Carry 6.45 LDA and Carry Companion 7.45 LDA
Best customer service	Smith & Wesson; SIGARMS; Glock; HK; Kahr Arms
Simplest to operate (Fewest mechanical controls)	Glocks; Kahr K9
Easiest to shoot	Glock 19 (9mm); Glock 30 and 36 (.45 ACP); S&W 3913 (9mm); HK USP Compact (in 9mm, .40 S&W, or .45 ACP); SIG P239 (.380), SIG P228 (9mm), P229 (9mm/.40 S&W), P245 (.45 ACP); Kahr K9

Compact Pistols Criteria	Manufacturers and Products
Easiest to clean	Glocks; SIGARMS; HKs; S&Ws; Kahr K9
Best performers	Glocks; SIGARMS; HKs; S&Ws; Kahr K9
Most affordable	Glocks; S&W 457
Most collectable	Kimber Ultra CDP II; Glocks; SIGARMS; HKs; S&Ws; Kahr K9
Fit and finish	Glocks; SIGs; HKs; S&Ws; Kahr K9
Accuracy	Glock 19/23/30/36; SIG P239, P228, P229, P245; S&W 3913 (9mm); S&W 457 (.45 ACP); HK USP Compacts (in 9mm, .40 S&W, or .45 ACP); Kahr K9

Full-Size Pistols Critieria	Manufacturers and Products
Quality and reliability	HK USPs; SIG Sauer P220/P226; Kimber Custom II TLE 1911 Government Model; Glock 17/21/22/31; Beretta 92 and 8000 Cougar series; Smith & Wesson 5900, 4000 and 4500 series
Most powerful caliber	Glock 21 (.45) Glock 31 (.357 SIG); HK USP .45; SIG P220 (.45); Kimber Custom II TLE (.45); Beretta 8045 Cougar (.45)
Most concealable	Kimber Custom II TLE; SIG P220 and P226; Glock 17/22
Best customer service	Smith & Wesson; SIGARMS; Glock; HK; Beretta
Easiest to shoot	Glock 17 (9mm), Glock 21 (.45); SIG P220/P226; Kimber Custom II; Beretta 92 FS and 8045 Cougar
Simplest to operate (Fewest mechanical controls)	Glock

Full-Size Pistols Critieria	Manufacturers and Products
Easiest to clean	Glocks, SIGs, HKs, S&Ws, Berettas
Best performers	HK USPs; SIG Sauer P220/P226; Beretta 8045 Cougar, Beretta 92FS; Kimber Custom II TLE 1911 Government Model; Glock 17/21/22/31; Smith & Wesson 5900, 4000 and 4500 series
Most collectable	SIG Sauer P220/P226; Kimber Custom II TLE; Glock 17/21/22/31; S&W 5900, 4000 and 4500 series; HK USPs; Beretta 92/96 series and 8000 Cougar series
Most affordable	Glocks
Fit and finish	Glocks; SIGs; HKs; S&Ws; Beretta 92 & 8000 Cougar series
Accuracy	Kimber Custom II TLE; Glock 17/21/22; SIG P226, P220, S&W 5900 series (9mm), 4000 series (.40 S&W) and 4500 series (.45 ACP); HK USPs (in 9mm, .40 S&W, or .45ACP); Beretta 92FS (9mm) and 8045 Cougar (.45 ACP)

Laser Aiming Devices Criteria	Manufacturers and Products
Most functional and reliable	LaserMax
Internal. No need to calibrate	LaserMax
Best Customer Service	LaserMax
Simplest to operate	LaserMax
Most integrated with gun	LaserMax

Tactical Flashlights Criteria	Manufacturers and Products
Most functional and reliable	Surefire; Streamlight; Mag Instrument Corporation ("Maglites")

Tactical Flashlights Criteria	Manufacturers and Products
Best Customer Service	Streamlight; Surefire
Simplest to operate	Surefire; Streamlight; Mag Instrument Corporation ("Maglites")
Most affordable	Surefire; Mag Instrument Corporation ("Maglites")

Weapon Mounted Tactical Lights Criteria	Manufacturers and Products
Most functional and reliable	Insight Technology (e.g., M3 Illuminator; M6TLI)
Best Customer Service	Insight Technology
Simplest to operate	Insight Technology
Most innovative	Insight Technology

Defensive Pepper Spray Criteria	Manufacturers and Products
Most functional and reliable	Spitfire
Best Customer Service	Spitfire
Simplest to operate	Spitfire
Most innovative	Spitfire

Defensive Ammunition	Federal "Hydra Shok" JHPs; Winchester SXT JHPs, Winchester Silver Tip JHPs; Speer "Gold Dot" JHPs; Remington "Golden Sabers" Fiocchi SJHPs
Range Practice Ammunition	Winchester FMJ; Fiocchi FMJ; American Eagle FMJ; Zero Ammunition Company

Remember President Theodore Roosevelt's turn of the last century motto. It is just as applicable, if not more so, in this century: *"Speak softly, and carry a big stick!"*

Well, folks. We hope you have enjoyed reading our book as much as we have enjoyed writing it. And we hope you have learned some useful things. There is always more to learn. So, keep an open mind, exercise good judgment, and don't forget what you know, if it works, as opposed to following every new trend that is in vogue and stylish. Keep learning, keep using what you know works, and survive! We wish you the best on your journey.

Our literal translation is:

STAY ALERT, STAY FOCUSED, STAY ATTENTIVE, STAY AWARE AND YOU'LL STAY ALIVE.

Index

OTHER TITLES OF INTEREST
FROM LOOSELEAF LAW PUBLICATIONS, INC.

Handgun Combatives
by Dave Spaulding

Defensive Living - 2nd Edition
Preserving Your Personal Safety Through
Awareness, Attitude and Armed Action
by Ed Lovette & Dave Spaulding

Use of Force
Expert Guidance for Decisive Force Response
by Brian A. Kinnaird

Instinct Combat Shooting
Defensive Handgunning for Police
by Chuck Klein

Condition to Win
Dynamic Techniques for Performance Oriented
Mental Conditioning
by Wes Doss

Citizens Terrorism Awareness & Survival Manual
by Col. Michael Licata (USAF, Ret.)

Path of the Warrior - 2nd Edition
An Ethical Guide to Personal &
Professional Development in the Field
of Criminal Justice
by Larry F. Jetmore

(800) 647-5547   **www.LooseleafLaw.com**

What the Experts Are Saying About
Essential Guide to Handguns

*...a definite **must** for all gun owners, novice to expert. It is one of those books that needs to be on the book shelf to be used as a reference manual and referred to often.*

—Steven Silverman, President
Firearms Research & Instruction

*Until now, there has not been a **one-stop-source of inform-ation** for the new defensive pistol shooter. This gap has been filled by "Essential Guide to Handguns." This book includes everything a new pistol shooter needs to know to select the right gun, as well as how to manage it, carry it, load it, and gives recommendations for obtaining the right equipment. It is one complete and thorough look at the modern defensive handgun. I seriously recommend it for my students.*

—Gabriel Suarez
Suarez International, Inc.
www.suarezinternational.com

*The information contained in this book is as good as it gets. For novices, advanced practitioners, plinkers, and those serious about self-defense, **I believe this book is the best and most complete reference I have ever read**. The book is filled with recommend-ations, choices, references and excellent advice for every level of firearms practitioner. Instructors and counselors can use the materials contained in this book to help in their class preparation and presentations. I personally will do so, and will also reference this book and recommend it to my students. Kudos to Stephen Rementer and Dr. Bruce Eimer. You have bested the best. Your book should be mandatory reading for anyone interested in or currently using firearms for any reason.*

—Kenny Woodward, Owner
Caswell Shooting Range
Certified Instructor and Training Counselor of the NRA

*...an excellent resource for beginners and experienced gun enthusiasts alike. The breadth and depth of the subjects covered was very impressive. **These guys did a great job of covering the basics**; choosing a gun, ammunition, maintenance & safety. However, the most exciting parts of the book are the chapters on psychological preparedness, gun myths and tactical survival. These are serious concepts that will save your life.*

—Tim Schmidt, Editor & Publisher
***Concealed Carry Magazine**, concealedcarrymag.com*